Catholic Fundamentalism in America

Catholic Fundamentalism in America

MARK S. MASSA, S.J.

OXFORD
UNIVERSITY PRESS

Oxford University Press is a department of the University of Oxford.
It furthers the University's objective of excellence in research, scholarship,
and education by publishing worldwide. Oxford is a registered trade mark of
Oxford University Press in the UK and certain other countries.

Published in the United States of America by Oxford University Press
198 Madison Avenue, New York, NY 10016, United States of America.

CIP data is on file at the Library of Congress

ISBN 978–0–19–775999–8

DOI: 10.1093/oso/9780197759998.001.0001

Printed by Sheridan Books, Inc., United States of America

To: Nick Lombardi., S.J.
Angela O'Donnell
Maria Terzulli
My dream team at the Curran Center at Fordham University

Contents

PART I
CATHOLIC FUNDAMENTALISM
AND THE FEENEY CASE

Part I of this study examines the emergence of Catholic fundamentalism in the late 1940s at the St. Benedict Center in Cambridge, Massachusetts.

1

What Is Catholic Fundamentalism?

A. The Emergence of Fundamentalism in American Culture

In the United States, at least since the second decade of the twentieth century, the word "Fundamentalist" (often capitalized) has usually been understood as something quite specifically Protestant, militant, and American. A host of perceptive scholars have attempted to explain why this phenomenon emerged in the early twentieth century, and why it still attracts significant numbers of believers today. George Marsden, one of the most respected historians of fundamentalism, has convincingly argued that, despite its cultural conflicts with modern mainstream US thought and practice, fundamentalism was (and is) exactly what it claimed to be: a *religious movement* that drew on specific theological traditions of Protestantism in the United States: evangelicalism, Pietism, premillennialism, revivalism, and well-established "orthodoxies" like the Calvinism taught by devotees of the "Princeton Theology." Its first centers of strength—despite popular perceptions of fundamentalism as the religion of uneducated southern "yokels"—were not among the uneducated working class of the American South. Fundamentalism initially drew more northern Presbyterians than Southern Baptists, and its intellectual birthplace was that bastion of Protestant establishment: the Princeton Theological Seminary. And despite its claim to witness to "that old time religion," it was very much a product of the late nineteenth and early twentieth centuries.[1]

In her insightful study of fundamentalism and gender, Margaret Bendroth has shown that fundamentalists were not naturally social outsiders: "nearly all of the movement's early leadership was white, male, middle-class, well-educated, and Protestant." Perceptive students of the fundamentalist impulse have thus been at pains to correct the misperception of fundamentalism as shaped in popular culture by films like *Inherit the Wind*, focused on the infamous Scopes "Monkey Trial" in Dayton, Tennessee in 1925, which portrayed adherents of the movement as small-town southern yahoos afraid of college-educated city slickers.[2] Marsden, and the succession of scholars who built on his work, trace the first significant appearance of what scholars now recognize as fundamentalist Christianity to 1919. That year, the Treaty of Versailles ended World War I, sending hundreds of thousands of American soldiers back from Europe, carrying with them European ideas and attitudes they picked up along the way. Joel Carpenter has also pointed out that 1919 was the year when the Interchurch World Movement—the forerunner of the (liberal) ecumenical movement in the US—generated something close to a "populist" reaction among conservative Protestants who disliked centralized bureaucracies and much preferred local control of their religious lives. For a number of cultural as well as theological reasons, then, 1919 was the year when a substantial number of white American Protestants of English and Scots ethnicity—formerly the ethnic backbone of mainstream culture in the US—experienced the first stirrings of a religious revolution.[3]

The cultural upheaval that followed World War I, as well as the threats of the emerging inter-church movement and what became known as "higher" criticism of the Bible—an approach, which had emerged in European universities, that did not take the Bible's truth for granted—created a new religious world for American Christians. And the immigrant experience of many old-line Protestants (who had always considered themselves to be part of the Protestant mainstream) profoundly shaped what became fundamentalism. But it was not the theological commitments of fundamentalist Christians that had changed—it was America itself. The fundamentalists' literal reading of the Bible ("biblical inerrancy") was not something fundamentalist believers invented out of whole cloth in 1919; just a few years earlier, the vast mainstream of American Protestants would have accepted it without a second thought. To adherents of the emerging fundamentalist movement, *they* had remained faithful to timeless principles. It was their progressive Protestant opponents, in accepting the new German theology of higher criticism and new-fangled ideas of a "super-church," who had apostatized.[4]

Likewise, fundamentalists were neither anti-intellectual nor anti-scientific, despite their rejection of Darwin and the resulting public perception. Indeed, one could make a very strong case that fundamentalist Christianity was, if nothing else, *extraordinarily* scientific. But it adhered to an older paradigm of science ("Baconian Realism") that, again, the vast majority of educated Protestants had accepted without question just four or five decades earlier. As Theodore Dwight Bozeman has demonstrated, Baconian Realism was about collecting hard and fast physical data that could be seen and tested—a model of experiment in which geology was presented as the normative science: rocks did not lie. Fundamentalist Christians were scandalized for *scientific* reasons when their opponents gave up on this approach in favor of Darwin's *theory* of natural selection (and they regularly put that word—"theory"—in italics).[5]

As fundamentalists consistently pointed out, even Darwin's most vocal supporters confessed that the Darwinian theory of natural selection couldn't be *proven* in any intellectually satisfying way that would meet the factual criterion of the older Baconian Realist model of science, which demanded that scientists confine their explanations to data that everyone could see and examine. How could it? Natural selection was a theoretical attempt to explain admittedly spotty geological evidence—often with gaps of millions of years in the chain of scientific explanation—that seemed to reveal significant evolutionary changes in creatures of the same species. But to fundamentalist believers such an argument—that science could be based on theories rather than proven data—was nonsensical and flew in the face of how educated American Protestants had always understood the word "science." Fundamentalists believed that those who embraced Darwin's *theories* were the unscientific ones.[6]

At stake was nothing less than the Bible itself.

Few Christian believers were more bound to a literal biblical understanding of revelation than those evangelicals, Pietists, premillennialists, and adherents of the Princeton theology who formed the nascent fundamentalist movement. For these Bible Believers (as they called themselves) Holy Scripture meant what it said and said what it meant. Its message was *self-evident* to anyone who read it in good faith. If Genesis asserted that God had created the world in seven days, it meant just that. And further, precisely as adherents of the Baconian Realist paradigm of science, they believed that the Bible—as real and trustworthy as the laws of gravity—was no less a storehouse of facts than the physical universe itself: the biblical account could be mined (like the physical world) to discover the origin and purpose of the physical universe, as well as the human place in it. From their point of view, then, they adhered to an extraordinarily scientific theology, grounded in the hard evidence of the Bible itself. "Go look at the evidence for yourself," they told opponents. "It's right there in black and white: it's God's word to us, and God cannot lie." Modern seminary professors in places like Harvard Divinity School or Union Theological Seminary argued that the Bible had to be *interpreted* in light of a new paradigm of science and a new theological approach to the Bible called "Higher Criticism." Fundamentalists jeered at such nonsense as merely the latest form of infidelity. They were being called to abandon an approach to Bible reading they had practiced for centuries—and for what? For a bunch of *theories* that couldn't be proven by hard evidence? Far from being intimidated, fundamentalist Christians thought their progressive theological opponents had lost their minds as well as their faith. They suddenly despaired of sending their young to educational institutions that had been founded precisely to educate Protestant ministers—Yale, Oberlin, the University of Chicago. In response, they founded a new network of colleges like Wheaton in Illinois and Gordon-Conwell in Massachusetts. They also established their own Bible Schools, places like Westminster Theological Seminary in Philadelphia, to train ministers unsullied by the nonsense taught at the older divinity schools.[7]

The movement itself came to be named after twelve paperback volumes of essays whose collective title—*The Fundamentals*—witnessed to its purpose as a "Testimony to the Truth." The authors of the dozens of essays in those twelve volumes were described as "the best and most loyal Bible teachers in the world," and they sought unapologetically to present a broad and united front of opposition to the kind of modernism now adopted by mainstream Protestants like the Methodists, northern Baptists, and Presbyterians. The volumes themselves provided the textual resources for (literally) hundreds of Sunday School teachers, adult education leaders, and summer Bible Conference speakers for many decades.[8]

Marsden's historical account offers two especially helpful interpretive tools for grasping the emergence and growth of fundamentalism. First, Marsden quite helpfully uses Thomas Kuhn's argument regarding paradigm revolutions in his classic work on the history of science, *The Structure of Scientific Revolutions*, to explain the fundamentalist dilemma. Central to Kuhn's famous thesis was the argument that science did not progress by a simple accumulation of new and more advanced theories as more facts are discovered by scientists, as though the history of science were one long, unbroken chain of facts from Aristotle to Heisenberg. Rather, science underwent periodic revolutions, in which old ways of thinking were eclipsed by new ones. Marsden cannily recognized that the older Baconian model of both science and Bible reading so prized by the fundamentalists rested *precisely* on such an older paradigm in which one could gather a "long, unbroken chain of facts" to understand both geology and the Bible. But, as Marsden recognized:

America between 1860 and 1925 [underwent] something like the general acceptance of a new perceptual model—or paradigm—in both the scientific and theological communities . . . The "modern" theological community adopted a model for truth that in effect stigmatized theologians who rejected evolutionary views as neither scientific nor legitimate theologians. The conservatives were equally dogmatic. No compromise could be made with a worldview whose proponents denied the fixed character of supernaturally guaranteed truth. Communication between the two sides became almost impossible. Fundamentalists, excluded from the community of modern theological and scientific orthodoxy, eventually were forced to establish their own community and sub-culture in which their ideas of orthodoxy were preserved.[9]

A paradigm revolution in the American Protestant mainstream had taken place after 1919. Modernist Christians embraced a new paradigm, while fundamentalists clung to the old one. And the result of that revolution was that while both groups used exactly the same words and phrases—the Bible as "God's revealed truth," a "scientific approach" to reading Holy Scripture, building a Christian civilization in the US—they meant completely different things by them. As Marsden recognized, fundamentalist and modernist Christians inhabited (almost literally) different universes when talking about God, redemption, and the Bible because they inhabited different—and to a large extent, mutually exclusive—paradigms.

Secondly, Marsden was at pains to emphasize that while theology and religion were the focus points for the Fundamentalist crusade against modern liberals, the cultural experience of post-World War I America had a great deal to do with shaping their theology. In the first two decades of the twentieth century, he observed, their expressions of cultural alarm were infrequent; but after 1919 leading Fundamentalists:

expressed alarm not only about modernism and evolution, but also about the spread of communism. Occasionally, even anti-Jewish sentiments were incorporated. At the same time unqualified fundamentalist patriotism was growing rapidly. [These observations] reinforce the point that American fundamentalism was not simply an expression of theology or concern about false doctrines. In the minds of most fundamentalists the theological crisis came to be inextricably wedded to the very survival of Christian civilization.[10]

Most scholars of American religion accept these careful—and often brilliant—explications of how, why, and when, fundamentalism (itself an unstable alliance of various militant conservative Christians) emerged from within the dominant Protestant establishment in America. That religious and cultural establishment was itself making significant moves to accommodate the new pluralist culture and the new evolutionary science that had emerged as the cultural norm after 1919. Fundamentalists, feeling like strangers in their own land, sought earnestly to counter those accommodations.

Catholic conservatives—similarly concerned about the accommodationist moves being made by their own Church to fit into the pluralist culture of the United States after World War II—would not be far behind.

B. Catholic Fundamentalism in the United States

There is no similar raft of scholarship on American Catholic movements of this stripe. Yet, an analogously reactive, militant, and sectarian "fundamentalist" movement emerged within American Catholicism in the decades after World War II for a similarly complex mix of theological and cultural reasons. Its emergence predated the Second Vatican Council (1963–1965) by several decades, although that council is itself often targeted as the reason for the rise of conservative American Catholic movements in the twentieth-century US. Its epicenter was the St. Benedict Center in Cambridge, Massachusetts, founded in 1940 to serve the growing number of Catholic students attending Harvard and Radcliffe Colleges. By the late 1940s, the Center—a block from Harvard Yard and across the street from the Harvard parish of St. Paul's—could boast of being an extremely successful operation, having produced two hundred converts to the Catholic Church, and regularly attracting over 250 students to the courses it offered in Greek, church history, hagiography, and philosophy (all of which achieved recognition by the G.I. Bill as legitimate courses that could be counted toward academic degrees). Originally the brainchild of a devout laywoman, Catherine Goddard Clarke, things took off—in both positive and negative ways—in 1943, when Leonard Feeney, S.J., sometime literary editor of the US Jesuits' weekly magazine, *America*, arrived.[11]

Feeney, by all accounts a charismatic person who could keep a large audience spellbound, almost immediately became a famous presence at the Center. People traveled from considerable distances for "Thursday nights at the Center," during which Feeney would hold forth for several hours, starting with hilarious imitations of famous people, like Theodore Roosevelt and Katherine Hepburn, before turning to extremely serious topics in theology that kept his audience on the edge of their seats. Soon, a famous phrase from third-century theologian and bishop Cyprian of Carthage became central to Feeney's performances: *extra ecclesiam nulla salus*, usually translated as "outside the church there is no salvation." The phrase itself was hardly controversial. But the all-important question of what that phrase actually *meant* was something else entirely.[12]

Feeney himself became the object of considerable concern to both his Jesuit superiors and to the Archbishop (soon to be Cardinal) of the Catholic archdiocese of Boston, Richard Cushing—so much so that he was eventually excommunicated from the Catholic Church and "exclaustrated" (dismissed) from the Jesuit order. The ironies here, of course, are deep and delicious, and were not lost on any of the participants at the time. Feeney, who had taken a hard line on the absolute necessity of being *inside* Holy Mother Church (more on the Freudian repercussions of that phrase in time), now found himself *outside* the Church, and therefore beyond the reach of saving grace. Moving forty-five miles west of Cambridge to the town of Harvard, Massachusetts, he and his several dozen followers formed a new religious order, the Slaves of the Immaculate Heart of Mary, who understood themselves to be the faithful remnant of a Catholic Church now mired in heresy.[13]

The "Boston Heresy Case," as it came to be called, was largely forgotten by the early 1960s, when Good Pope John (XXIII) called together Catholic bishops from around the world for the first ecumenical council in a century. But despite its marginalization in the American Catholic consciousness, the Boston Heresy Case was extremely important, and not just for what happened in and around Harvard Square in the 1940s and early 1950s. Feeney and his Slaves crafted the paradigm for American Catholic fundamentalism—an anti-modern, reactive, and sectarian impulse that has been with us ever since. Indeed, it is alive and well in the twenty-first century, and shows no sign of disappearing. The Feeney case modeled the five characteristics that have marked all Catholic Fundamentalist movements since.

First, the Feeney episode embodied a strong *sectarian* impulse that characterizes all the Catholic Fundamentalist movements that followed. As the University of Chicago religion scholar Mircea Eliade observed five decades ago, in his famous encyclopedia entry on Catholic Christianity, what is most directly opposed to Catholicism is not Protestantism (which, in any case, has many Catholic elements within it) but *sectarianism*, the movement within Christianity that holds that the church is a community of true believers, a precinct of righteousness within and yet in opposition to the unredeemed world of sin, pronouncing judgment upon it and calling it to repentance, but never entering into dialogue with it, much less collaboration on matters of common social, political, or religious concern. For the sectarian, dialogue and collaboration are invitations to compromise, and compromise is anathema.[14]

Eliade had this exactly right. Catholicism, since its emergence in the third and fourth centuries after Christ, has always been Christianity's big tent. As James Joyce famously observed, "Catholicism means here comes everybody." Unlike Protestantism, which generated innumerable spin-off groups that evolved into still more break-away churches, each claiming to be purer than the last, Catholicism has always insisted on *communion* as basic to its identity. Indeed, the Latin version of that term, *communio*, referring to the communion of believers with each other—saints with sinners, the pure with those considerably less pure, the converted with the not-quite converted—witnessed to the fact that *all* of those groups were "inside the true church." And, therefore, Catholic Christianity has always condemned sectarian movements—movements that seek to break away from the larger church to become more pure and less contaminated by the world—as deeply suspect and even foreign to the Catholic impulse. It is for that reason that Eliade's observation points to something basic at the very core of the Catholic tradition: sectarianism is the polar opposite of the very word "catholic" (from the Greek, *katholikos*, meaning "universal"). The very core of Feeney's crusade to draw a tight circle around those who accepted Feeney's own strict (and painfully small) band of believers as alone constituting the true Catholic Church was profoundly sectarian, and to that extent unCatholic—perhaps even anti-Catholic. Feeney's sectarianism created the template for all the Catholic fundamentalist movements that followed.[15]

Second, Feeney and the Slaves of the Immaculate Heart of Mary did not invent their particular (and increasingly, after 1945, peculiar) take on Roman Catholic faith and practice out of whole cloth. Rather, like their Protestant fundamentalist second cousins, they held on to an earlier paradigm of Catholic identity that was in the process of being swiftly replaced by a newer paradigm, one that would receive official status in the years after 1965, when the teachings of the Second Vatican Council were received and implemented in the United States. But that revolution had already begun well before the bishops of Vatican II had even gathered in Rome. In a word, the Feeneyites found themselves staking out the wrong side of a paradigm revolution after World War II.

The older, and quite revered, paradigm of Tridentine Catholicism—a highly clerical and hierarchical model of Catholicism crafted at the Council of Trent that identified the *institution* of the Roman Catholic Church as itself the "perfect society" mirroring the Kingdom of God—was quietly unraveling as the grandchildren of Catholic immigrants left urban ghettos that separated "us" from "them" for the verdant pastures of the suburbs. They now found themselves surrounded not by Irish, German, or Italian fellow-believers, but by friendly Methodist, Presbyterian, and Lutheran neighbors, with whom they hosted backyard dinners and car-pooled. The older paradigm of the church as the *societas perfecta*—a paradigm that had scoffed at the very idea that Methodist or Baptist believers were even really Christians—now seemed quaint, or even ridiculous. And that sense of the older paradigm being quaint (or worse) received something like a formal stamp of approval when the documents published by Vatican II started referring to the Protestant and Orthodox faithful as "our separated brethren" and "fellow laborers in the Vineyard of the Lord."[16]

When Feeney and his followers claimed that their strict reading of the phrase "outside the church there is no salvation" was, in fact, the orthodox and correct understanding of that phrase, they were not being disingenuous. In the papal bull *Unam Sanctam*, issued in 1302, Pope Boniface VIII had famously stated that "we declare, define, and pronounce that it is altogether necessary for salvation for every human creature be subject to the Roman pontiff." Not too much ambiguity there, Feeney and his followers pointed out, especially as Boniface had used the canonical formula ("declare, define, pronounce") for offering infallible teaching. And the great Jesuit missionary Francis Xavier wrote that he had undertaken his heroic Mission to the Indies in the sixteenth century precisely because he had a vision of thousands of lost (heathen) souls being cast into hell—like autumn leaves being blown off trees during a November storm—precisely because they had died outside the church.[17]

The Feeneyites were at pains to point out that they were simply echoing earlier (and quite orthodox) church teaching: wasn't the solemn teaching of a pope solid ground for "orthodox" doctrine? They had not changed; Holy Mother Church—or at least those claiming to speak for her—had. And like the Protestant fundamentalists who thought that the liberal seminary professors who now embraced theory instead of facts for understanding both the Bible and the physical world had betrayed the faith of their fathers, so Feeney and his Slaves saw the formal condemnation of their teaching by the Archbishop of Boston and their eventual excommunication by Rome as proof positive that Catholic leaders had abandoned one of the core teachings of Catholic orthodoxy, and were now in heresy. And the Feeneyites' own traumatic experience of being on the wrong side of a paradigm revolution would be replicated by the Catholic Fundamentalist movements that would follow them.

Third, Feeney's consistent return to the literalistic teaching of earlier popes (like Boniface VIII) witnesses to his *a-historical* understanding of the Catholic past. For Feeney, church teaching (and more importantly, the meaning of church teaching) *could not change*. The past was frozen in aspic. Feeney resolutely refused to even consider the possibility that the doctrine, worship, or ethical guidelines of Catholicism could develop and change over time. Like the Protestant Fundamentalists who preceded him—who insisted that biblical teaching *had* to be interpreted as it had been interpreted by evangelical Protestants throughout the nineteenth century—Feeney insisted that Boniface VIII's pronouncements had to mean the same thing in the twentieth century as they did in the fourteenth.

Among church historians this tendency is usually referred to as "primitivism," a heresy that insists that church structure, worship, and teaching had achieved its perfect (and eternally true) form at some moment in the primitive past. The name itself was coined to explain why the British and American Puritans insisted that their churches in the sixteenth and seventeenth centuries *had* to model themselves on the primitive church described in the fifth book of the New Testament, the "Acts of the Apostles." If "Acts" never mentioned organs, set prayers, kneeling to receive the eucharist, clerical vestments, or bishops, then they were bound by the exact same guidelines fifteen centuries later. The only way that Puritans believed that they could claim to be the pure (and therefore true) church was by pointing to the fact that they worshiped and structured their church order exactly as the early first-century church had done in the decades after Jesus's death. Any change to that worship and governance was not development, it was apostasy. Church worship, structure and teaching would always be the same, as it was in the beginning, is now, and ever shall be, world without end.[18]

Feeney and his disciples, of course, had no such primitivist reading of the New Testament, but they espoused a primitivist reading of the Catholic past, especially of the Catholic medieval past, when they believed the True Church had achieved its perfect (and for them, final) form under popes like Boniface VIII. Theirs was a resolutely a-historical reading of Catholic Christianity, in which development was not possible because it represented apostasy from a faith once delivered.

Fourth, like the Protestant fundamentalists, Feeney and his followers really were, just as they claimed, focused on theology and doctrine, and not primarily on cultural or political issues (although these did play a secondary but important role). And also like their Protestant cousins, they used the essentially political monikers of "conservative" and "liberal" to delineate their own position vis-à-vis mainstream American Catholicism. But unlike the Protestant Fundamentalists, their usage of these left/right political markers was actually noteworthy in the Catholic subculture of the 1940s and 1950s, and it is precisely the use of those political monikers in presenting church teaching that constitutes the fourth characteristic that Feeney bequeathed to many of the fundamentalist movements that followed him. Until the immediate postwar era, there were really only two terms Catholics used to describe fellow believers: "faithful" and "lapsed." Lapsed Catholics weren't necessarily liberal in any American political sense, any more than faithful Catholics were necessarily conservative. The idea that one could use the American political label of liberal to describe a group undermining the True Church was a startlingly new and arresting phenomenon, which gained currency only after Feeney and his Slaves started using it to mark out who was "in" and, especially, who was not. Feeney consistently said that the Liberal Catholic (the former word always in capital letters) is one who always knows how God *should* behave:

> God's behavior is invariably made to conform with the Liberal's own fine feelings in any situation. A Catholic Liberal tries to make the Jesus described in Holy Scripture square with his own pre-conceived notion of how an incarnate God should talk and behave. A Liberal Catholic does not like the statement "No salvation outside the Church" because "it isn't nice."[19]

There had, of course, always been parties within the US Catholic community who debated what the correct relationship of the Church to American culture should be: one might contrast the urban Irish Jansenism of the Eastern Corridor, concerned with maintaining tribal loyalty against Yankee outsiders by emphasizing church's rules, especially regarding sexuality, over against the German farmer immigrants who settled in the "German Triangle" (Cincinnati/Milwaukee/St. Louis), whose understanding of Catholicism as a "public faith" incorporated the rich Rhineland traditions of music and art that welcomed "outsiders" to Catholic worship. Or one could contrast the "Americanist" program sponsored by Archbishop John Ireland of St. Paul, who sought to acculturate Catholic immigrants as soon as possible to the traditions of the US, against the ultramontanist vision of Bishop Bernard McQuaid of Rochester, who believed that American Catholicism should reflect the structure and values of the "Home Office" in Rome, and therefore opposed any effort to acculturate immigrants too quickly (or maybe ever). Or, then again, one might contrast the historicizing scholarship of Jesuit John Courtney Murray, who believed that American Catholic theology needed to incorporate the best insights of contemporary scholarship into its systems, over against the neo-scholasticism of Monsignor Joseph Fenton of the Catholic University of America, who believed that Catholic thought had achieved its perfect form in the theology of St. Thomas Aquinas in the thirteenth century, and saw no need to look further than that medieval thinker. The list is long and lively, and worthy of study in its own right.

What was new in the Feeney episode was the easy adoption of American political labels, especially the use of "liberal" to describe their enemies in the battle for the soul of American Catholicism. This new usage witnessed to their deep fear of what was happening in postwar American culture. The feeling of a cultural displacement—much like the experience of so many English and Scottish-stock Protestants after 1919—overwhelmed Feeney and his followers after 1945, making them feel like aliens in their own land, as well as in their own church. And they blamed Catholic Liberals for buying into a culture that had won its war against the Axis powers by dropping the atomic bomb on Hiroshima, thus ushering in an apocalyptic age.[20]

But equally important for the future growth of Catholic fundamentalism in the United States was the fact that Feeney's usage of "Liberal" to describe the enemies of Christ's True Church paved the way for the gradual wedding of Catholic fundamentalism with conservative politics in the United States by the twenty-first century. That wedding was still inchoate and largely unexplored during the Boston Heresy Case itself, but over the next several decades that merger of theological and political impulses would emerge into the bright light of day. As John Deedy observed in his fine study of the Feeneyites, the sense of chaos that seemed to engulf North American Catholicism with the reception of Vatican II "was all the evidence the community needed that theirs was the right course; for them, the onus was on the 'salvation liberals' and those who dealt with them so harshly." As Deedy explained, adapting a phrase from Barry Goldwater, "In their hearts, they know they were—and still are—right."[21]

And finally, Feeney—like the Protestant fundamentalists several decades earlier—gave voice to a rhetorical style marked by apocalyptic urgency. And that urgency embodied the fifth characteristic that would define the Catholic fundamentalist movements that followed: the almost breathless, accusatory, militant tone of their denunciations of others, especially fellow Catholics. There would not be—there could not be—any question of compromise or respectful conversation with those who disagreed with Feeney's embrace of an earlier paradigm of Catholic belief and practice. For Feeney and his followers, anyone who questioned that paradigm had to be denounced in apocalyptic tones. And it was the militant tone—as much as the message— that defined the group's interactions with fellow Catholics, including with the cardinal archbishop of Boston.

What generated that urgency for Feeney and his followers was not any particular biblical text, but American Catholic complicity in bringing about the atomic age, an age that Feeney was certain would end in apocalypse. Catherine Clarke—easily Feeney's most devoted follower, and the founder of the St. Benedict Center—famously observed that "we were never the same after the dropping of the atomic bomb. It seemed to have shocked us awake." And part of that shock was her sense that the leaders of both her Church and her nation had failed her in the Japanese bombings that ended the war:

> We waited and we listened, but no new strong voice arose above the noise of the world. There was only the jubilant announcement of a new age, the atomic age, born out of the abandonment of a Christian principle![22]

Feeney shared Clarke's sense of dread. But he believed that he didn't have to look far to find the culprits who ushered in the threatened apocalypse: Harvard itself—just across Massachusetts Avenue from the Center. "The bomb" was simply the logical conclusion of the kind of secularism Harvard taught and instilled in its students. Indeed, Feeney claimed that Harvard's scientist president, James Bryant Conant, who had been a significant figure in the Manhattan Project that developed the bombs dropped on Hiroshima and Nagasaki, had even told his guests at one of his dinner parties in the university president's house that "to make a more interesting experiment," the United States should have dropped ten atomic bombs on Japan. Feeney therefore repeatedly voiced his belief that "there'll be a Third World War and another after that because of these 'skeptical chemists' like Conant."[23]

But as withering as Feeney's aspersions on Conant were, they couldn't compare with his fury against Catholic leaders like Boston's Archbishop Cushing, who began showing up at Lowell House High Table dinners at the invitation of President Conant himself. Cushing and Catholic leaders like him were putting their imprimatur on the road to the apocalypse paved by Conant and other "33rd degree Masonic brutes." Fraternizing with non-Catholics who had put the very future of the world at risk was the bridge too far for Feeney and for his followers. Cushing and his ilk were not to be challenged or questioned; they were to be *denounced* in the most militant and pointed way. And that militant, pointed style of denunciation would characterize most of Feeney's public pronouncements, and those of his closest followers.[24]

Feeney reserved his loudest and harshest denunciations for fellow Catholics, which was less counterintuitive than it might appear. The fiercely militant tone of Feeney's message *had* to be focused on fellow Catholics. As Samuel Heilman insightfully observed in his fine study of Jewish fundamentalism, Jewish fundamentalists—like fundamentalists of all religious groups—saw the greatest threat, paradoxically, *not* from those who were completely different from themselves, but rather from those who have staked out a middle ground within Judaism:

> the absolutely different represent an unthinkable evil; but those who occupy a *moderate* middle ground without abandoning [orthodoxy] represent the insidious and thinkable alternative to the Fundamentalist way of life . . . Thus [Jewish Fundamentalists] save their greatest contempt *not* for those who are altogether different from them, but rather for those who are "partially Orthodox," who make their peace with modern culture, and thereby lend legitimacy to acculturation and contemporary secular culture.[25]

This militant and oftentimes savage denunciation that Feeney directed toward his own kind was often frightening to fellow Catholics. When acclaimed British Catholic novelist Evelyn Waugh visited the Center in November 1948, he found Feeney "surrounded by a court of bemused youths, and he stark, raving mad." When Feeney launched into a violent attack on Monsignor Ronald Knox (a much respected British Catholic intellectual and a friend of Waugh's) for his attempt to mediate between Catholic theology and modern thought, Waugh stalked out of the Center: "It seemed to me he needed an exorcist more than an alienist. A case of demonic possession, and jolly frightening." But oftentimes that militant denunciation of fellow Catholics could be unintentionally amusing as well, as when a group of Feeneyites provoked a scuffle during a Notre Dame football game when one of them yelled out to the crowd, "the first sign of your approaching damnation is that Notre Dame has Protestants on its football team."[26]

But it would, in fact, be unhelpful to dismiss that bitter, militant tone as simply the product of Feeney's mental state, or to the peculiarities of "Domer" devotion to the Fighting Irish football team. It was that very militancy—often frightening to those, like Waugh, who witnessed it first-hand—that defined Feeney's fundamentalism over against the kind of intellectual conservativism that marked neo-scholastics and ultramontanists critical of mainstream progressive culture, but who were most decidedly *not* fundamentalists.

Bendroth, in studying the role of women in the Protestant fundamentalist movement, offers a key insight for understanding the militancy and fierce anger that defined Feeney's denunciation of his Catholic enemies: although many of Feeney's most fervent disciples were women (Clarke first and foremost among them), a significant element of his militancy "was generated [by] the masculine persona that fundamentalists identified as the true hallmark of the Christian *warrior*." Feeney believed, as the male Protestant leaders studied by Bendroth believed, that he was undertaking a crusade within an:

> institution that was predominantly female in membership *and in its watered-down doctrine*. Masculine language and comradery became a common rallying point for those who chose to do battle with the devil in modern Babylon.[27]

If Bendroth was correct in positing this important source for the overdrawn anger and militancy in male fundamentalist leaders' rhetoric (and I believe that she was spot on), then there is a gendered subtext to Feeney's fierce denunciation of his opponents: his liberal enemies were somehow less manly in their witness to the Faith. They had somehow become softened or feminized by lush temptations of an indulgent culture and had to be called to account for their degeneracy.

It was, then, these five characteristics marking the Boston Heresy Case—
its sectarian impulse, its championing of an older paradigm of Catholic identity just then being rejected by the American Catholic community, its use
of American political monikers, its militant tone in denouncing its enemies
and the enemies of the True Church, and its appeal to apocalyptic urgency
in denouncing *fellow* Catholics—that would define the American Catholic
fundamentalist movements that would emerge in the wake of the Feeney episode. These five characteristics also separate Catholic fundamentalism from
mere traditionalism and conservative theology. Far from being a "comic
opera heresy," as Cardinal Cushing's biographer famously termed it, the
Boston Heresy Case gave birth to a militantly reactive rejection of modern
Catholic and American history that is still alive and well—and very much
flourishing in the land of the Pilgrim's pride.[28]

While each of the subsequent Catholic movements that followed the
Boston Heresy Case embodied *some* of its characteristics, they did so in different ways, and in different registers. The chapters that follow will explore
these movements in detail. But we will begin where it all began, near the intersection of Bow and Arrow Streets in Cambridge, Massachusetts.

2

The Comic Opera Heresy at Harvard

The Birth of Catholic Fundamentalism

A. The Clear Voice of an Earlier Catholic Paradigm

On the afternoon of September 6, 1952, the readers of the Catholic Archdiocese of Boston's newspaper, *The Boston Pilot*, were startled to find on the front page of their usually staid weekly—normally chock full of accounts of the archbishop's visitations to local parishes to administer the sacrament of confirmation or to bless May Processions—the text of a stern letter from the Holy Office in Rome. It is a safe bet that, in 1952, the vast majority of faithful Catholics in Boston had only the faintest idea of what, exactly, the Holy Office was or did; but it is also a safe bet that the vast majority knew that receiving a letter from it was probably not a cause for celebration. And the text they read in the *Pilot* was, in fact, a difficult document to understand, even for seasoned Vatican watchers. The text of the letter, emblazoned in English as well as in the original Latin on the front page of the paper, seemed to take away with one hand what it offered with another. But what was as clear as the bad news it seemed to deliver (why else emblazon it on the front page of the *Pilot?*) was its deep ambivalence.[1]

The letter began with the seemingly unequivocal assertion that all believers were bound in faith to assent to the proposition that "no one will be saved who, knowing the church to be divinely established, withholds obedience from the Roman Pontiff, the Vicar of Christ on earth." But it then asserted that a person might be in the church by no more than "implicit desire" (an interpretation of the phrase that had achieved almost universal acceptance among Catholic theologians by the mid-twentieth century). But that doctrinal interpretation—however unremarkable among seminary professors in the United States—receded to the deep background when the letter moved on to an angry denunciation of the disobedience of a group of self-proclaimed "orthodox Catholics"—then in Cambridge, Massachusetts— a group which taught that anyone who stood outside communion with the bishop of Rome (i.e., all non-Catholics, Protestant Christians as well non-Christians) risked facing eternal damnation when they died. Whatever ambivalence the text seemed to exhibit, that letter sought to end, four years after the furor in Harvard Square began, one of the most ironic as well as one of the most revealing episodes in twentieth-century Catholicism. But the longer-term effects of the letter from the Holy Office also marked and defined what would be an ongoing impulse within American Catholicism that has continued to thrive into the twenty-first century.[2]

The first appearance of that impulse within American Catholicism—usually referred to by historians as the "Boston Heresy Case"—still excites debate among historians and scholars studying the post-World War II American Catholic experience. Clearly, as a number of very smart scholars have pointed out, the case accompanied the social move of a largely immigrant group leaving their areas of first settlement into the verdant pastures of suburbia. And that sociological move offered a new identity for the Catholic faithful, who could no longer stand on their front porches and look down the block onto the front porches of fellow believers, all under the shadow of their parish church. And in a certain sense, the experience of that religious pluralism—bringing first-hand interaction with good and generous non-Catholic neighbors—was part and parcel of the geographical move itself, an experience well described by Gibson Winter as the "suburban captivity of the churches." The once-high walls of the Catholic ghetto were being dismantled because of the GI Bill (allowing hundreds of thousands of Catholic ex-GIs to attend college on the government's nickel), as well as the postwar economic boom that helped working-class Catholics to ascend into the middle class. The Boston Heresy Case unfolded just as that move was beginning on a very large scale. Clearly, those two historical events *had* to be related in some way.[3]

Another darker and more apocalyptic—and perhaps even prophetic—version of the interpretation above presents Feeney as more prescient than his contemporaries about the downside of Catholic arrival into the verdant pastures of suburban affluence. In this version of the story, Feeney himself—although undoubtedly sharp-elbowed, resentful, and most probably paranoid—was nonetheless the prophet without honor who correctly predicted what has happened *within* the American Catholic community as he viewed the scene from the high battlements of a Catholic fortress undergoing collapse. The accommodationist gestures made by US Catholics as they moved into the broad mainstream of American middle-class culture—a move that began in earnest after World War II as a result of many factors, not least of which was the GI Bill—held distinctive dangers that were ignored (or, at least, underappreciated) in the giddy embrace of adaptation and affluence. As scholars like Will Herberg, R. Laurence Moore, Roger Finke, and Rodney Stark have convincingly argued, standing apart from the bourgeoisie middle-class mainstream held certain benefits, as well as drawbacks. But from a historical point of view, those high-tension religious groups which have refused to fully embrace the broad mainstream view of pluralism as beneficial without remainder have endured longer, and fared somewhat better over the long haul, than those groups which have opted for a low-tension relationship with US public culture. Yes, Feeney appeared to be saying at the opening of a new era, there would be definite economic, social, and educational benefits from such an embrace of middle-class affluence and values, but at what cost? And Feeney's fears of a divided Catholic community, at least viewed from the twenty-first century, have more or less come to pass, even if the cultural embrace that brought US Catholics into a first-hand experience of religious pluralism was both inevitable and unavoidable.[4]

Likewise, the Feeney episode appears to offer a classic example of the insider–outsider tension studied by one of the founders of the discipline of sociology, Émile Durkheim. Feeney, himself the child of Irish immigrants (and therefore by definition an outsider in the Yankee Boston of the 1920s and 1930s) loudly denouncing all those Brahmins across the street in Harvard Yard made perfect sense from the point of view of Durkheimian social theory. For Feeney, Harvard College itself—the jewel in the crown of patrician Boston—became the special object of his wrath, especially after increasing numbers of Catholic men and women started attending "that godless place." Fair Harvard, moreover, was presided over by the great-great-grandson of one of the original Puritan settlers, James Conant, whom Feeney regularly referred to as a brute and "thirty-third degree Mason" (although it was never clear that Conant had ever actually belonged to the Freemasons). For Feeney, that latter detail was very much of second-order importance: how could the children of Irish immigrants entrust their children to the Church's ancient enemies? From Feeney's point of view, Catholic students (us) attending Harvard (them) was not an educational opportunity: it was rather an "unclean mixing" that portended grave consequences for the Catholic community. Being inside Holy Mother Church—an image that Freudian scholars would undoubtedly go to town with—had to be insulated against the pollution of mixing with the outside world. And as Durkheim had reminded his readers, deviance (outsider-hood) was not a quality inherent in any group or cause; it was, rather, *invented* by one group or person to show where the line existed between the safe inside and the extremely dangerous outside. Thus Feeney's constant appeal to the ancient phrase of St. Cyprian—*extra ecclesiam nulla salus* ("outside the church there is no salvation")—to demarcate the safe inside (Holy Mother Church) from the damned outside (everyone else) was a way of having his cake and eating it too: far from being the unwashed *arrivistes*, it was the devout attendees of the St. Benedict's Center who were actually God's chosen, not those affluent sons of the Brahmins across the street. In this reading, if Durkheim had not existed, Feeney would have had to invent him.[5]

All of these readings of the Feeney episode are smart, and they uncover important impulses that undoubtedly defined the Boston Heresy Case. And this study will use all of these in examining the complex (and sometimes deeply buried) impulses that lent energy—sometimes demonic energy—to the Feeney Episode that unfolded from 1945 well into the 1950s. But the fundamental theory that will guide the application of those other interpretive strategies (like those previously discussed) in understanding the birth of Catholic fundamentalism at the St. Benedict's Center will be based on Thomas Kuhn's famous theory of "paradigm revolutions" in his classic work, *The Structure of Scientific Revolutions*. That work, generally regarded as a landmark study in the history of science, took on one of the most widespread assumptions regarding the progress of science. Indeed, Kuhn strenuously argued that science actually didn't progress at all. Kuhn argued that scientists had been misled in fundamental ways about how science explained the functioning of the physical universe. Basic to Kuhn's argument was his belief that the older model of science he had learned as a graduate student had posited a cumulative process in which the great discoveries in science stood on the shoulders of their scientific predecessors in advancing knowledge. For example, that older model presumed that Galileo had built on and extended the insights of ancients like Aristotle in exploring what made falling bodies fall, while Isaac Newton in turn built on Galileo's insights in explaining gravitational forces. The progress of science advanced by this older model extended backward to the very beginnings of Western speculation about the physical universe in ancient Greece, and all the way forward to contemporary explorations into the gravitational forces affecting superconductors. This "grand march of science" approach thus posited an unbroken masternarrative that stretched over centuries and a wide variety of cultures. And it took as axiomatic the belief that Aristotle, Galileo, Newton, and the scientists working in laboratories adjacent to Kuhn's office were all engaged in the very same scientific pursuit, seeking answers to the same kinds of questions regarding the physical universe (albeit with ever-more sophisticated instruments), and all contributing to the same scientific project.[6]

But Kuhn argued that in the several decades before the publication of his book historians and philosophers of science had come to have significant doubts about the validity of the grand march of science model. In its place, Kuhn proposed a far more disjunctive and far less cumulative model for explaining how science *actually* worked: this was his first crucial insight. Yes, he allowed, Aristotle, Galileo, and Isaac Newton had all studied falling bodies. And all three had indeed sought to arrive at a theory to explain why such bodies did fall. But they were *not* engaged in the same scientific pursuit, nor was their understanding of the laws governing such bodies in any way cumulative, or even analogous, to each other's speculations. And the crucial theoretical key to understanding Kuhn's quite revolutionary assertion was Kuhn's (now famous) distinction between "normal science" and "paradigm revolutions"—his second insight.[7]

Normal science, in Kuhn's reading of how scientists plied their trade, referred to the day-to-day work of scientists and graduate students exploring questions of how "nature" (a word that Kuhn tended to put in scare quotes) actually operated. Basic to normal science was a shared understanding of the basic laws governing the physical universe. And Kuhn argued that it was normal precisely because it rested on a somewhat arbitrary agreement reached among a majority of scientists in any given discipline (biology, physics, chemistry, etc.) that they could articulate an overarching model of the real world based on their experiments in normal science. And Kuhn called that overarching model that lent intelligibility and coherence to the experiments in normal science the "paradigm." Basic to Kuhn's argument about the foundational nature of the paradigm was his assertion—supported by numerous examples from the history of science—that this paradigm or overarching model *never* claimed the support of all the scientists in a field: there would always be outliers in any scientific discipline who rejected the coherence of the reigning paradigm. This point about outliers seems unimportant; however, it is, in fact, quite crucial for understanding Kuhn's model.[8]

And the reason why this point is crucial is because science could never legitimately claim to offer a *definitive and final* model of the world. And that was because of his third (most crucial) insight: the laws of nature were not a set of rules "out there" waiting to be discovered, like prospectors discovering gold in the ground. Rather, the laws of nature were human-constructed theories advanced by scientists to explain how the real world seemed to operate. From Kuhn's perspective, then, the laws of nature were *not* nature's laws, somehow embedded in reality, already complete and only waiting to be discovered, dusted off, and applied. The laws of nature were, rather, human laws—predictive strategies (based on many previous experiments) that could correctly predict (for the most part, anyway) what would most probably happen in a scientific experiment. The laws of nature, therefore, were *provisional, partial*, and *human-constructed*. But they were—in another now-famous line from his book—"good enough for now." And they were good enough for now because they could reliably explain the thousands of daily experiments of normal science, an endeavor Kuhn termed "fitting nature into the conceptual boxes constructed by human scientists."[9]

But—and this is the crucial "but"—there would always be parts of reality studied in normal science that didn't fit neatly into the conceptual boxes provided by the paradigm, and Kuhn called these exceptions that didn't fit neatly (or often-times, at all) "anomalies." And this constituted Kuhn's fourth insight. Scientific anomalies—outcomes of experiments that did not conform to what the paradigm predicted would happen—happen every day in every laboratory on earth and did not constitute any kind of crisis for the scientists undertaking the experiments. Exceptions to the expected outcomes of scientific experiment were either explained away as being due to faulty equipment, or to inexact measurements, or to the broad array of errors to which all human beings (even scientists) are heir. Equally often, anomalies are initially missed or overlooked entirely because scientists (like all humans) tend to look for what they already expect. It is only later, when a pattern of unexpected outcomes emerges from repeated experiments, that an awareness develops that something has gone wrong, or at least that the outcome of the experiment seems to defy (repeatedly) what the paradigm said *would* happen. But for an anomaly to evoke a genuine crisis of confidence in a paradigm's utility as the guiding model of scientific research, the number of anomalies must become widespread, and must appear to raise questions about the fundamental assumptions on which the paradigm rests. At that point, Kuhn argued, the most respected scientists in the field began to consider that perhaps their reigning paradigm of how the universe functioned didn't actually provide the kind of verifiable predictive map they had thought. "Perhaps the paradigm itself—and not just the experiments of normal science based on it—needed to be rethought."[10]

Kuhn himself admitted that widespread perceptions of fundamental problems with the *entire* paradigm are rare, but they do happen, and they mark turning points in the history of science. The adoption of a new paradigm, however, doesn't happen quickly, or by the unanimous agreement of all the scientists in a given field. Rather paradigm revolutions occur after a long period of intellectual insecurity, when different paradigms are, in a sense, "tried on for size," and the debates that mark that often prolonged and insecure time frame are fierce and sometimes even personal, as much of a scientist's life's work was tied to a particular paradigm now deemed obsolescent or even irrelevant. Kuhn called this fractious time frame between paradigms the "period of crisis" (his fifth insight), and it is precisely here that Feeney comes in.[11]

Read through the lens of Kuhn's theory of paradigm revolutions, Feeney might be helpfully understood as a particularly sharp-elbowed apologist for an older paradigm of Catholic orthodoxy that was unthinkingly accepted by the vast majority of the Catholic faithful for centuries after the Council of Trent in the sixteenth century, but that now seemed under threat during the period of crisis that followed World War II. That paradigm—often labeled "the Church as *societas perfecta*" (after the phrase coined by Cardinal Robert Bellarmine)—was most probably the dominant one carried to the New World by Catholic immigrants from the Old, even if it was largely unarticulated or only partially understood by the faithful, who tended to be more schooled in orthopraxy than orthodoxy in any case. That ecclesial paradigm of the institutional church as the perfect society posited that the Catholic Church was the sole ark of salvation, outside of which was almost-certain damnation. Hammered out in the decades after the Council of Trent—itself gathered to answer the protestant heresies of Luther, Calvin, and other heresiarchs—this perfect society, whose institutional form was the Roman Catholic Church *itself*, had no need of amendment or development because it was perfect from its inception. It was Feeney's fealty to *that* understanding of what the Catholic Church was that shaped the episode now named after him; it also explains his almost pathological repetition of the phrase from Pope Boniface VIII's encyclical *Unam Sanctum* (which to Catholics like Feeney seemed infallibly declared)—that it was "altogether necessary for salvation for every human creature to be subject to the Roman Pontiff."[12]

Finding himself in the period of crisis that always occurs between the final replacement of the older paradigm by the newer—in this case, the replacement of the older (Tridentine) paradigm with the more biblically based paradigm of "People of God," which deemphasized the hierarchical, institutional aspects of Catholicism to advance a more egalitarian (democratic) understanding of Church on pilgrimage—Feeney enunciated a powerful reactive "no" to what he saw as an abandonment of Catholic orthodox teaching. In Feeney's eyes, the forces of modern American life were the engines driving that betrayal, and thus his message was (by design) anti-modern, especially targeting modern liberals within the Catholic community who were leading Catholic lambs astray. And while it is unlikely that Feeney was fully aware at the time of the bridge that the use of the political label "liberal" offered in creating common cause between Catholic theological conservatives and their more politically oriented fellow believers, the utility of that label would be recognized in time by the latter group (who had no interest in being part of Feeney's "comic opera heresy").

And an important component of Feeney's fiery denunciations of traitorous liberals within God's very household was a distinctively gendered take on those quislings, who by implication had been "feminized" by yielding to the blandishments of all-too-comfortable cultural circumstances—circumstances in which the pampered House System of Harvard College, with its maids making beds every morning and white-tied waiters serving High Table to male students in evening clothes, might serve as a prime example. Instead of fighting like hardened and faithful crusaders (the latter term evincing uncomfortable implications of *real* manhood when uttered by Feeney), those feminized liberals were betraying the Church from within. As Margaret Bendroth argued so persuasively in her study of Protestant fundamentalists earlier in the twentieth century, the male leaders of that analogously reactive movement:

> saw their world as dangerously "feminized," [and] sought other-worldliness through assertive masculinity. "The world is a proud, cold, haughty, attractive woman. Just as Salome won the heart of Herod, when the world dances before a soul, the voice of the true preacher sounds fainter and fainter." The world might scoff at righteous zeal, but the true man stood for his faith without compromising an inch.[13]

And as the Feeney episode would testify, not compromising an inch to the blandishments of a hedonistic society was one of the chief distinguishing marks of the true crusader—battle-scarred but unbowed by fighting the Good Fight against a culture more dedicated to the values of Salome than to those of John the Baptist.

But arguably the most tragic aspect of Feeney's crusade against Church Liberals was his seeming lack of awareness that the reactive, sectarian model of church that he crafted to repel the modernist assaults on Holy Mother Church from within was itself a profoundly uncatholic, sectarian construct, recognized as such at the time by the leaders of Feeney's own Jesuit order, and even by the Archbishop of Boston himself. If, indeed, the center was not holding for the older Catholic paradigm of church as perfect society in the United States well before Good Pope John even thought of calling Vatican II—an interpretation given serious historical heft by the recent work of Joseph Chinnici, among others—then the search for a new paradigm was already well underway before the St. Benedict Center was even founded, and the Feeney episode can be helpfully understood as an especially unpleasant but memorable moment in the period of crisis that extended over many decades and which, among other things, elucidated a new form of fundamentalism in the United States. And thereby, as they say, hangs a tale.[14]

B. At the Corner of Bow and Arrow

It all began uneventfully enough in a nondescript building across the street from the much-grander Romanesque façade of St. Paul's, the parish that served Catholics in central Cambridge. St. Paul's impressive early medieval architecture (obviously chosen to contrast with the more sober, red brick Georgian buildings in Harvard Yard) certainly served the sacramental needs of Catholic students at Harvard, but the idea of anything like a "Catholic student center" in the modern sense was the brainchild of a pious Catholic laywoman named Catherine Clarke. In 1940, with several undergraduates (including Avery Dulles, son of John Foster Dulles, soon to be Secretary of State), Clarke approached the Archdiocese of Boston to set up a gathering place for Catholic students attending Harvard and Radcliffe—a seemingly novel idea, or at least one that had never been acted on before. Clarke had her eye on a vacant furniture shop at the corner of Bow and Arrow Streets, the rent being remarkably cheap (something current Cambridge residents would find difficult to believe).[15]

It was clearly an idea whose time had come, for in short order the Center became a lively social scene that included afternoon teas hosted by Mrs. Clarke (surprisingly popular) and courses in ecclesiastical Latin and Catholic literary works like Dante's *Divine Comedy*, often taught by Catholic scholars on the Harvard faculty. Word spread quickly, so that students from around Boston began showing up to hear Catholic luminaries like Dorothy Day and Clare Booth Luce. Among the luminaries invited was Jesuit Leonard Feeney, albeit a luminary in a somewhat more parochial sense. During the late 1930s, Feeney had served as literary editor for *America* magazine (the weekly published by the Jesuits in the United States), an appointment generated in part by Feeney's 1934 "bestseller," *Fish on Fridays*. A loose collection of sketches, poems, and stories, that book would become a staple in Catholic primary and secondary schools and in parish book clubs around the country, making Feeney something of a minor literary celebrity among the faithful. By 1940, Feeney was elected president of the Catholic Poetry Society, and was transferred from *America* in New York City to the order's seminary in suburban Boston, Weston College, where he was to teach homiletics to the Jesuit priests in training. The new appointment was both a recognition by his order of Feeney's talent with words, and also an attempt to help him to dry out in an environment decidedly different from midtown Manhattan: in Jesuit seminaries of the time, alcohol was only provided to mark first class feasts in the Church's liturgical calendar, and it was most assuredly not a regular evening event.[16]

But Feeney was less than thrilled by his work as a seminary professor in a leafy suburb of Boston, far from the pulse of New York, and occasional radio interviews on *The Catholic Hour* failed to make up the difference. Thus, he found the thriving social scene at the St. Benedict Center (a short thirty-minute drive from Weston College) a welcome distraction: he started attending lectures and social events regularly, but also volunteered his time and energy counseling students on their spiritual lives. Indeed, Feeney himself gradually emerged as one of the attractions drawing students to the Center, so that, by 1945, Clarke formally asked that Feeney be assigned to the Center full-time. Thanks to crucial support of Monsignor John Wright (himself a frequent visitor to the Center and a rising star in the archdiocesan firmament of "those soon to be bishops"), Feeney was so assigned. In one sense unremarkable, Clarke's request also marked a revolutionary turn in Harvard's then-three-centuries-old religious history: Harvard now had (even if only unofficially) a Catholic chaplain.

When Dulles returned to Harvard from the Navy just a year later, he reported that St. Benedict's was the place to be on Thursday nights in Cambridge: that was the night when Feeney held several hundred people jammed into the cramped space spellbound. As Dulles would later recall, at those performances, Feeney "would tell anecdotes, recite poems, and in various ways seek to gain the attention and good will of all his hearers." And in winning them over, Feeney would offer side-splitting parodies of the famous:

> He would deliver with mock solemnity imaginary speeches such as [Governor] Al Smith on the fallacies in Descartes' philosophy ("putting Descartes before the horse"), Fulton Sheen on the merits of Coca Cola ("Ho, everyone that thirsteth for the pause that refresheth"), Katherine Hepburn reporting a championship prizefight, and Eleanor Roosevelt broadcasting the events of Good Friday.[17]

As Dulles remembered it, Feeney would only launch into the main part of his Thursday evening presentations when "he had satisfied himself that every member of the audience was disposed to understand and accept his message." But the main part of his Thursday evening talks was a meaty intellectual affair—on the integration of nature and grace, on the sacrifice of reason in the act of faith, on the primary role of the senses and the imagination in understanding the sacramental life. The light-heartedness that had defined the introductory part of his presentations was soon replaced with serious intellectual forays into the dense forest of neo-scholastic theology, forays that were not for the faint of heart. Thus, to call the Thursday talks "popular" is both correct and not quite true: yes, they were open to all comers; but they also contained dense theological expositions of often-complex doctrinal points. That is why it is perhaps quite counter-intuitive that the audiences grew week by week: every seat would be filled, and groups of listeners could be seen gathered around the open doors and at the window to catch whatever fragments they could.[18]

And part and parcel of the counter-intuitive popularity of the Thursday talks was the fact that the words and phrases that defined the content of Feeney's lectures were marked by a form of neo-scholasticism that (both ironically and imperceptibly) was passing into obsolescence among Catholic theologians just as Feeney was introducing it to his young audience. The theological superstructure in which Feeney himself had been schooled three decades earlier was "rational" (superficially, at least), and was based on an older classicist model of god-talk in which truth was primarily propositional and objective. Neo-scholasticism prided itself on the fact that the mysteries of Christianity were banished to the margins of theological study; indeed, mystery was replaced by minutely defined concepts that did not evolve or develop; instead, they were true all the time, for everyone, everywhere. And the concepts:

> came embedded in formulae ("imperfect contrition") and distinctions: mortal sin and venial sin, matter of sin and intention of sin, occasion of sin ... To know the terms was to know the thing, to solve the problem. So we learned, and used, a vast vocabulary.[19]

Well before the fracas at Bow and Arrow became the subject of front-page newspaper stories, Feeney was presenting a paradigm of Catholic theology as normative that was already dated and was being supplanted by newer understandings of the Catholic theological tradition. The *Nouvelle theologie*—a broad Catholic theological movement that had emerged in France in the 1920s, but that came into its own in the 1940s and 1950s—sought to return to the sources of western theology in the Fathers of the Church (writing from the fourth to the eighth centuries); that is, well before the nineteenth-century neo-scholasticism that was presented by Feeney as a timeless statement of Catholic belief. Scholars of the stature of Josef Fuchs (on the Jesuits' theological faculty at the Gregorian University in Rome) and Bernard Haring at the Redemptorist-sponsored Roman seminary—both influenced by the historical studies produced by the *Nouvelle theologie*—had already come to the conclusion that the static, propositional theology of the kind being presented by Feeney to his packed audiences in Cambridge produced too many anomalies to be a useful paradigm for a working Catholic theological system, and were experimenting with other models during what was already perceived (in Europe, at least) as a "period of crisis" for twentieth-century Catholic theology. All of this, quite poignantly if disastrously, seems to have been invisible to Feeney. For Feeney, Catholic Christianity was timeless and eternally true only because he seemed totally unaware of the intellectual onslaughts on the older paradigm of the Church as a *societas perfecta* being undertaken by the giants of Catholic theology, even as he was giving the St. Benedict Center the reputation of being the place to be on Thursday night in Cambridge.[20]

But Feeney himself did not perceive those presentations of his timeless theology to Thursday night crowds as the true heart of his mission at the Center. Rather, the heart of that mission was focused on a much smaller, closer coterie of students, on what Dulles termed his "inner group of disciples" (a phrase that was either inspiring or chilling, depending on one's point of view). From Feeney's standpoint, as gratifying as the huge Thursday night crowds were, his main business was in shaping a group of followers who "made the Center their principal occupation in life—those for whom it was a kind of family, school and parish all rolled into one." For this group, Feeney would make himself available every afternoon, hearing confessions and offering spiritual direction. And it was with *that* group that he would "pile into Catherine Clarke's decrepit sedan so that conversations could continue over hamburgers in a restaurant." And as Dulles added at the end of his recollection of those dinners, "conversation was never known to lag."[21]

And Feeney's words fell on fallow ground: it was estimated that at least two hundred attendees at the St. Benedict Center converted to Catholicism, and dozens entered the seminary or convent, in the process withdrawing from Harvard and Radcliffe to pursue lives in religion in the safer context of Catholic institutions. This, in itself, became something of a cause for concern across the street at the meetings of the Harvard Corporation. Once the educational pinnacle of Yankee arrival, Harvard College was unaccustomed to being the halfway house to other academic institutions—institutions it did not consider to be its intellectual peers. But those early worries—no larger than a man's hand on the horizon in 1946—would come to be dramatically overshadowed by other concerns, concerns focused on a new and growing polemical edge in Feeney's public and private utterances that would become sharper and more bitter by the end of the 1940s. Even Dulles himself, one of Feeney's most devoted disciples and headed into the Jesuit order in the summer of 1946, perceived something new and darker in Feeney's message by the time he left Cambridge:

> I did notice, toward the end of my stay, that Leonard Feeney was becoming increasingly polemical. His attacks on materialism, skepticism, and agnosticism became sharper and more personal. He used bitter invective against Hume and Kant, Marx and Freud. At times, he denounced the "liberal Catholics" who had failed to support Generalissimo Franco. Even Jacques Maritain was in his eyes infected by the poison of liberal culture. Father Feeney's attitude toward the Jews was ambivalent. He felt that they could not achieve their true vocation except in Christ.[22]

Dulles—who was never accused of being a liberal at any point in his long life—sought to offer possible reasons for Feeney's darker, more condemnatory turn in his memorial essay published on Feeney's death in 1978: perhaps, Dulles averred, it was the result of rebuffs Feeney experienced from the non-Catholic institutions around him (and from one non-Catholic institution in particular); perhaps he was led into doctrinal exaggerations by his own mercurial poetic temperament or as the result of his exhaustion from meeting so many students for so many hours every day at the St. Benedict Center. Or—quite telling and insightfully for one so devoted to the Center's project—Dulles observed that perhaps Feeney "may have been intoxicated by the dramatic successes of the Center, and [from being] too much isolated from opinions coming from outside his own narrow circle." Dulles, who knew the man well, was undoubtedly correct in positing all of these factors as influences shaping the new tone emanating from the corner of Bow and Streets.[23]

But there were larger, more culture-wide factors that also undoubtedly helped shape Feeney's new tone and message—factors arguably far more important in decoding the events that would lead to the comic opera heresy. As Robert Colopy, himself one of the inner corps of disciples, would later recall, "after the war everything was chaos, and all the boys were returning to college. But the secular teachings were equally confusing." Academic institutions were very much aware of the chaos and confusion that greeted its new crop of more mature students returning to their quads, chastened by battle and the rigors of war. Robert Hutchins, a major educational figure at the University of Chicago, famously presented his Great Books program as a way of organizing a more coherent program focused on the western intellectual tradition. But Harvard sounded a more uncertain trumpet in response to the educational chaos that its students encountered in its Yard: in 1946, Harvard College inaugurated its much-touted program in General Education to fill in for a core curriculum it had banished several decades previously. But the study of religion appeared nowhere in that widely publicized report, a somewhat shocking omission in an institution that had been founded precisely to train Protestant ministers. Indeed, as historian Mark Silk observed, even "the Bible could not secure a place in [Harvard's] general education curriculum, even as great literature." Did the resolutely secular turn at the institution across the street from the Center send many young perplexed and anxious people to Feeney seeking a deeper kind of education that included spiritual and religious resources not available in Harvard Yard?

Undoubtedly. And were Feeney's deep suspicions about the dead end toward which the American Protestant culture appeared to be heading confirmed, making him even more resolute that Catholicism not make the same disastrous choices? Equally undoubtedly.[24]

And the new terrors unleashed by the postwar nuclear age also played a part in the Feeney episode: as Clarke herself observed:

we were never the same after the dropping of the bomb. It seemed to have shocked us awake. It was almost as if we saw the life around us for the first time. The scales fell from our eyes, and we beheld clearly as actualities many things which we had dreaded might one day be the outcome of our exclusively humanitarian society. We waited and we listened, but no strong voice arose above the noise of the world.[25]

The tone of Feeney's increasingly biting and urgent commentaries on the dire state of American culture after 1945 does indeed sound like it proceeded from one who had been shocked awake to the situation of a civilization perched precariously on the precipice of disaster. Like those mainline white Protestants who suddenly discovered in 1919—the year of the Great Reversal—that they were now aliens in their own culture, the message coming out of the St. Benedict Center after Hiroshima seemed like an apocalyptic warning pronounced by strangers in a strange land, pilgrims in the alien world of postwar American culture who could see more clearly than the native population the precipice toward which western culture seemed to be hurtling. And just like those evangelicals who would quickly form the nucleus of what would become Protestant fundamentalism, Feeney and his disciples could not help but believe that the silence that greeted the promise of such a disaster testified to the fact that those silent leaders had lost their faith as well as their minds. Did Feeney himself, then, believe that he was called to be that strong voice speaking above the "noise of the world"? Again, undoubtedly.

Add to that mix the lingering ethnic resentment of an Irish Catholic in Boston—where "No Irish Need Apply" signs still appeared outside shopfronts within living memory—and one can safely assert that many social, cultural, and religious factors combined to adversely affect a priest whom even one of his most devoted followers described as possessing a "mercurial poetic temperament." In a sense, all of those factors are easily discernable in the story that would unfold. What is more difficult to explain, or at least more counter-intuitive in the narrative, is why Feeney and his disciples turned so resolutely against the leaders of their own church, a church they professed to love more than others, as the real villains in the story. Harvard and James Conant as *bêtes noires*? Easily accountable. The horrific nuclear threat after 1945? Ditto. The desire for a bigger platform than a teacher of homiletics in a seminary for a former Manhattan celebrity? Obvious. Archbishop Richard Cushing and Feeney's own Jesuit superior as part of the "synagogue of Satan"? *That* demands a more complex explanation. And it is precisely here that appeal to Thomas Kuhn's theory of paradigm revolutions offers some important insights into the Feeney affair.

In a sense, the beleaguered tone of being under attack was present from Feeney's first appearance at the St. Benedict Center. In the very first issue of *From the Housetops*—the St. Benedict Center's journal published sporadi-cally over a number of years—Dulles had written that "every culture which is not Catholic is in some degree anti-Catholic . . . The belief that one can with impunity consort constantly with heretics and atheists, and casually exchange ideas with them, is a dangerous product of modern liberalism." Thus, from the outset, the St. Benedict Center had drawn something like a line in the sand about the danger of "consorting constantly with heretics and atheists." That kind of rhetoric was still within the bounds of accept-able Catholic orthodoxy regarding religious pluralism (although admit-tedly at its boundaries in postwar Catholicism, which had already begun to process a different understanding of religious pluralism). But by the end of 1947, Feeney's rhetoric—and that of his disciples—became much harsher and more judgmental and began to worry even friends of the St. Benedict Center, like Dulles himself. Increasingly Feeney's Thursday night lectures returned week after week to what he repeatedly called "the teaching of twenty-nine Doctors of the Church": that it was "wholly necessary for sal-vation for every human creature to be subject to the Roman Pontiff." The laughter and good humor that had marked his earlier Thursday night talks soon disappeared, as Feeney increasingly focused his talks both on those without (like Conant) as well as those within (like Archbishop Cushing) who appeared to be deliberately making light of church doctrine. Indeed, Cushing himself, as well as Auxiliary Bishop Wright (who, as previously mentioned, had personally effected Feeney's appointment to the St. Benedict Center) and even fellow Jesuit William Kelleher (the president of neighboring Boston College) increasingly emerged as the special objects of Feeney's wrath.[26]

The previous archbishop of Boston, William O'Connell, would have enjoyed Feeney's edgy comments about both Harvard and Catholic "appeasers." Indeed, O'Connell was in favor of forbidding sacramental absolution to Catholic mothers who placed the education of their children in the hands of "infidels and heretics." He had frowned on Catholic students attending secular schools like Harvard, and he loved to show up in full regalia at events like the Harvard Commencement, demanding his due as a prince of the church, and requiring a place of honor on the dais from discomfited Yankees. But Cushing had little time for such doings that highlighted the outsider image of the church. Cushing possessed both the shrewdness and the warmth of a politician from South Boston, where he was born and raised. Further, he seems to have been particularly influenced by the happy marriage of his sister to a Jewish man. The loudly proclaimed otherness of his predecessor (and the antics that accompanied it) was not for him. For Cushing, that older model of the Catholic fortress had already died, and he wanted nothing of it.[27]

On February 16, 1948, Cushing decided to cut short what he perceived to be an emerging public relations storm and called for an end to religious feuding in a much-publicized speech. Americans, he announced, could no longer afford the luxury of "fighting one another over doctrines concerning the next world, though we must not compromise on these." Rather, he called on all Americans of good will (regardless of their religious affiliation) to "unite their forces to save what is worth saving in this world." Feeney and his disciples were, of course, appalled by Cushing's speech, and immediately denounced what they took to be the publicly announced moral compromise from their own ordinary. Further, just a month later, in March 1948, Cushing's auxiliary bishop, Wright, gave an even more publicized speech before Harvard's (famously progressive) Liberal Union, to state the Catholic case against universal military training. Then, on Monday evening of April 5, 1948, Cushing came to dine at "High Table" at the invitation of Elliott Perkins, the master of Lowell House.[28]

Perkins had his own reasons for inviting the Archbishop of Boston to the quintessentially Oxbridge ritual of High Table: Temple Morgan (of the powerful Yankee Morgan clan) had resided at Lowell House before his conversion and baptism by Feeney, and subsequent withdrawal from Harvard College to matriculate as a student at the St. Benedict Center. The invitation to a Catholic archbishop (surely something unusual at Unitarian Harvard) was a strategic move to get Cushing involved in an increasingly messy matter.

When Perkins overheard Cushing questioning the students sitting on either side of him (both Catholics) about the St. Benedict Center, he apologized for their bringing up dirty linen at a festive occasion (although bringing Cushing on board regarding the increasingly messy doings going on at the St. Benedict Center was undoubtedly the very reason for Perkins inviting him in the first place). It was, therefore, no surprise that the very next day, Harvard Yard buzzed about the unusual visitor to the Lowell House High Table, while the St. Benedict Center sent a delegation to the archbishop's residence in Brighton, partly in response to one of the rumors buzzing in Cambridge that the St. Benedict Center was about to be closed. Once there, Cushing himself confirmed the story of his presence and questioning at the previous night's dinner, and told the delegation to meet with his auxiliary, Wright, who much more of a scholar than Cushing but nonetheless unsympathetic to both the tenor and content of Feeney's emerging theology.

By early August, when both Cushing and Wright boarded a ship to Rome to promote the beatification of Pope Pius X, things appear to have developed off stage, like a good play by Aristophanes: on August 25, the Jesuit Provincial of New England, John McEleney, S.J., sent a letter to Feeney, ordering him to leave the St. Benedict Center and report to the College of the Holy Cross (thirty-five miles west in Worcester, Massachusetts) by September 8. Both Feeney and his flock at the St. Benedict Center strongly protested this order both in missives and by picketing Cushing's residence across the river from Cambridge in Brighton, all to no avail. The stage thus set—in retrospect, anyway—reads like a Hollywood grade-B movie: bags packed and car waiting at intersection of Bow and Arrow, Feeney held a final (and, as it would turn out, eventful) meeting with his disciples. "The competing claims of Truth and Obedience were hung in the balance." But quite ironically, Feeney, the self-proclaimed defender of *real* Catholic teaching, opted for what was the quintessentially "protestant" position taken by Martin Luther at the Diet of Worms in 1521: obedience to legitimate religious superiors would have to be sacrificed to the claims of Truth. And while Feeney himself never spoke exactly the same words, his decision to disobey his provincial (in the Jesuit world the very serious sin of disobedience) mirrored that of Luther himself, who had refused to submit to a papal directive to obediently return to his Augustinian monastery and stop teaching heterodox doctrine. Luther is reported to have responded: "Here I stand. My mind is held captive by the Word of God: I cannot do otherwise."[29]

In the meantime, Feeney's teaching had spread to the Jesuit-run Boston College: David Walsh and Fakhri Maluf, devout followers of Feeney's teaching philosophy there, were called before the college president to be questioned about statements they had made regarding Feeney's famous position on salvation. Maluf, something of a classroom bully, had gained the reputation of failing students who disagreed with his reading of the philosophy of St. Thomas Aquinas on this topic. Kelleher, Boston College's Jesuit president, ordered Maluf to include other readings of Aquinas that offered a different understanding of those outside the church, which Maluf refused to do. He therewith accused Kelleher himself, as well as the Jesuits at Boston College generally, of teaching heresy, and he was promptly dismissed from the faculty. In response to these outrages against Catholics propounding orthodox doctrine, Feeney and his disciples wrote to the Pope, complaining that the possibility of salvation outside the church—"an insidious heresy" in his estimation—was receiving support both by the leaders of the archdiocese and by the Jesuits at Boston College. Just two weeks after that they sent a letter to the superior general of the Jesuits in Rome, similarly accusing the Jesuits of Boston College of heresy. But well before the reception of that second letter, Jesuit leaders in Rome had already decided to act (undoubtedly from pressure exerted by both Cushing and the local Jesuit provincial, McEleney): Vincent McCormick, an American Jesuit who served as assistant to the Jesuit's general superior, had already been dispatched from Rome to confront Feeney for his disobedience. On April Fools' Day (no less), McCormick met with Feeney at Boston College (not the St. Benedict Center), where McCormick challenged Feeney on what (from the Society of Jesus's point of view) amounted to contumacious disobedience, Feeney having just recently refused to move from the St. Benedict Center a second time. Feeney held firm and refused to leave his disciples at the St. Benedict Center without its shepherd.[30]

At the very same time—and in response to Maluf's charge of heresy—the Boston College theology faculty circulated a four-page position statement on salvation outside the church written by a respected Jesuit theologian, Philip Donnelly, then teaching at the same seminary in Weston to which Feeney had originally been assigned when he first arrived in Boston. Donnelly, who knew the Catholic theological tradition considerably better than Feeney, laid out the mainstream Catholic position on the topic, arguing that the church had not understood the phrase *extra ecclesiam nulla salus* to mean that "salvation is impossible for anyone who does not believe explicitly in the

Catholic Church." However orthodox such an interpretation may have been in the past, the church now had a somewhat more nuanced understanding of that ancient and revered phrase, especially in light of the religious pluralism in cultures like that of the United States. Whatever Boniface VIII's intention in 1302, the church's understanding of that phrase had evolved over the course of the centuries. And while Donnelly himself never referred in his position paper to John Henry Newman, the famous nineteenth-century convert who wrote *An Essay on the Development of Christian Doctrine*, the tenor of his argument agreed perfectly with Newman's most famous observation in the *Essay*: "To live is to change, and to have lived long is to have changed often."[31]

What was now being called "The Boston Heresy Case" broke in the newspapers during Holy Week, 1949, and the firings made front page news well outside of Boston: the *New York Times* began a series on the theological debate (surely a singular turn for so resolutely secular a New York cultural icon), and *Time*, *Life*, and *Newsweek* all offered stories. The question of the salvation of non-Catholics was soon being debated in Boston bars and at newsstands by customers eager to hear what others were thinking. But on Easter Monday (the day after churches were packed with Catholics making their "Easter Duty"), Archbishop Cushing formally silenced Feeney and removed his faculties (his permission to preach, say mass, and hear confessions). Further, the archbishop announced that Catholics attending the St. Benedict Center were to be denied the right to receive communion or go to confession (arguably the most famous imposition of interdict ever applied in the United States). "Weighty points of dogma," Cushing wrote, "are not debated in headlines nor made the occasion of recrimination and inordinate attack on constituted authority." On that very same day, Feeney also received word that formal (canonical) proceedings were underway to dismiss him from the Society of Jesus—a complex and rare procedure for dismissing solemnly professed Jesuits who were deemed the cause of public scandal or heterodox teaching.[32]

And then, on April 21, the Confraternity of Christian Doctrine (a select group of Catholic scholars and prelates appointed by the bishops of the United States) issued a new official *Catechism of the Catholic Church* for US Catholics, which supported the position of both Archbishop Cushing and the Jesuits of Boston College on the sticky issue of salvation outside the church. The publication of the 426-page catechism was certainly not issued in any kind of direct response to the Feeney dust-up, being the result of twelve years of research and debate by the members of the Confraternity to update the much older *Baltimore Catechism*. But its publication was certainly timely, and not in a good way for Feeney and his disciples.[33]

But the new *Catechism* itself might be read as mirroring the ambivalence of a church now in what Kuhn would have called a "period of crisis," caught between an older paradigm and a newer one not yet completely elucidated. This new edition of the older catechism announced that the "basic doctrine is unchanged, but the *tempo of the times is mirrored in added text and new shifts in emphasis.*" The new document certainly reiterated the older teaching of the *Baltimore Catechism* (1885), which had stated that "he who knows the church to be the true church and remains outside of it cannot be saved. This applied to men [*sic*] of bad faith who sin against the truth; it does not apply to men of good faith that belong to the soul of the church." And it reaffirmed the older Catechism's definition of the soul of the church as "all who possess God's grace even if they are not actual members [of the Catholic Church]." Slipped in among its reiteration of a position that had become normative by the twentieth century among Catholic theologians—that anyone who followed their conscience belonged mystically to the "soul of the church," whether they were Catholics, or even Christians, or not—it had also announced that non-Catholics (and non-Christians) who followed their consciences to the best of their ability were people of good faith. This somewhat more "nuanced" reading of the Church's official doctrine (what it described as a "new shift in emphasis") was thus laid at the door of the tempo of the times. But it is important to note that this new shift in emphasis in explaining the doctrine went somewhat further than previous pronouncements, opening the door to salvation just a crack wider—a door which would be flung wide open several decades later by the Second Vatican Council.[34]

Feeney's dismissal from the Jesuit order came on October 28, a process that had been long, involved, and somewhat expected, despite Feeney's regular expressions of shock and outrage at the result. By that date, Feeney's followers—organized into the "Slaves of the Immaculate Heart of Mary"—were (from the point of view of Catholic Church authorities, anyway) considered outside the church themselves, an anomalous situation when considered from the view of Feeney's ferocious insistence on salvation itself being dependent on church membership. But Feeney's expulsion from the order also seems to have unleashed a desire for more public exposure for his theological views, especially given the canonical prohibition forbidding him to preach or give public lectures as a priest. The result led (arguably) to the most disturbing manifestations of the Boston Heresy Case: every Sunday, rain or shine, for forty-five consecutive Sundays after his expulsion from the Jesuits, Feeney appeared on the Charles Street Mall of the Boston Common, disrupting the normally quiet and peaceful Sunday traffic with harangues and *ad hominem* attacks on Jews, Protestants, and the Catholic leaders of the Boston archdiocese that quickly attracted large crowds, consisting mostly of hecklers and mocking auditors who egged on the priest and his disciples. The appearances invariably began with a procession of seventy-two stern, black-suited young people who marched silently onto the Common; once in place, several would give:

> wild and defamatory speeches. Finally their leader [Feeney] speaks, pouring out a stream of invective particularly aimed at Roman Catholic Archbishop Cushing of Boston, but also at Protestants, Jews, and the "filthy adulterous" people who came to the Common to heckle him.[35]

Counter-intuitively, that corps of seventy-two "witnesses" on the Boston Common on Sunday afternoons was made up of young women as well as young men—despite the hyper-masculine tone of Feeney's vituperative rhetoric—women who themselves addressed the crowd of "filthy, adulterous" people gathered to heckle them. Or perhaps it was less counter-intuitive than at first appeared. Among that corps was Evelyn Uberti, a sometime student at both Radcliffe and Emmanuel Colleges, but finally a student enrolled in the St. Benedict Center. But Ms. Uberti was a disciple of Feeney's who seemed to appear in a wide spectrum of venues other than educational institutions, witnessing to her teacher's message of salvation. Among the more surprising of those venues was not only the Boston Common, but also the Brighton District Court. In a report to Monsignor Walter Furlong, the Chancellor of the Boston Archdiocese, entitled "Memoranda on Extra-Curricular Activities of the Feeney Group," Isabel Currier reported that, along with Clarke of the St. Benedict Center, Maluf of Boston College, and Morgan and William Smith (both formerly of Harvard College), Uberti and Ellen Beneway were also present in the Brighton District Court for a hearing on December 10, 1952.[36]

That appearance was occasioned by a physical assault on the father of Uberti, who had presented a formal legal complaint against both of her parents in that district court. Mr. and Mrs. Uberti had grown increasingly concerned when Evelyn transferred from Radcliffe to Emmanuel College, a women's college in Boston's Fenway, because of the "godless Atmosphere" she had found at Radcliffe. But two days before her graduation from Emmanuel, Evelyn withdrew from Emanuel as well, refusing to take her degree. Evelyn, it turned out—deeply influenced by the teaching of Feeney while at Radcliffe—had found Emmanuel College (run by the Sisters of Notre Dame, a religious order of nuns famed for the quality of the Catholic schools they ran) to be as godless Radcliffe:

> I transferred to Emmanuel in order to get certitude and the Faith [sic]. Instead I found secularism, liberalism, and confusion . . . I've known for some time that Emmanuel was teaching heresy, but it wasn't until recently that I realized that if I accepted my degree I would be supporting their teachings.[37]

The Uberti's efforts to reclaim their daughter finally inspired a member of Feeney's seventy-two witnesses—Hugh MacIsaac—to physically assault Evelyn's father for harassing her into compliance with false teaching and urging her to stay and graduate from Emmanuel. Currier, writing up an account of that December court appearance for Monsignor Furlong, reported that "I sat with Mrs. Uberti, who suffered acutely from her daughter making a great business of presenting a document of complaints against her parents." McIsaac had appealed that assault charge; but on that particular December day in court, Chief Justice John Higgins refused to accept that appeal, and ordered MacIsaac to reappear on December 23 to face those very same assault charges. (He was found guilty). Evelyn, along with several other young women who had begun their college careers at Radcliffe, ended up at the St. Benedict Center, some of whom subsequently entered the Slaves of the Immaculate Heart of Mary.[38]

The disturbing reminiscences left by people present at those Sunday afternoon encounters, as well as witnesses to court cases brought by Feeney's young disciples against their parents, have led some scholars of the American Catholic past to dismiss Feeney as simply an unbalanced bigot, a megalomaniac, or an antisemitic simpleton. Thus Currier, present on a succession of Sundays on the Boston Common, regularly narrated a succession of unsettling interactions of Feeney and his seventy-two disciples, with crowds making fun of both Feeney and his followers. In response to one such onslaughts, Feeney and his followers gave as good as they got:

Shut up you Jew! And you evil filthy, adulterous Protestants can go back and tell your ministers what I say. The Catholic Archbishop of Boston has his stooges here. God help a so-called Archbishop who associates with Protestants and Jews as he does![39]

Feeney was very much still at it several years later, when *Time* magazine reported on his continued appearances on the Boston Common, surrounded by his disciples, many of whom would soon become Slaves of the Immaculate Heart of Mary. And the magazine opined that the isolation of Feeney and his followers had seemingly caused their cult to grow narrower—and angrier—at the world of unbelievers outside. The sheer vituperation of the exchanges on the Common was—then and now—shocking, and (if anything) made Feeney and his disciples appear to be cartoon-like fanatics, easily dismissed as theological voices to be taken seriously: in recounting one such Sunday afternoon encounter, Feeney reportedly took to the platform provided for him by two of his burly disciples to announce that "Archbishop Cushing is a heretic!" A heckler in the crowd—such heckling at Feeney having become something of a Sunday afternoon sport in Boston—stopped Feeney mid-sentence, to which Feeney responded:

"I came here to preach the love of the Blessed Virgin Mary, and I found nothing but filthy adulterous faces, who attacked her." He pointed to a newspaperman making notes in the crowd. One of the girl slaves [*sic*] turned, scowling, and sprinkled some holy water in the reporter's direction. "I preach hatred of those who hate Jesus," Father Feeney continued. "Am I a hate-priest when I want to be a child of Mary? Mother of God, I ask you to include those who hate me among your enemies."[40]

Feeney's growing antisemitic and anti-Protestant rants on the Boston Common only deepened his rift with the Archbishop of Boston, who at the Second Vatican Council would famously speak very forcefully in favor of changing church reaching that held the Jews responsible for the crucifixion of Jesus, perhaps most famously expressed in the Solemn Prayers read on Good Friday, in which the faithful asked God to soften the hearts of the "perfidious Jews" in light of their role in the death of Jesus. Long before Vatican II, Cushing spoke regularly in Boston's synagogues, so the situation was rife for conflict when Brandeis University, in Waltham, Massachusetts, announced plans to construct Protestant and Catholic chapels on campus, as well as a synagogue for its Jewish students. Feeney and his followers were outraged by the very prospect of such a chapel on the grounds of a Jewish-sponsored university. Physical interchanges became something of a regular feature on the Boston Common on Sunday afternoons; and the rhetoric fanning those physical interchanges became more and more focused on "Jewish dogs" after it was announced that Archbishop Cushing intended to conse-crate the Bethlehem Chapel (as the Catholic space was called) to mark its opening. The Slaves of the Immaculate Heart of Mary publicly condemned Cushing as a traitor to the Faith and called on the city's Catholics to stop such a blasphemous ritual, even with physical violence if need be. The Jewish Telegraph Agency began to regularly report such interchanges in a weary, if laconic, voice:

> Police here intervened yesterday to break up a scuffle which resulted from a placard message exhibited on Boston Common by the followers of Leonard Feeney charging desecration at Brandeis University. The placard read "Catholics of Boston, stop the Jews from dishonoring and desecrating the Blessed Sacrament at Brandeis University."[41]

Boston's Jewish Community Council convened a panel of psychologists and public relations experts to help it discern between two possible courses of action: to either completely ignore the antics of Feeney and the Slaves of the Immaculate Heart of Mary on the Boston Common rather than draw atten-tion to his hate-filled rants, or to launch a public information campaign to counter his accusations. The Council chose the former option of ignoring Feeney, not surprisingly only adding to his rage. At the event, police guarded the Brandeis campus both before and during the chapel's blessing, and Cushing consecrated the chapel (with a number of rabbis present) without incident. The Slaves of the Immaculate Heart of Mary protested the event, but off campus and closely monitored. A large portrait of Cushing still hangs in the sacristy of the Bethlehem Chapel, witness to his important role in the event. And when Cushing died several decades later, a number of rabbis and administrators from Brandeis came to Holy Cross Cathedral to sit shiva for him.[42]

But even as these wars of religion were being acted out on the Boston Common, Rome finally and definitively weighed in on Feeney, undoubt-edly at the urging of the Archbishop of Boston, fully a year after the stern letter from the Holy Office had been published on the front page of the archdiocese's paper, the *Pilot*. Feeney had, of course, petitioned Rome for clarification on the question of salvation outside the Church over the course of four years, and Rome had responded to his request in a number of letters over the course of those years: on August 8, 1949, and again on September 6, 1952, and yet again on October 25, 1952. The Holy Office had declared in each of these pronouncements that it "rejected the extremely rigorous view defended by the members of St. Benedict's Center," and expected Feeney to submit to duly-constituted church authority—indeed, in this case, to the highest such authority. Finally, Rome sent a telegram to Feeney on November 22, 1952, requiring him to appear in Rome to answer questions both about his teaching and his consistent refusal to appear before the Holy Office. Feeney had refused to comply with any of these letters requiring his "submission of mind and will" to the highest teaching office in the Church, and he refused to even consider an appearance before church officials at the Vatican until it had addressed his theological question.[43]

It came as no surprise to anyone, save to Feeney himself, therefore, that on February 19, 1953, the news service of the National Catholic Welfare Conference (the official Washington-based voice of all the bishops in the United States) issued a special bulletin from Rome that was to be published in every US diocese, announcing that on February 13, the Holy Office (the official voice of the Pope) had issued a disciplinary statement, "declaring that the Reverend Leonard Feeney had incurred the penalty of excommunication." But the announcement itself evinced the tensions that had undoubtedly shaped its composition: while the letter stated overtly that the Holy Office "rejected the extremely rigorous views entertained and defended by the members of the St. Benedict Center," the reasons offered for the excommunication were not heterodoxy—that is, teaching false doctrine—but rather disobedience to his religious superiors, both Jesuit and Roman. The letter never addressed the question as to how Feeney's interpretation *was* "extremely rigorous." Did the rigor that was denounced result from his admittedly sharp-elbowed application of that famous phrase from St. Cyprian without nuance? Was it the result of Feeney's failure to read the tempo of the times in applying such teaching? Was it the result of his stubborn refusal to acknowledge the "new shifts in emphasis" in applying church teaching in pluralist cultures like that of the United States? The news release of February 19 simply declared that:

the Reverend Leonard Feeney of St. Benedict's Center, Boston, Mass., to have automatically incurred excommunication. The Rev. Father Feeney has shown stubborn disobedience to an order legitimately enjoined upon him to appear in Rome before the authorities of the Sacred Congregation [of the Holy Office]. This action of the Holy See is the climax and concluding act of a controversy that has done considerable harm to souls and disturbed the peace of mind in Catholic circles . . . [This] penalty puts him out of communion with the faithful and deprives him of the right to administer and receive the Sacraments.[44]

This ambivalent excommunication of Feeney is the more noteworthy because it occurred just a decade after the 1943 publication of Pius XII's famous encyclical, *Mystici Corporis* during World War II, which had equated the "mystical body of Christ" with the Catholic Church itself. Jews, heretics, and the worthy pagans, according to such an identification, could be saved only if they were, in effect, unwitting Roman Catholics, marked by an "invincible ignorance" of the necessity of belonging to the Roman Church as the sole path to salvation. But Feeney and his disciples thought it risible to accuse President Conant of Harvard, the Jewish professors of Brandeis, and Protestant Yankees in Boston of being invincibly ignorant about the necessity of Catholic Church membership. Such an understanding of "baptism of desire" (that is, of being in the Church through unconscious desire due to ignorance of Church teaching) had been worked out in the early modern period of the sixteenth and seventeenth centuries, when Catholics were just beginning to send missionaries to the New World and the Indies; that is, to places where Catholic missionaries had never set foot. It was, for Feeney and his disciples, at best disingenuous to claim that the non-Catholic residents of Harvard's Adams House (literally across the street from the St. Benedict Center and St. Paul's Church) were invincibly ignorant of Catholic teaching on this matter.[45]

The very question of invincible ignorance would become irrelevant by 1965, when the Second Vatican Council promulgated its most important document, the "Dogmatic Constitution on the Church" (*Lumen Gentium*). That document offered a two-word revision of the older understanding of the relation of the institutional Church to the "Mystical Body of Christ," but two words that would revolutionize Catholics' understanding of their relation to other believers. In place of Pius XII's famous identification of the institutional Catholic Church itself with the Mystical Body, the Council's "Dogmatic Constitution" announced that the True Church "subsists" in the Roman Catholic Church. With that seemingly minor substitution of two words—asserting that the Church of Christ *subsistit in* rather than *est* ("is") the Catholic Church—the entire question being debated by Feeney became something of an irrelevant point. Thus, paragraph 8 of *Lumen Gentium* simply declared:

> The [True] Church constituted and organized in the world as a society subsists in the Catholic Church, which is governed by the successor of Peter and by the Bishops in communion with him, *although many elements of sanctification and truth are found outside of its visible structure. These elements, as gifts belonging to the Church of Christ, are forces impelling toward catholic unity.*[46]

Those two Latin words in Vatican II's "Dogmatic Constitution"—*subsistit in*—came to represent the very heart of what Feeney and the American Catholic "Traditionalists" who would follow him saw as a heterodox abdication of the institutional Catholic Church's responsibility of understanding itself—and proclaiming to others—its identity as the sole ark of salvation. More of this in time. But Feeney had drawn a line in the sand a decade before the Second Vatican Council even convened, a line that would serve as a boundary marker for others who would follow him.[47]

C. A Prophet Without Honor

The closing of the St. Benedict Center was nowhere near as noteworthy or public as the high drama that defined Feeney in his heyday: in 1957, partly in response to pressure from Cambridge building inspectors pressing Clarke and Feeney for code violations, Feeney and one hundred of his disciples moved from Cambridge to the rural village of Harvard, Massachusetts (about forty-five miles west of Boston). The profound ironies that marked his excommunication and exclaustration moved with him as well, as the farm he and his followers settled into was directly adjacent to Bronson Alcott's famous Transcendentalist communal experiment at Fruitlands, and very close to the Shaker village at Hancock, at one time one of the largest communities of that "United Society of Believers in Christ's Second Appearing," which believed that Mother Ann Lee (their founder) was the second incarnation of the Christ Principle. Given Feeney's loudly proclaimed contempt for all things Protestant, the irony of living so close to two of the most famous ultra-Protestant communal experiments in New England could not have been lost on him. It was certainly not lost on his critics at the time. But whatever he made of his local Protestant landscape, by that time Feeney and the Slaves of the Immaculate Heart of Mary had also become synonymous with social pathology: interrupting Notre Dame Football games, demonstrating against interfaith chapels like that at Brandeis, and denouncing the prince of Satan's legions, Archbishop Cushing himself.[48]

On strictly theological grounds, Feeney's teaching about church membership was not as outrageous or pathological as might appear from the vantage of the twenty-first century. Catholic propagandists in Counter-Reformation Europe believed that their Protestant opponents, no less than Moslem infidels, were well beyond the reach of grace, and a rigorist interpretation of St. Cyprian's phrase (condemned by the Vatican itself in 1953) clearly uncovers the motives of Catholic as well as Protestant missionaries in the early modern period. The urgency of snatching souls from the jaws of hell motivated Jesuit Francis Xavier in India no less than seventeenth-century Puritan John Eliot, founder of the Native American Praying Town in Natick, Massachusetts, to go out and preach the good news to the "people that walked in darkness" (Isaiah 9:2).

With the establishment of his religious community at Harvard into two separate communities—one for men and another for women—the Slaves of the Immaculate Heart of Mary double-downed on precisely the features of their teacher and mentor that had taken shape over the course of a decade at the St. Benedict Center: the pronounced emphasis on a sectarian purity that renounced the ("feminine" and degenerate) accommodation that postwar Catholicism seemed to be making with mainstream American culture. Feeney's own call for such sectarian purity led, of course, to the group's rupture with arguably the defining impulse in Catholic Christianity itself: the emphasis on *communio*—the necessity of communion with the hierarchy and with other believers, however sinful they may be.

Likewise, Feeney's increasingly frequent denunciation of Liberals (especially Catholic Liberals) set up an open-ended invitation to discontented Catholics later in the century to use the same nomenclature in denouncing subversives in the Church and more broadly in American politics and culture. Faithful Catholics, in their estimation, anyway, came increasingly to mean conservative Catholics, and perhaps even "masculine Catholic crusaders," an identification that would become solidified in the last several decades of the twentieth century. Likewise, the accusatory, militant tone of Feeney and the Slaves of the Immaculate Heart of Mary's denunciation of Jews, Protestants, and even of Catholic leaders like Archbishop Cushing, exactly mirrored the apocalyptic urgency of Protestant fundamentalist believers decrying the apostasy of mainstream Protestantism in the years after the Great Reversal of 1919. That militant tone of Feeney and his disciples, lamenting the apostasy of Holy Church, strikes any reader familiar with Protestant Fundamentalist history with the sense of familiarity: "I've heard this before," one notes with the shock of historical recognition, "in a different part of the denominational forest." The one major difference being that, for Feeney and his followers, the tone was tied to the very real threat of nuclear terror after 1945. And Feeney himself was not shy about naming those responsible for the nuclear cliff on which the world now perilously perched: "thirty-third degree Masons" like Harvard's President Conant and those ostensibly Catholic leaders who cooperated with him.

But what lends genuine pathos to the Feeney affair is the fact that Feeney *correctly* recognized in his primitivist, a-historical understanding of Catholic Christianity that the older paradigm of the Roman Church—that of the *societas perfecta* embraced by the Council of Trent and elaborated by post-Tridentine theologians like Bellarmine—was being jettisoned by Catholics in the pews as well as by members of the hierarchy because it was no longer helpful in defining the self-identity of postwar Catholics both in North America and in Europe. As Kuhn would phrase it, the anomalies that resulted from the application of that paradigm to the mid-twentieth-century cultural circumstance were too many, and no longer had the ring of truth. What most defined the state of theological scholarship in mid-century, both in Europe and America, was that realization, making Kuhn's famous phrase "period of crisis" an apt label to describe the search for a new paradigm that could replace it. The paradigm that, in the event, did replace it was forged at the Second Vatican Council: the older preferred model of Church as the perfect society was replaced as the preferred metaphor by the metaphor of Church as the "People of God" on pilgrimage, struggling as best it could to witness to a truth *subsisting* within Catholicism, but transcending institutional exclusivity.

It might even be argued that Feeney himself saw that displacement of the older paradigm better than others, and he sought to halt that displacement by loudly witnessing to its eternal validity precisely because it had been elucidated at the Council of Trent, and further buttressed by the documents of the First Vatican Council in the nineteenth century, under the direct inspiration of the Holy Spirit. For Feeney and his disciples, the model of church as perfect society and "sole ark of salvation" did not change precisely because it *could not change*: it was true everywhere, all the time, regardless of cultural circumstance. The anomalies that both theologians and laity discovered in the attempt to apply it to their own cultural conditions were optical illusions: like their Protestant predecessors in the second decade of the twentieth century, the old-time religion was true because it was God's truth, not theirs. But what Feeney and his Protestant forebears couldn't see was that "reality"—including religious reality—"is always more complex than any model we can construct to explain it" (one of Kuhn's favorite phrases). And we can never access that reality directly (precisely because of its complexity) but only through models—paradigms, if you will—that in fact do change over time. One might even say that church history itself is simply the record of those paradigm changes over the centuries.

While one might very well argue that Feeney himself recognized the fraying assent to the older paradigm on the part of Catholics better than others; what he didn't see was that the fraying itself witnessed to the fact that many other Catholics, in both the United States and Europe, had realized that the Catholic theological world was already in the period of crisis that would inexorably lead to a new paradigm. But Feeney would not be the last Catholic in the United States who would rage against the dying of that paradigm.

PART II
"CHRIST AGAINST CULTURE"

Part II of this book examines figures and movements who adopted what H. Richard Niebuhr, in his book *Christ and Culture*, described as the "Christ against Culture" model of Christianity, eschewing cultural influence in order to remain "pure" from the defilements of the world.

3

Gommar DePauw and the Schismatical Worship of the *Novus Ordo*

A. "Undermining the Church from Within"

On April 24, 1967, Gommar DePauw announced to a capacity crowd in an auditorium in Nyack, New York, that he was starting a liturgical reform movement, not only to "save" the Latin Mass, but to save the very identity of the Catholic Church itself. His audience responded with a minutes-long standing ovation. But much more was to come, as DePauw spoke to the large crowd for another three hours. His message that Saturday evening was hardly new, for the predictability of his public talks was precisely part of what drew hundreds of people to his public appearances. And on this particular Saturday evening DePauw rang yet again the changes of that well-known carillon: the "damnable Robber Council of Vatican II" under the control heretical liberals; that Council's replacement of the "true mass" contained in the Missal of 1570 with the (Protestant) "new mass" (the *novus ordo*) promulgated by Vatican II, which spread heretical beliefs; the systematic silencing of disaffected lay people, "60% of whom are violently opposed to the liturgy changes" (at least according to DePauw, although the source for that statistic was never actually revealed).[1]

However bizarre these points may have sounded to his own bishop, Cardinal Lawrence Shehan of Baltimore (who had, in fact, already formally suspended DePauw from speaking at events precisely like the one that evening in Nyack), DePauw did not begin his career as a renegade: indeed, he was viewed as something of a hero by Belgian Catholics earlier in his life. Born in 1918 at the end of World War I, he graduated with high honors from the College of St. Nicholas in Louvain, from which he entered the diocesan seminary in Ghent. When the World War II broke out, he left his seminary studies to volunteer as a combat medic with the Belgian military, and was captured and imprisoned by the Nazis at the Battle of Dunkirk. But DePauw managed to escape from his captors, which he took to be a sign regarding his future vocation. He did not return directly to the army but to his seminary studies, being ordained to the priesthood with thirty-seven others in 1942, at the tender age of twenty-three. Now a functioning priest, only then did he return to battle as an underground chaplain to the famed Belgian Resistance, for which he received both the (Belgian) Cross of Honor and named honorary chaplain by the Polish Free Forces at the Annual Polaski Parade in 1946. DePauw's battles against the principalities and powers of a fallen world had begun early in life.[2]

But both the object and the tenor of DePauw's courageous ministry underwent something of a sea-change (both literally and figuratively) in 1949, when DePauw joined family members in the US, where he was immediately put to work as a pastoral assistant in the archdiocese of New York in two parishes in Manhattan and the Bronx. However fulfilling those pastoral assignments might have been, DePauw had his sights on a bigger Catholic audience than could be gathered parochially on Sunday mornings. For while still serving in those parishes he enrolled in the graduate program at the Catholic University of America, from which he was awarded a doctorate in canon (church) law in 1953. But being as indefatigable in study as in everything else, DePauw was invited to teach canon law in the seminary located on the rural campus of Mount St. Mary's University in Emmitsburg, Maryland, in 1952, while he was still working on his degree. Once there, DePauw proved himself almost indispensable both in and outside of class, and he was named academic dean shortly after his arrival (to no one's surprise, least of all his). DePauw remained at Mount St. Mary's until 1963. Now clearly at home in America, he requested that his incardination (the official marker of his home diocese) be transferred from the diocese of Ghent (Belgium) to the Archdiocese of Baltimore in 1955, the same year he became an American citizen. But DePauw left his highly successful seminary deanship (and his new home diocese) in 1963 for an even more visible position: to serve as a *peritus* (theological advisor) to the bishops gathering in Rome for the Second Vatican Council. His careful canonical advice to the bishops gathered there caught the eye of one of the most powerful clerics inside the Vatican, the ultratraditionalist Amleto Cicognani, Cardinal Secretary of State, who made him a domestic prelate of the Papal Court (and thus able to be addressed as "Right Reverend Monsignor," and not just Father.) But this steady climb inside the institutional bureaucracy of the Church would encounter some turbulence when DePauw returned from Rome to his adopted diocese and country.[3]

While still serving as a *peritus* in Rome, DePauw began to have grave misgivings about the "reforms" (a word he regularly put in scare quotes) being passed by the Council, most especially the reforms mandated by what would turn out to be one of its most far-reaching documents, "The Constitution on the Sacred Liturgy" (*Sacrosanctum concilium*). That epochal document, passed by the astonishing lopsided vote of 2,147 bishops to four at the end of the very first session of the Council in December 1963, called for the replacement of the Latin Mass that had been published after the Council of Trent in 1570 with a new liturgy (the *novus ordo*, the new order of mass). That new order of mass, allowing for readings of scripture in the vernacular, was to be implemented in the US in November 1964, causing some confusion to the faithful gathered that day to celebrate the First Sunday of Advent (the beginning of the Church's liturgical calendar). And among the new guidelines added to the original Conciliar document in 1964 was a directive allowing the altar to be free-stranding, and not flush with the back wall of the sanctuary. Of the many new rubrics implemented for the celebration of the eucharist on that Advent Sunday, arguably the most disorientating was the one re-arranging the placement of the altar, causing considerable disorientation to at least to some of the faithful, who were unaccustomed to seeing their parish priest facing *them*, and not the east wall of the church (and, presumably, God).[4]

Just part of the confusion that would come to define DePauw's later career in denouncing the reformed liturgy emanating out of Vatican II in favor of the *Missale Romanum* (the Roman Missal) of 1570 was his seeming a-historical and static understanding of the unique status of that latter book. The *Missale*, formally promulgated five years after the close of the Council of Trent in 1565, was an attempt by Pope Pius V to put into one volume the unwieldy collections of rubrics, prayers, scriptural readings, and chants—often in separate books—that priests needed for the proper celebration of the eucharist. Besides being confusing just in terms of keeping track of where the correct pages were in the collections to properly celebrate the mass, there was also a fair amount of overlapping repetition and duplication as well. As Josef Jungmann, the dean of Catholic liturgy scholars, famously remarked in his 1950 magisterial study, *The Mass of the Roman Rite*, the bishops assembled at Trent had recognized that a reform of Catholic worship was essential to any larger reform of the Catholic Church:

taking cognizance of the Mass books [in the plural], which had in many ways become a jungle . . . At the same time, there was a hue and cry for a unified missal in which only the special diocesan saints' masses would be added as a sort of appendix. But the idea was not shared everywhere.[5]

In fact, the 1570 Roman Missal was an effort—never really finished or set in stone in the centuries after its promulgation—to unify the rubrics of the Roman Rite, streamlining the additions that had accumulated in the western church over the course of a millennium. Originally, the "*Roman* Rite" was literally just that—the order of mass proscribed for celebrating the eucharist by members of the Roman Curia in the Vatican. But many Roman Catholics in the centuries before the Council of Trent followed rites that were different from that Vatican rite, both in rubrics and prayers. Indeed, a number of the older religious orders (priests and nuns who were nothing if not model *Roman* Catholics) had developed their own rubrics for celebrating mass, oftentimes various in terms of the details of liturgical practice. Thus, one could cite the "Carthusian Rite," the "Cistercian Rite," and the "Dominican Rite" (among others) as distinct variations of the rite celebrated in the Roman Curia. And in Italy itself there were other missals containing rites that were as old—and as revered—as the curial rite in Rome. In Milan, an ancient diocese with a distinguished history because of its saintly fourth century bishop, Ambrose, who was considered one of the Doctors of the Western Church, celebrated the eucharist according to the "Ambrosian Rite," which differed from the Curial Roman Rite in a number of ways. And when St. Augustine (at the time living in Milan and a close friend of Ambrose) visited Rome, he was unsettled to encounter the differences in how the Romans both worshipped and fasted. Writing back to Milan asking for advice as to how he should proceed, Ambrose responded with a famous quip which most people have heard of, but of whose origin they are largely ignorant. Anselm responded to him: "When in Rome, do as the Romans do." Augustine wisely followed that advice (although he always thought that the Roman way was odd in a number of ways). But no Roman Christian ever accused him or Ambrose of being somehow less Catholic for not worshipping according to all the details of the "Roman" Rite.[6]

There were, then, variations in how Catholic Christians celebrated the mass, even after the promulgation of the Roman Missal of 1570. *Quo Primum*, Pius V's bull introducing the 1570 mass book, announced that any local church which could demonstrate a ritual eucharistic custom of at least two hundred years before 1570 could retain their local rite, and a number did just that: about five million Catholics in northern Italy continued to worship according to the Ambrosian Rite even after the implementation of the 1570 Missal. And there were other Catholic rites that could demonstrate just such a two-hundred-year-old tradition that have continued into the present: the Braga Rite in Portugal; the Lyonese Rite celebrated in the area of Lyon, France; and the Mozarabic Rite in the dioceses of Toledo and Salamanca in Spain. There were, as well, the luxurious collection of rites of the Eastern Catholic Church—the Maronite Rite and the Syro-Antiochene Rite among many others. All of those Eucharistic rites were recognized as both licit and valid for the celebration of mass by both the Roman Curia and the Pope.[7]

Thus, DePauw's fanatical insistence that the 1570 *Missale Romanum* was the *only* valid rite for the Catholic celebration of mass was actually not supported by the historical record of the Catholic Church itself, which appeared to witness to the *pluralism* of Catholic worship as much as to its uniformity. Similar to Leonard Feeney before him, orthodoxy—or in this case, orthodox worship—seemed to be defined by DePauw in a singular and a-historical way that was not borne out by the history of Catholic worship among widely scattered local churches which had used other rites for centuries, all of whom claimed to be loyal Catholic Christians, and were indeed perceived to be such by the Bishop of Rome.[8]

Further, and equally to the point, Pius V's Missal itself had undergone revisions well before the twentieth century, so that what DePauw referred to as the "timeless" Roman Missal of 1570 used in the twentieth century was not, in fact, what had been promulgated in the sixteenth century: both Pope Clement VIII (in 1604) and Pope Urban VIII (in 1633) ordered revisions in the text (especially in the collects) to clarify what, exactly, was being asked of the Holy One in the prayers said by the priest during mass. Likewise, Pope Leo XIII (in 1884) ordered a new "typical edition" (the edition that provided the model for future printings of the mass text) to incorporate the changes introduced into the Roman Missal since Urban VIII. Pope Pius X likewise undertook a revision of Leo's text: and while few of Pius's changes dealt with the prayers said during mass (as Clement VIII's changes had), Pius's edition introduced modifications in the rubrics (the actions of the priest during the celebration of the eucharist), which in fact made for some changes in what the congregation saw. And even Pope Pius XII, never accused by anyone of being a theological liberal, ordered the Sacred Congregation of Rites (the Vatican office charged with overseeing Catholic worship) in 1948 to simplify the rubrics of the Easter Vigil liturgy (and eventually of the entire Easter Triduum) so that the simple and dignified structure of the Roman Rite might emerge in clearer form, bringing it closer in form to what historians were then discovering about the worship of the early church.[9]

There were, then, significant portions of the *Missale Romanum* as it was celebrated in the US before the convening of Vatican II that Pius V had *not* approved of in 1570, representing undramatic but continuous liturgical change over the course of the four centuries after its initial promulgation. The "pure text" that DePauw championed in his crusade after 1964 was largely a product of his own wishful thinking rather than of historical evidence.

In this, DePauw—like Feeney before him—pressed his own form of primitivism—the historical heresy that believes that religious traditions achieve their perfect (and eternally valid) form at some moment in the religious past. For Protestant fundamentalists, that perfect moment had been embodied in the worship and ministry of the primitive church in Jerusalem, described in the "Acts of the Apostles." For Feeney and his disciples in Boston, that perfect moment had been achieved in Pope Boniface VIII's famous encyclical of 1302, *Unam Sanctam*, which had declared that salvation itself was dependent on membership in the Roman Church. For DePauw and the small group of disciples who became faithful members of the Catholic Traditionalist Movement (CTM) that he founded in 1964, the perfect (and, again, eternally true) form of Catholic worship had been embodied in the Roman Missal of 1570. That "primitive" order of mass (which privileged an understanding of the eucharist as a renewal of Christ's sacrifice on Calvary) had been promulgated "for all time"; indeed, in light of the papal bull which had published that Missal, DePauw strenuously argued that Vatican II's new order of mass was "schismatical, sacrilegious, heretical, and possibly invalid."[10]

Further, the CTM (centered around the Ave Maria Chapel which DePauw established in Westbury, Long Island) provided DePauw with the platform he sought for delivering a message that was startlingly similar to that of Feeney: like the excommunicated head of the Slaves of the Immaculate Heart of Mary, DePauw consistently denounced what he termed the "Americanization of the Roman Catholic Church." And in that Americanization, liberalism—defined in an analogous way to Feeney—played a leading role. The very fact that DePauw turned to a political moniker to identify his (and the True Church's) enemies put him in the direct line of Feeney and his equally strenuous denunciation of Catholic liberals: the church was being undermined from within, most scandalously even by church leaders like the archbishop of Baltimore (DePauw's former archbishop), an ecclesiastical analogue to Boston's Archbishop Cushing, whom Feeney regularly denounced in unmeasured terms on the Boston Common.

For DePauw, the destruction of the Latin liturgy was only a symbol of the *real* rebellion: the cabal by a handful of *liberal American* bishops, who had pushed through a liturgical revision because "Latin was a symbol of our link with Rome, and therefore they say it must go." Their liberalism consisted in precisely taking the standards of American culture as normative, to which Catholic worship had to conform. And the destructive designs of those liberal American bishops so decried publicly, was oftentimes revealed graphically in the press, as in a photograph published in *The Washington Post* on July 17, 1966, in which one of DePauw's followers picketing outside the resident of the Apostolic Delegate in Washington carried a large sign declaring "We are Americans who are Roman Catholics, *not American Catholics*, who are One-World Socialists."[11]

In all of this, DePauw constructed a sectarian, anti-liberal, and primitivist understanding of Catholicism analogous to Feeney: only those several hundred faithfuls who drove from all over the New York metropolitan area to his chapel were actually worshiping according to true Catholic rubrics. The millions of American Catholics who participated in the *novus ordo* eucharist in their local parishes were actually taking part in a sacrilegious and "new" rite that was in schism from the true Catholic Church—a Catholic Church largely limited to DePauw himself and his followers. For DePauw:

> the "liturgical beatniks'" striving to de-Romanize the Catholic Church for the collective madness which has taken possession of the establishment of our *once* Catholic Church in America [have], as their ultimate goal, a one-world religion by a one-world government.[12]

Likewise, DePauw himself was not mistaken in claiming that the normative (but much re-edited) status of the *Missale Romanum* of 1570 was based on a directive of an ecumenical council of the church and had been promulgated by the pope himself (a double imprimatur reflecting the highest form of definitive Catholic teaching). But, again like Feeney, DePauw's fatal mistake was in the fact that he found himself fighting on the wrong side of a paradigm shift in Catholic practice that had been mandated by a later ecumenical council and promulgated—equally authoritatively—by a later pope.

Likewise, DePauw was not mistaken in believing that a new ("radical") model of Catholic worship was being implemented on the First Sunday of Advent in 1964. What did elude him, however, was the fact that "radical" in this instance reflected the etymological base of that word, as *radix* is the Latin word for "root." Vatican II's "new rite" sought its model not in the 1570 *Missale Romamun*, but rather in the eighth-century *Ordo Romanus Primus*, a form of the Roman Rite that predated the Tridentine liturgy by eight centuries, and which liturgical scholars believed reflected the liturgy of the early church much more faithfully than the Tridentine liturgy. In doing so, it was not advancing a eucharistic liturgy in discontinuity with the history of Catholic worship. If anything, the Second Vatican Council was restoring the worship style that had defined the liturgy of the first centuries of Christianity: a less ritualized liturgy in the vernacular, which called for active congregational responses during the liturgy itself. It was a liturgy which reflected, as well, Vatican II's non-hierarchical understanding of the Church itself as the "People of God," which included the entire congregation: *all* of them—priest and people—were now understood as "celebrating the eucharist," an understanding that was taken for granted in the first six centuries of the Christian era.

The *novus ordo*, in other words, implemented a form of worship that early Roman Christians would recognize as reflecting the worship assemblies they themselves attended in both house churches and in the early basilicas taken over for worship during the first centuries of Christian worship. One could, in fact, argue that it presented a liturgy that was actually "radically old" rather than radically new, based on the careful retrieval of the Christian past that had been undertaken by liturgical historians like the German Jesuit Jungmann during the 1930s and 1940s, as well as by scholars in the *Nouvelle theologie* movement.[13]

Far from attempting to Americanize the Catholic rite of the eucharist, then, the new paradigm of liturgy outlined in *Sacrosanctum Concilium* was an attempt to restore the oldest liturgical traditions of the Church in Rome for contemporary worship, along with additions that the contemporary culture seemed to call for. In contrast to DePauw's a-historical, static understanding of Catholic worship, Paul VI's promulgation of the Council's constitution on worship revealed that the Vatican's understanding of Catholic tradition was worlds removed from the agenda of the Catholic Traditional Movement. To use the famous distinction outlined by Canadian Jesuit theologian Bernard Lonergan, over against DePauw's classicist understanding of Catholic worship, Vatican II's "Constitution on the Sacred Liturgy" embodied a far more historicist approach to genuine Catholic worship: in place of the model of the mass advanced by DePauw, the Council Fathers and the Pope called for a reform of liturgical practice based on the best historical research. The latter approach understood that changing historical circumstances demanded new liturgical rubrics and practices. And that latter approach, in fact, had always been the genius of the Roman Rite—a rite which had undergone many changes over the course of millennia. It was precisely that genius that had been recognized by Cardinal John Henry Newman in the nineteenth century, which he elucidated in his famous *Essay on the Development of Christian Doctrine*, commenting on the "plastic" nature of the Catholic tradition.

The "dirty little secret"

Before DePauw left for the first session of the Second Vatican Council, he simply presumed that after its close he would return to his post as Professor of Theology and Canon Law and Academic Dean at Mount Saint Mary's Major Seminary in rural Maryland. But his experience in Rome as a *peritus* had unsettled him, especially his insider's view of what he took to be the spurious historical arguments for overturning the mass that almost all US Catholics witnessed week after week in their parishes before 1964. But, in fact, upon his return after that session of the Council, he had determined that God was calling him to a new work—a work of God focused on agitating to retain what he took to calling "the completely unchanged [*sic*] Roman Catholic Mass." And even before he began that crusade in Westbury, Long Island, he believed that he found the rallying cry and justification for that crusade in *Quo Primum*—the papal decree in which Pius V had promulgated the 1570 Missal. For in that decree the pope had announced that:

> by this our decree, to be valid *in perpetuity*, we determine and order that *never* shall anything be added to, omitted from, or changed in this Missal . . . At no time in the future can a priest . . . ever be forced to use any other way of saying mass. We herewith declare that it is in virtue of our Apostolic Authority that we decree and determine that this our present order and order is to last *in perpetuity and never be legally revoked or amended at any future date.* And if anyone would nevertheless ever dare to attempt any action contrary to this order of ours, *given for all times,* let him

know that he has incurred the wrath of Almighty God and of the Blessed
Apostles Peter and Paul.[14]

DePauw believed that Pius V's decree had provided him with the smoking
gun he needed to launch his crusade against the new mass emerging out of
Vatican II. Far better than he expected, *Quo Primum* offered the definitive
grounding for his sense that *Sacrosanctum Concilium* was stillborn on de-
livery. From the mouth of a Successor of Peter himself, DePauw's deepest
loyalties had been confirmed in a (literally) infallible way: just as he had always believed, the 1570 Missal was binding on Catholics *forever* ("in perpetuity" and "for all times"). And much like Feeney—who also had never
experienced what has been wonderfully termed the "grace of self-doubt"—
DePauw never looked back.

DePauw did return (briefly) to his post as academic dean at Mount Saint
Mary's, but while there he formed an organization called the Catholic
Traditionalist Movement (CTM) in 1964, dedicated to fighting the implementation of Council's new order of mass. But within a month of that
group's founding, his ordinary, Archbishop Shehan of Baltimore, informed
DePauw that CTM was in fact disseminating teaching that was seriously at
odds with the mandate of the highest authority known to Catholics—the
pope in union with an ecumenical council of the universal church. Shehan
demanded that DePauw immediately disband the group or officially dis-
sociate himself from it. Rather than comply with an explicit directive from
his own bishop, DePauw moved his base of operations from Maryland to
New York City, refusing to return to Maryland. Therewith, "the loathsome
Lawrence Shehan" of Baltimore" (as DePauw and his disciples came to call
him) immediately revoked DePauw's faculties (the permission to say mass or
celebrate the sacraments) and declared that the CTM was a renegade group
formally condemned by the Baltimore archdiocese. Undeterred (as always),
DePauw decided to undertake a traveling ministry—in public disregard for
the explicit command of his own bishop—undertaking a wide-ranging lecture tour (like the one in Nyack, New York) to concerned Catholics in the
greater New York area and much further afield. Indeed, DePauw attracted so
much public attention during the next several years (not least because he was
a canonically silenced priest lecturing in flagrant public disobedience to his
own bishop) that the media took to calling him the "rebel priest."[15]

But DePauw's actual canonical status itself became something of a canonical issue: a priest deprived of faculties by his diocesan ordinary but

whose primary mission focuses on the public celebration of the "true mass" presented something of a conundrum, even for a cleric accustomed to maintaining many balls in the air like DePauw. While Cardinal Shehan maintained that the rebel priest *was*, in fact, a cleric incardinated in Shehan's own Archdiocese of Baltimore (even if not exactly a priest in good standing), DePauw undertook to fix that arrangement. In September 1965, DePauw managed to elicit permission from Rome to attend the fourth session of the Council as advisor to Blaise Kurz, an exiled bishop from China. On arriving in Rome, DePauw took his case as a rebel priest to Cardinal Alfredo Ottaviani (secretary of the Vatican's Holy Office—the old "Office of the Holy Inquisition"), who arranged for DePauw's transfer from the Archdiocese of Baltimore to the Italian diocese of Tivoli, which was under the direct supervision of Ottaviani himself, thus removing DePauw from the supervision of Shehan. This was (to understate the case by half) extremely irregular, both because the decision was made without any real input from Shehan (to whom DePauw had promised "obedience and respect") and because of the terms of that transfer. As the *New York Times* described those terms on its front page in January 1966:

> The move, according to Father DePauw, was a technical necessity. [DePauw] will not be expected to work in the diocese of Tivoli but will center his activities in the United States as president of the traditionalists. The movement is now a corporation under the laws of the State of New York.[16]

Once freed from the oversight of his ("loathsome") American bishop, DePauw undertook a speaking tour that became something of a crusade, although a crusade whose original message was surprisingly moderate: DePauw presented himself as the defender of the rights of ordinary Catholics over against the efforts of an overweening hierarchy out of touch with the piety and sentiments of the folks in the pews—the folks who actually paid the bills. Thus Michael Cuneo, one of the most perceptive students of DePauw, has noted that DePauw tried hard to present himself as an enlightened moderate—a "theological democrat"—whose crusade was really about protecting the rights of ordinary Catholics against the tradition-bashing undertaking of liturgists unconcerned with the piety of ordinary Catholics. The CTM's real complaint, DePauw insisted, "wasn't with the Second Vatican Council or its Constitution on the Liturgy, but rather with the almost pathological fanaticism displayed by our Litnicks [liturgical beatniks] in their fight against Latin in the liturgy." DePauw proposed what he took to calling "full and complete freedom of choice" in choosing which parish mass one would attend. Why not, he proposed, offer both the older Latin Mass *and* the new vernacular mass, and let people decide which one to attend? If such an option were put into operation, no one would feel oppressed or outraged.[17]

That moderate message, organized around what sounded like a very American freedom of choice option, however, would quickly change after November 1971. In April 1969, the new vernacular mass (the *novus ordo* liturgy) officially replaced the Missal of 1570 as the normative rite of the church in canon law, making that Vatican II liturgy standard throughout the Catholic world, but still allowing exceptions for pastoral need, for "extraordinary circumstances," or for other rites already recognized by Rome (e.g., the Ambrosian Rite in Milan, the Braga Rite in Portugal, etc.). But even that small loophole for Catholics of the Roman Rite was formally closed in November 1971, when Paul VI narrowed the "wiggle room" for using the 1570 mass book to a very small group of British Catholics who sought a clearer demarcation from the Anglican liturgy, elderly priests celebrating without a congregation, etc. It was in outraged response to that 1971 Vatican directive that DePauw started regularly referring to the vernacular mass as "schismatic, sacrilegious, and *heretical.*" And it was that last word that would come to effectively cut DePauw off almost entirely from the Roman Church. Paul VI and the universal body of bishops who followed him in outlawing the 1570 Missal in all public Catholic worship now had proven *themselves*—at least in the eyes of DePauw and his disciples—to be in schism from the true church, a true church incarnated in one very small chapel in Westbury, Long Island.[18]

Just one instance of the heresy being promulgated in the new rite (and a favorite hobbyhorse referenced in almost all of DePauw's public talks after 1971) was the English translation of the Latin phrase spoken by the priest during the consecration of the bread and wine at mass. In the 1570 Missal, the priest declared in Latin that the sacrifice of Jesus on the cross (and remembered at every Catholic mass) was done "*pro vobis et pro multis.*" *Multus* (the root for "multis") is a Latin word with many meanings: it can correctly be translated as "all," "many," "great," "much," or "some," depending on the context or on the intention of the author. The International Commission on English in the Liturgy (ICEL, as liturgy scholars referred to it) translated the word as "all," thus constructing the English phrase spoken by the priest at the consecration during mass as "[this is the cup of my blood, shed] *for you and for all men*," as opposed to "for you and for many," the translation DePauw believed to be the orthodox one. In DePauw's estimation, ICEL's translation of the 1570 Missal's Latin words of consecration was outrageous, as well as being heretical, for it implied that all people (and not just "the elect" chosen by God) would be saved by Christ's sacrifice on the Cross. That belief—that eventually all people might be saved—is known among theologians as "universalism," and while not formally heretical (who, after all, could know how many people might be saved by God?), was not exactly the mainstream Catholic understanding either. But for DePauw and his disciples at the Ave Maria Chapel, ICEL's English liturgy, now the text spoken in most Catholic parish masses in North America, was proof positive—if further proof was needed—that the entire *novus ordo* rite was both invalid and schismatic.[19]

In 1971, therefore, from DePauw's viewpoint anyway, the CTM's small chapel in Westbury, Long Island, formerly a Ukrainian Orthodox Church about an hour's drive from Manhattan, was the sole outpost of the Holy Roman and Apostolic Catholic Church on the entire east coast of the US. Ave "Maia" Chapel was the little oasis of true Roman Catholicism in an age of widespread spiritual and liturgical apostasy. But that chapel was soon to be only the mother church of DePauw's movement, as dozens of other Tridentine Mass chapels began popping up across the US, many either formally tied to DePauw's CTM or in sympathy with it.

And the faithful attracted to the Ave Maria Chapel made up for in fervor for what they lacked in numbers. The *Long Island Press* reported on July 1, 1968, that "more than 120 Catholics from as far away as Bridgehampton gathered yesterday at a prim, modestly decorated little church in Westbury" to witness DePauw's Latin Mass, despite the fact that the Long Island diocese has "denied the legality of both the church and the priestly powers of the man who led the services." But the members interviewed after the mass were strident supporters of the renegade priest, despite his suspended status in the eyes of the institutional church. Thomas Zawislak (from Jackson Heights, Queens) announced that he had made the seventeen-mile trip because of his deep desire "to hear [*sic*] a mass where I truly believe Christ is present. I feel closer to Christ when mass is celebrated at an altar rather than at a table." And Mrs. Leonard Britting had traveled from the Bronx with five members of her family:

I came here because I'm a Roman Catholic and I don't believe in what's going on in the church today. On Good Friday I was so disgusted at what they've done to the mass that I walked out of the church in my home parish.[20]

The observations made by Mr. Zawislak and Mrs. Britting, in fact, were repeated by several others among the hundred or so worshippers present in the Ave Maria Chapel. And they mirror the repeated themes that DePauw made both in his homilies during mass and at his public lectures outside of church: that the abandonment of the Latin liturgy was an "outward and visible sign of the inward and invisible *lack* of grace" (parodying the famous answer of the *Baltimore Catechism* regarding how the Church understood the sacraments, which the *Catechism* described as "outward and visible signs of invisible grace"); that authentic Catholic identity had been diluted and minimized in an unseemly effort to Americanize the true Roman faith; that Pope Paul VI had been duped by the unscrupulous scheming of a cabal of liberal American bishops into betraying the Church's most valuable gift, the sacrifice of the mass; that Catholic identity had been hijacked by heretical theologians (whom he regularly referred to as "ecumaniacs") dedicated to propagating "junkumenism"; that the implementation of the decrees of Vatican II constituted a frontal assault on the true faith: "the pressure is on to bring the Catholic Church down to the level of the Reformation—the Deformation!" And DePauw regularly ended both his homilies and his public talks by reading the "Third Revelation" purportedly delivered at Fatima (Portugal) by the Virgin Mary earlier in the twentieth century, announcing (at least according to DePauw) that "Satan will even succeed in infiltrating into the highest positions in the Church in the second half of the twentieth century." And in delivering that last piece of information (a revelation that regularly drew gasps from his audience), DePauw read from a sheet of paper that most audience members took to be some kind of official document that DePauw had managed to procure through his contacts in the Vatican; but DePauw never revealed either how he managed to secure such a document or how authoritative the Vatican understood the three revelations supposedly revealed by the Mother of God to be.[21]

DePauw's solitary crusade on behalf of orthodox worship and prayer received something of a major boost in the 1970s from the crusade launched by French bishop Marcel Lefebvre against the teachings of the Second Vatican Council. Lefebvre had first garnered wide public attention when he refused to sign the Council's "Decree on Religious Liberty (*Dignitatis humanae*) and its "Constitution on the Church in the Modern World" (*Gaudium et spes*), both promulgated in December 1965. Lefebvre believed that both documents offered weighty proof that the Council itself had capitulated to the heresies of modernism and secularism, and like DePauw believed that the institutional church itself was now in schism from the true Catholic Church, which he himself represented. In 1970, in fact, he established his own seminary for the training of priests in Switzerland and announced that he had every intention of ordaining those priests himself, according to the ordination rite that had been promulgated by the Council of Trent. He did precisely that in 1973 and 1974, when his clerical products arrived in the United States, and set about setting up traditionalist chapels—much like DePauw's on Long Island—in California, Texas, and New York. By that time, Lefebvre had organized his movement into a "priestly confraternity" called the Society of St. Pius X (SSPX), canonically (at least) in formal schism from the Bishop of Rome. By the late 1970s, SSPX had eclipsed DePauw's CTM both in numbers and in visibility as the leading traditionalist movement in the United States.[22]

As Ken Briggs reported on the joint crusade of DePauw and Lefebvre in a *New York Times* story over a decade after DePauw had launched his CTM crusade, the widespread disaffection regarding the "new mass" on the part of the Catholic faithful had actually failed to appear. Indeed, Briggs reported on a very different reception on the part of US Catholics than what DePauw himself (and his French fellow-warrior) had reported to the press:

> The ultra-traditionalists have as yet to demonstrate a large following in the United States or Europe, despite indications of some growth and publicity surrounding Archbishop Lefebvre's dramatic acts of rebellion. The Rev. Gommar DePauw, the flamboyant founder of the Catholic Traditionalist Movement, now in its 12th year, estimates that there are 10,000 activist traditionalists among 40 million Catholics in the United States, but believes that millions more are sympathizers. [But] data from other sources indicate that the recently introduced new order of the mass has gained overwhelming acceptance.[23]

Indeed, Briggs quoted statistics from the National Opinion Research Center (NORC) at the University of Chicago that offered a counter-narrative to DePauw's claim that sixty percent of American Catholics "violently opposed" the *novus ordo* mass: according to the careful polling of the NORC, eighty percent of American Catholics polled reported being "somewhat" or "very" satisfied with the new vernacular mass, and evinced very little or no desire to return to the Latin Mass in their parish.[24]

B. The House of Arrested Clocks

As Garry Wills observed in his (often brilliant) 1971 account of the changes wrought by the Second Vatican Council, especially the changes to Catholic prayer life and worship, what the First Sunday of Advent in 1964 actually did was "let out the dirty little secret, in the most startling symbolic way, that the *church changes.*" Wills was, of course, exactly right in this, although DePauw never accepted the fact that such a thing was possible, or even thinkable.

Wills used one of the most famous scenes from Charles Dickens's novel, *Great Expectations*, to explicate what coming to church on that First Sunday in Advent in 1964 felt like for Catholics unaware of the liturgical changes that had been going on for centuries. In setting up his argument, Wills set the scene when Dickens's young hero, Pip, is summoned to Satis House, the dilapidated mansion of an old spinster, Miss Havisham, for an unknown reason. What Pip finds there is truly frightening: a house in which all the clocks had been stopped at the exact hour when Miss Havisham's groom had failed to appear many decades before on her wedding day. As Pip looks around him, he spies an uneaten wedding cake— long since collapsed and rotting on the table where the wedding banquet was never held. Terrified, Pip pulls open the windows that had been nailed shut decades before, resulting in blinding streams of sunlight pouring into the house, to the horror of Miss Havisham, who preferred "death's security" to an uncertain future, one in which the clocks are reset. As Wills tells the tale, what that Advent Sunday in 1964 really revealed was that Catholicism's dirty little secret was not about either sex or money, but rather about change itself:

> No more neat historical belief that what one did on Sunday morning looked (with minor adjustments) like what the church had always done, from the time of the catacombs. All that lying eternity and arranged air of timelessness (as in Mae West's vestmented and massive pose) was shattered. The house with arrested clocks, like Miss Havisham's Satis House, collapsed by reverse dilapidation, out of death's security into uncertain life.[25]

But Wills' metaphorical use of Dickens's dramatic account of Pip's visit to Satis House limps if used to emphasize the "timeless" text of the 1570 Missal: Catholic liturgical practice, in fact, had never been housed in a house with arrested clocks. For many centuries before Trent, the *Missale Romanum* had gone through continual revisions and emendations. And even after 1570—the magic date when DePauw believed the Roman Church achieved its perfect worship form "for all time" in Pope Pius V's missal—many other rites (the Ambrosian, the Lyonaise, etc.) thrived within the Catholic Church (even within Italy itself). DePauw's simplistic and a-historical reading of the liturgical betrayal embodied in the *novus ordo* was simply not borne out by the long history of Catholic liturgy. No pope after Pius V believed that the 1570 Missal was sacrosanct and beyond revision, and a number of them did, in fact, call for changes to that rite—some of them significant. Thus, the missal that DePauw used to celebrate mass both in Belgium and in the United States before 1963 was a re-edited and re-ordered rite based on the 1570 text, but containing many changes added after 1570.

But the larger point that Wills makes in using that famous Dickensian scene is true nonetheless: what the implementation of *Sacrosanctum Concilium* undoubtedly did was let out the dirty little secret that both the church and its worship has changed, and probably would continue to do so. On that point, at least, Wills's use of the famous Satis House scene was spot on: for Catholics like DePauw, the real shock was not hearing mass in English, or the rearranged furniture in the sanctuary, or seeing the priest face the congregation instead of the east wall of the church. The real shock was rather the realization that the church had adopted a new paradigm for worship (as it had done many times in the past) that was now normative in a way that changed the definition of that word.

Thomas Kuhn's famous insight regarding paradigm revolutions, in fact, can help us understand both the implementation of the documents of the Second Vatican Council and DePauw's crusade against those very documents. Much like Feeney a decade earlier, DePauw believed that the belief and practice of the Holy Catholic Church—precisely because Jesus had declared that the gates of hell would never prevail against it—were fixed and sure, unchangeable because they embodied the True Faith, established by Jesus Christ himself when he walked the earth. DePauw's constant reiteration in his public talks was to Pope Pius V's decree *Quo Primum*, which had established how Catholics were to worship in the wake of the Council of Trent. In the rebel priest's estimation, that document offered (literally)

infallible proof that both Vatican II and its new mass had departed from orthodox Catholic teaching. PiusV had announced in that decree that the 1570
Missal was "valid in perpetuity," and ordered that "*never* shall anything be
added to, or omitted from, or changed in [his] Missal." Further, Pius had
declared that at "no time in the future" could any Catholic priest "ever be
forced to use any other way of saying mass," and that his promulgation of that
Missale Romanum was to "last in perpetuity, and never be legally revoked
or amended at any future date." But that is easier said than done: at the time
of the Reformation, the Catholics had opted for an infallible pope while the
Protestants had opted for an infallible Bible, and over the years it has proven
easier to change popes.

Exactly analogous to Feeney's a-historical reading of the papal bull *Unam
Sanctum*, DePauw believed that there could be no change in the rite of mass
because a pope had solemnly declared that the 1570 Missal was valid forever,
and popes don't lie (or, at least, not often). But one of Pius V's successors in
the Chair of Peter, Pope Paul VI, in fact *did* promulgate a new rite for the
saying of mass for Catholics four centuries later, a rite which retained some of
the older rubrics but added new ones—and new payers—as well. This was a
theological scandal for DePauw in the literal meaning of that word (from the
Greek root word, *Skandalon*, meaning "stumbling block"), because it challenged the very foundation of the paradigm on which he operated: that once
established by papal teaching, sacred rituals (and most especially Catholic
Christianity's most sacred ritual, the eucharist) were unchanging and unchangeable ritual actions, fixed forever in their 1570 forms because the pope
had declared them valid in perpetuity. But that understanding was based on
an earlier paradigm that posited that truth was propositional and formally
static. But the foundational reality that had changed by 1964 was not the
mass ritual itself, but rather a new understanding of the historical process itself, and of Christianity's place in that process. Starting in the late nineteenth
century, a succession of popes had declared that Catholic scholars were now
free to use the methods of historical criticism in studying Christianity's past,
and that permission unleashed a new paradigm for understanding Catholic
Christianity's place within the historical process.

An important resource for understanding what that new paradigm was
about was Lonergan's famous 1967 address to the Canon Law Society
of America, "The Transition from a Classicist Worldview to Historical
Mindedness." In that short but epochal address, Lonergan had argued that
the battles going on after Vatican II were *not*, at bottom, about the vernacular

mass, the arrangement of church furniture, or the condemnation of birth control. What was *really* going on was the clash of two paradigms for understanding both Catholic Christianity and its place in the world:

> One may be named classicist, conservative, traditional; the other may be named modern, perhaps historicist (though that word is unfortunately ambiguous). The differences between the two are enormous ... [for] they are differences in horizon, in total mentality.[26]

For Lonergan, the real energies fueling the battles between traditionalists like DePauw and his "loathsome" ordinary was a paradigm revolution that had begun early in the twentieth century, but which achieved major public attention among Catholics in dramatic ways in the decades after the close of Vatican II. For the classicists (a category in which both Feeney and DePauw might be presented as prime exemplars), the real world rested on unchanging laws. The Truth (oftentimes in caps for such believers) remained substantially the same throughout history. For classicist believers, human nature and right (orthodox) belief were necessarily static realities because they rested on the laws and dictates of God, who revealed these things through scripture, and for Catholics through the teaching of Christ's Vicar on earth, the Bishop of Rome. Ritual action (like the mass) as well as ethical activity were guaranteed to be both unchanging and unchangeable, and declared to be such by Christ's Vicar on earth, Pope Pius V.[27]

But over against this classicist paradigm of how the real world operated, Lonergan laid out another paradigm, which he termed historical mindedness. Adherents of this paradigm believed that everything—human persons and institutions, no less than the physical universe itself—was shaped by the changing circumstances of history. This second approach, in Lonergan's estimation, had won the day in Western culture during the Enlightenment of the eighteenth century, and had even won the day among Catholic scholars (especially among Catholic scholars of the liturgy) in the early decades of the twentieth century. In this "historical mindedness" paradigm, the presentation of the Gospel message was shaped by the processes of history; and while the truths underlying the Christian message didn't change, the way in which the Church witnessed to those truths of necessity did, because different cultural traditions demanded a new way of bearing witness to them, precisely to be faithful to them in new historical circumstances. Indeed, one of Lonergan's most famous statements in that 1967 address was that

Jesus's message of redemption (eternal in its import) nonetheless had to be framed within the "context of historicity, for it is on this level and through this medium . . . that divine revelation had entered the world, and [through this medium] that the Church's witness is given to it." Lonergan's point is a crucial one, even if it is one that eluded DePauw: Jesus's preaching of the Gospel was encased in first century Semitic metaphors and presuppositions. To be faithful to that message centuries later, the Church had to translate those metaphors and propositions into modern terms. For while Catholics believed that Jesus of Nazareth was indeed God's son, he was also a real man ("true God and true man" in the language of the creed) shaped by the cultural beliefs and practices of his time and place.[28]

Read from Lonergan's point of view, then, while Christ's presence in the bread and wine of the eucharist was part and parcel of the Church's unchanging message—always true and witnessed to by the Christian community—the manner in which the Church ritually celebrated that eternal truth (i.e., the shape and rubrics of the mass itself) had evolved and changed over the course of the centuries, precisely to make that truth clearer and more easily understood by people who lived in very different cultures and whose cultural presuppositions differed from other believers—sometimes dramatically.

What Lonergan had so brilliantly limned, then, was the contours of a new basic model for understanding the real world (a real world that included the Roman Catholic Church). In that new paradigm, human institutions and their message were "*not* fixed, static, and immutable, but shifting, developing, going astray [but] capable of redemption." And this was obviously the case (obvious, at least, to those who ascribed to historical consciousness) because everything was immersed in the stream of history—including the worship of the Catholic Church.

From the viewpoint of Kuhn's theory of paradigm revolutions, then, Pius V in 1570 could very well announce that, magisterially speaking, his missal was to be "valid in perpetuity," without a second's hesitation, because Pius had lived in a classicist paradigm in which the Truth always stayed the same, a Truth that included the eucharist. But that static paradigm had begun to unravel long before the calling of the Second Vatican Council. And a number of factors had contributed to that unraveling: the historical research undertaken by liturgical scholars like Jungmann, whose publications pointed (chapter and verse) to the long historical evolution of the mass rites (in the plural) starting in the first centuries of the Christian era as well as the publications of the French theologians in the 1920s and 1930s, collectively known as the *Nouvelle theologie*, who documented the fact that theological discussion of the mass, in particular, and sacraments, in general, had evolved as the discipline of ecclesiology (the part of theology studying the church itself) had evolved.

Indeed, the research of revered Catholic scholars like Jungmann and the members of the *Nouvelle theologie* movement illustrated how the church had lost its fullest sense of celebrating the eucharist during the early Middle Ages, localizing that celebration on the priest "saying mass." But such an understanding of who, exactly, celebrated the eucharist flew in the face of the understanding of the early centuries of Christian history, during which the Christian community had understood that *everyone* present in the church celebrated the mass, not just the priest at the altar. As a result, it became increasingly evident decades before the first session of the Vatican II that the 1570 Missal would have to be reshaped and revised, precisely to regain the fuller ecclesiological understanding of the eucharist that had informed the earliest centuries of Christian worship. For these scholars, living in the second of Lonergan's paradigms that took historical-mindedness as one of the givens for living in the real world, Pius V's solemn declaration regarding the perpetuity of the 1570 Missal had to be contextualized in its time and place: what made perfect sense in 1570 now appeared nonsensical, or at least historically naïve. Precisely to witness to the perpetuity of Christ's sacrifice memorialized in the mass, the mass rite itself had to be reshaped and changed.

DePauw's primitivist casting of the 1570 *Missale Romanum* simply witnessed to his unfamiliarity with serious Catholic scholarship that had been going on for several generations before he started prophetically witnessing to the "timeless" Missal of 1570: if Pope Paul VI's promulgation of the *novus ordo* constituted a serious act of schism and heresy, did the same judgment apply to his predecessors, who had also made reforms in the mass rite (some of them significant)? Where did one draw the line? But much like Feeney, DePauw lived in solipsistic universe hermetically sealed against history and its changes—indeed, a world in which history and its changes could be ignored, because the Truth had already been achieved in its pristine form at an earlier moment.

It could be argued that it might have benefited DePauw to read through Newman's classic work *An Essay on the Development of Christian Doctrine*, one of the classic works in nineteenth-century Catholic theology. In that famously long and complex, but important text, Newman (himself a major influence on the events that occurred in the Second Vatican Council) had famously observed that "to live is to change, and to have lived long is to have changed often." And the Roman Rite has lived long.

4

The Old-Time Religion in Alabama

Mother Angelica and the "Authentic Magisterium"

A. "I'm So Tired of You, Liberal Church in America"

The world's largest, most-watched religious media network—reportedly reaching 250 million people in 140 countries around the globe—began, singularly enough, in a garage in Irondale, Alabama, in 1981. And it was the brainchild of a Poor Clare nun, Mother Angelica, who had founded Our Lady of the Angels Monastery in Irondale in 1962, initially with the aim of recruiting more African American women to the (Catholic) religious life. Mother Angelica and the sisters who came with her initially kept their mission of ministering to the African American community low key, so as not to attract the hostile attention of the Ku Klux Klan in Alabama, where the Klan still seemed to be flourishing. The Alabama Klan at the time was only *slightly* less hostile to Catholics than to African Americans. And that initial decision to sin on the side of discretion (rare, as it would turn out, in the nun's media career) was buttressed by a number of violent incidents in the American South attributed to the Klan, most notably the Klan bombing of the Sixteenth Street Baptist Church in Birmingham, Alabama, in 1963. That bombing killed four young Black girls inside the church the year after she established her monastery, and the incident only confirmed her growing sense that the original purpose for the foundation might not be the reason God had led her to Ironside.[1]

But other avenues for missionary outreach had already opened up for the nun: she quickly became a sought-after lecturer on personal spirituality and prayer, while also producing accessible pamphlets and even audio and video tapes and appearing on a number of local and national television stations, including the Christian and Trinity Broadcasting Networks. Her remarkable success as a plain-spoken and pungent media presence convinced her that she and her monastery needed to start their own network. Recalling an interview she gave on the Chicago then-Christian station WCFC, she recounted that:

> I walked in, and it was just a little studio, and I remember standing in the doorway and thinking, "It doesn't take much to reach the masses." I just stood there and said to the Lord: "Lord, I've got to have one of these."[2]

And thereby began an extremely unlikely media career with global outreach. Mother Angelica purchased satellite space and began broadcasting on August 15, 1981—the Feast of the Assumption of the Virgin; the starting date clearly was not random. Initially the broadcasts consisted of four hours of daily programing, which included her own show (*Mother Angelica Live*), which aired bi-weekly, a recorded Sunday mass, and selection of older "Catholic programming" like Fulton Sheen's famous television program from the 1950s, *Life is Worth Living*. The remainder of the time on-air was filled with shows produced by various dioceses across the country, as well as shows from Protestant networks that Mother decided would not offend Catholic sensibilities. Also aired were reruns of the *Bill Cosby Show*, public domain films, and cooking shows. In time, EWTN increased its daily programming to six hours, and, by 1986, to eight hours daily. In 1987, the network began broadcasting around the clock, which included daily recitation of the rosary. By 1991, a daily mass was broadcast from the chapel in her monastery.[3]

Mother Angelica's media empire did not stop there: in 1992, EWTN established the largest privately owned short-wave radio station, WEWN in Vandiver, Alabama, and four years later announced that WEWN would make its radio signal available via satellite to both AM and FM radio stations throughout the United States free of charge. By 1999, the radio programs (heard by thousands of listeners) included the show *Open Line*, during which live callers could have their questions regarding Catholic belief and practice answered online. In 2004, Mother Angelica's network announced an agreement with Sirius Satellite Radio; by 2020, EWTN Radio was affiliated with 384 stations in the United States alone, and more than five hundred stations globally. In January 2011, she acquired the *National Catholic Register* (originally a local Catholic paper published out of Denver, but developed into a national paper by 2014), as well as the Catholic News Agency, a Catholic news service with bureaus in the United States, Latin America, and Europe.[4]

Mother Angelica herself, born Rita Antionette Rizzo on April 20, 1923, in Canton, Ohio, was raised in a single-family home after her father abandoned the family when she was five years old, "home" being an admittedly hard-scrabble community of African American and Italian immigrant mill workers. As she later recalled, "we were poor, hungry, and barely surviving on odd jobs until Mother joined the dry-cleaning business as an apprentice to a Jewish tailor." Despite their poverty, young Rita Rizza attended parochial school, but intensely disliked the nuns who were her teachers there ("the meanest people on earth"), and she switched to the public high school. By her own admission she was a poor student at Canton's McKinley High School, partly explained by the continual abdominal pain she experienced, which seemed impervious to medical treatment. Her mother took her to Rhoda Wise, a local self-described mystic who claimed to receive regular visions of St. Therese of Lisieux. Wise instructed the young girl to pray a novena (a course of nine consecutive days of prayer): on January 17, 1943, (the day after the novena ended), Rita woke up to find that the pain had vanished, leading her to believe that God had performed a miracle: "at that point I knew that God knew me and loved me and was interested in me. All I wanted to do after my healing was to give myself to Jesus."[5]

As a result of that experience, Rita began exploring various orders of religious women, finally finding an order that felt like the perfect fit at St. Paul's Shrine of Perpetual Adoration in Cleveland, Ohio. That shrine was operated by the Poor Clare nuns, the Second (i.e., women's) Order of Franciscans founded by the spiritual companion of St. Francis, Clare of Assisi, in the thirteenth century. The Poor Clares were famous in the Church for both the austerity of their lifestyle (thus their name) and for the intensity of their prayer life She subsequently entered, and on November 8, 1945, Rita was given her new "name in religion," Sister Mary Angelica of the Annunciation, eventually making her Solemn Profession in January 1953. But her intense prayer life in the Poor Clares gradually led her to believe that God was calling her to a more ambitious work: establishing a community in the American South to serve African Americans. That sense seemed to be confirmed by Archbishop Thomas Toolan, who suggested that she establish a new Poor Clare community in his own diocese of Mobile-Birmingham, Alabama. In 1961, Mother Angelica and the nuns who accompanied her bought a building and land in Irondale (a suburb of Birmingham), naming their new foundation Our Lady of the Angels Monastery.[6]

During their first year in their new monastic home, Mother Angelica began recording her talks to her community—which sold surprisingly well to the lay public. She then began taping a regular radio show for broadcast on Sunday mornings. Her radio show became something of a local hit, such that, by the 1970s, she began videotaping her talks for television, which were broadcast via satellite on the Christian Broadcasting Network, founded by television preacher Pat Robertson in 1960 and well known as the home of the *700 Club*. But it was after her famous visit to Chicago's WCFC television studio ("it was just a little studio") that she formed the nonprofit EWTN corporation, and began broadcasting from a converted garage on the monastery's property.[7]

Within very short order, EWTN became one of the most powerful voices for American conservatism in both its political and cultural forms as well as for traditionalist Catholicism, to some extent offering a much more accessible and plain-spoken version of the kind of "culture warrior" stance of higher-brow Catholic media voices like *First Things* and *Crisis* magazines. Charles Chaput, sometime archbishop of Philadelphia and himself a culture warrior of impeccable credentials who served on EWTN's Board of Governors, famously noted how "Mother's" rhetorical style (variously described as plain-spoken or unlettered, depending on one's viewpoint) succeeded at a task that the nation's bishops themselves couldn't achieve. She:

> founded and grew a network that appealed to everyday Catholics, under-stood their needs and fed their spirits. She had a lot [*sic*] of help, obviously, but that was part of her genius.[8]

Mother Angelica's "rightward turn" in both her personal messaging and in her televised events on EWTN was gradual but consistent when viewed with a backward glance. It was by no means anomalous that a "who's who" of conservative bishops turned out to preside at her funeral: Archbishop Chaput himself presided at her funeral mass, while renegade archbishop Carlo Maria Vigano (at the time Apostolic Nuncio in Washington, DC, but shortly to become famous—or infamous—by publicly calling on Pope Francis to re-sign for his purported role in covering up the sexual misdeeds of Cardinal Theodore McCarrick, among others) showed up as well. The nun's funeral mass, in fact, reflected her consistent ideological commitments throughout her television career.[9]

Mother Angelica's increasingly visible rightward career turn also included a distinctly cozy relationship with a number of very conservative Catholic funders and donors who also served as board members for the network, as well as political pundits engaged in the larger culture war being fought both inside and outside the Catholic Church. This fairly large group of "reliably right" individuals who supported the nun's programming in financial and in other ways included Frank Hanna III, a devoted member of the Legion of Christ's lay movement Regnum Dei and a generous supporter of conservative political and religious causes. Also included among Mother Angelica's friends was Tim Busch, who sat on the EWTN Board and was co-founder of the Napa Institute, which charges $2600 a head for his "retreats" that bring together conservative Catholic theologians, other members of the right-of-center "donor class," and Republican politicians like Lindsay Graham and former Wisconsin Governor Scott Walker. Busch believed that a truly Catholic faith takes a dim view of labor unions and raising the minimum wage. He has publicly stated that "Capitalism and Catholicism can work hand-in-hand," and greeted the inauguration of Donald Trump with the declaration that a "time of light" had finally arrived in Washington, DC, in contrast to the "time of darkness" of the Obama presidency (an observation apparently made without irony). At the Napa Institute, therefore, one is hard-pressed to decide where to draw the line between conservative theology and the political loyalties of the right wing of the Republican Party.[10]

And in a similar "rightward" gesture, Mother Angelica made sure that her network was part of a network of "authentically Catholic" media and publishing outlets like the Sophia Institute Press, publisher of Taylor Marshall's genuinely bizarre book, *Infiltration: The Plot to Destroy the Catholic Church from Within*. That work offered a somewhat breathless account of betrayal and conspiracy that reads like a blend of Maria Monk's nineteenth-century *Awful Disclosures of the Hotel Dieu Monastery* and Senator Joe McCarthy's revelation of communist spies inside the State Department in the 1950s— a revelation that McCarthy himself had described as "a conspiracy so immense" as to defy reason (as indeed it did).[11]

According to Taylor's book—which made it to the number one spot in the "Christian Church History" category on Amazon.com—after more than a century of plotting, a diabolical group of Freemasons and Communists (the usual suspects in this literary genre) abetted by liberals, modernists, and other church "reformers," were able to elect a corrupt pope (Francis) as part of a much larger diabolical plot for world domination. But at least as interesting as the book's fantastical plot was the press that published it. Sophia Institute Press was, in fact, a small press located in Manchester, New Hampshire, affiliated with EWTN: Mother Angelica's network announced in 2015 that the press would produce publications that "supported the mission and values of Mother Angelica." That same year Dan Burke (who would become president and chief operating officer of EWTN News) joined Sophia Institute's Board. By 2011, the Sophia Institute Press became the publishing arm of two colleges: Thomas More College in New Hampshire and Holy Spirit College in Atlanta, the latter founded by EWTN board member and donor Hanna.[12]

How *Infiltration*'s narrative is related to the Sophia Institute Press's "Mission Statement," which declares its purpose to publish books "in conformity with the authentic teachings of the Catholic Church," is difficult to discern—as difficult to discern as EWTN's relationship with it. And that question only becomes more insistent when one takes a look at the Sophia Institute Press's backlist of books, among which is *Vigano vs. Vatican: The Uncensored Testimony of the Italian Journalist Who Broke the Story*, an ostensibly "unvarnished expose" detailing the courageous crusade of Archbishop Vigano to force Pope Francis to resign from the papacy because of his supposedly leadership role within the Vatican in covering up the sexual depredations of Washington Archbishop McCarrick, among other degenerates living inside the walls of the Vatican. How either of these two works are related to the mission of defending the "authentic teachings of the Catholic Church" remains somewhat opaque.[13]

Considerably less opaque is what the interlocking relations between the Sophia Institute Press and EWTN's founders, donors, and board members reveals about the Catholic alt-Right. Not surprisingly, it reveals the Catholic version of what American religious historians term the "interlocking directorate" of individuals and organizations which had founded and maintained the nineteenth-century evangelical Protestant empire in the decades before the American Civil War. And the key to the nineteenth-century interlocking directorate, what Charles Foster called "The Evangelical United Front" had been—as it is in its Catholic analogue in the twenty-first century—money, lots of money. Then, as now, a distinctive ideological vision of what both religion and American culture should look like was pressed by a network of very wealthy donors, journalists, and conservative Protestant clergy, dedicated to protecting a Protestant America over against assorted "others." And chief among those "others" were Catholics, beginning to pour into country in the 1830s and 1840s. The one outstanding anomaly in that analogy is that the interlocking directorate on the American Catholic right today poses the Bishop of Rome himself as the central figure threatening the "authentic teachings of the Catholic Church."[14]

All of this is grist for the mill in considering Katherine Stewart's article in 2021 for *The New Republic*, "How Big Money is Dividing American Catholicism," which noted both that American Catholics were theologically and culturally diverse, and that where they stand out from other similarly diverse groups in the ecology of American religion is the financial imbalance between the Catholic "left" and "right." Stewart argued that *that* imbalance between the Catholic left and right in the United States is extreme—and growing. And in Stewart's telling, that financial imbalance is not just one of a number of factors: it is *the* cause of the cultural war going on inside the American Catholic Church: "the intellectual world of the extreme [American] Catholic right today is the world that big money made." And the American Catholic world that "big money made" includes a network of individuals and groups, one of which was most assuredly EWTN itself. Other players in that world which merged conservative political and theological ideologies are the Becket Legal Advocacy Group (which played a central role in extending religious privileges to corporations in the famous *Burwell v. Hobby Lobby Stores* case), the journal *First Things* (a journal that "reinvented itself as a center for pro-Trump theology"), and The Acton Institute in Michigan (which champions the union of libertarian ideology and what it confusingly calls the "Judeo-Christian tradition").[15]

And by no means least important in Mother Angelica's quiver of individuals fighting the good ideological/theological fight was the increasingly visible figure of Raymond Arroyo: besides being the host on EWTN's weekly show *The World Over*, he also regularly appeared as a guest host on the Fox Network's *The Ingraham Angle*, one of Fox's most popular news shows. But on EWTN itself, Arroyo regularly brought in figures who combined Catholic identity with uncompromisingly conservative (and even libertarian) "takes" on overtly political issues like migrants on the US border; marriage equality; and Pope Francis's encyclical on the environment, *Laudato Si*. Regular guests on *The World Over* included the soon-to-be-indicted Trump "fixer" Steve Bannon; Bishop Thomas Paprocki of Springfield, Illinois, who would publicly accuse Cardinal Robert McElroy of heresy in the pages of *First Things* for saying that denying people communion for sexual sins was a now-dated practice that needed to be rethought; and Cardinal Gerhard Mueller, whom Pope Francis removed as Prefect of the Vatican Congregation for the Doctrine of the Faith, both for his vigorous public rebuke of the entire German bishops' conference for considering blessing gay couples ("to bless homosexual couples is blasphemy") and for more than implying to the press that the pope himself was personally blocking investigations into the clerical abuse of children. Bannon, Paprocki, and Mueller were known critics of the pope and of various aspects of his teaching, and some of them more than implied that the pope himself might be guilty of heterodoxy. For the host of a "Catholic" television program to regularly bring in such figures to interview was, at the very least, singular, and arguably considerably more than that.[16]

B. "Zero Obedience"

In the early 1990s, EWTN began producing more of the shows for its network in place of using programming produced for other media sites, a move which witnessed as well to a marked conservative shift in practice and worship. In place of earlier "borrowed" shows on issues of social and racial justice, Mother Angelica's programming began to increasingly focus on issues of Catholic doctrine and "faithful practice" (more on this, too, in time). And that shift was reflected as well in its daily televised masses, which, in 1992, began to incorporate increasing amounts of Latin and the gradual elimination of contemporary religious music in favor of Latin hymns and older Catholic music from the (pre-Vatican II) *St. Gregory Hymnal*. After 1992, when Pope Benedict XVI allowed the celebration of Latin Masses for "pastoral need", the masses broadcast from the EWTN chapel regularly started using Latin in saying or singing the *Gloria*, the *Sanctus*, and all of the prayers and responses after the "Great Amen" of the Mass Canon (i.e., the *Agnus Dei*, the *Domine non sum dignus*, etc.). And on Christmas Eve, 1993, Mother Angelica and all the nuns of her monastery appeared in the older Poor Clare habit of coif and full veil. But Mother Angelica's increasing emphasis on her own (somewhat singular) understanding of "Catholic tradition" led to famously public feuds, not only with American Catholic church leaders, but even with the pope.[17]

All of this portended the jeremiads that Mother Angelica would deliver on her show, although at the time when these changes appeared few put all the pieces of the puzzle together. But it was not exactly lightning in a cloudless sky when, in an August 1993 episode of *Mother Angelica Live*—broadcast live from World Youth Day, which was then taking place in Denver, Colorado— she strongly criticized a re-enactment of the Stations of the Cross performed by young people in which a woman played the part of Jesus. She categorized that ritual as an "abomination to the Eternal Father [*sic*]," a pronouncement followed by thirty minutes (live) of a denunciation of the "liberal church in America":

> I'm so tired of you, liberal church in America. Your whole purpose is to destroy . . . It's time somebody said something about all these tiny little cracks that you have been putting for the last 30 years into the church . . . We're just tired of you pushing anti-God, anti-Catholic and pagan ways into the Catholic Church. Leave us alone. Don't pour your poison, your venom, on all the church.[18]

Who, exactly, the "us" was in her request to be left alone would be become clearer in fairly short order. Rembert Weakland, the Archbishop of Milwaukee, who is generally considered one of most astute episcopal theologians in the American hierarchy (and one of the most progressive), responded to Mother Angelica's denunciation of the Youth Day event by labeling her rant as "one of the most disgraceful, un-Christian, offensive, and divisive diatribes I have ever heard." Hardly cowed by a reprimand by one of the most respected and visible bishops in the American Catholic Church, Mother Angelica simply added Weakland's name to those pouring poison and venom into the community: "he didn't think a woman playing Jesus was offensive? He can go put his head in the back toilet as far as I'm concerned."[19]

Even the most ardent champions of Mother Angelica and the EWTN would freely confess that no one would ever have described her public persona as either demure or restrained: indeed, it was her plain-spoken, pungent rhetorical style and simple, practical approach to Catholic faith and practice that constituted a large part of her attraction to many Catholics. But the exchange with Archbishop Weakland in 1993 represented a new stage in her participation in the US culture wars, in her case resolutely on the side of the conservative Catholic phalanx. And part and parcel of that new stage was a clear willingness to take on major figures in the American Catholic hierarchy. What was considerably less clear was the authority she believed she possessed to "take on" those church officials. Mother Angelica had never studied either theology or canon law, and her explication of the *Catechism* on which she regularly expounded on-air revealed a naïveté (either charming or frightening, depending on one's viewpoint) that allowed her to ignore the gradations of authority in Catholic teaching.

Mother Angelica thus sometimes offered a mixed bag of "faithful" Catholic belief and practice, largely without the benefit of formal study and research.

For instance, devotion to the Blessed Virgin Mary—a significant component of Mother Angelica's own personal prayer life—was given strong visual references during the televised masses from the monastery chapel (during which the camera paused for significant periods of time on the chapel's statue of Mary), and during Mother Angelica's direct-on-camera conversations with her viewing audiences during her own EWTN show, *Mother Angelica Live*. During these "one-on-one" conversations with her viewing audience, Mother Angelica talked about both Catholic devotion to the Blessed Virgin Mary (a several millennia-old tradition within Catholic Christianity) and Marian apparitions at Lourdes, Fatima, and elsewhere. But her discussions of the latter phenomena sometimes veered off-course, at least from a theological point of view. Her fervent explanations of the "secrets of Fatima" or the miracles at Lourdes steered very close to implying that these were intrinsic parts of Catholic doctrine and belief, to be placed on the same—or similar—level of authoritative teaching as the doctrines about the Trinity and the dual natures of Christ.

But the *Enchiridion Symbolorum* (the "Handbook of Symbols"—the official compendium of Catholic belief) always made it perfectly clear that there were explicit *levels* of authoritative teaching, distinguished by the "Theological Notes" attached to them. Those doctrines, which were labeled *de fide definite* ("defined of the faith"), were given the theological note of "1," and represented core doctrinal teaching to which all of the faithful were obliged to give assent. But none of the Marian apparitions so dear to Mother Angelica could be found in that category as being "defined of the faith." Indeed, none could be found in the next level of authoritative teaching either. Concretely, that meant that they could be "voluntarily embraced" (or not) on the part of faithful Catholics: there was no required assent on the part of Catholics as to whether the Virgin Mary did, or did not, appear at Lourdes, Fatima, and other locations. But many of her viewers undoubtedly would have been surprised to learn of that fact: Mother Angelica's spiritual conferences with her viewers seemed to either ignore those levels of authoritative teaching (perhaps in a moment of Marian fervor) or perhaps because she was not familiar with the idea of "Theological Notes" in the first place. These distinctions—so central to theologians in explaining Catholic belief and practice—took a back seat in Mother Angelica's efforts to explain a complicated theological tradition as simply as she was able to a largely theologically untrained viewing audience.[20]

That larger context goes a considerable way toward explaining Mother Angelica's public critique of Cardinal Roger Mahony, the Archbishop of Los Angeles. On November 12, 1997, Mother Angelica publicly denounced a pastoral letter Mahony had written to the Catholics of his far-flung archdiocese. In her opinion, that pastoral letter, "Gather Faithfully Together: A Guide to Sunday Mass," denied Catholic teaching on the Real Presence of Christ in the eucharist.

But there were many levels of reflection in Mahoney's document so it difficult to say what exactly the nun took exception to: Mahony opened his thirty-one-page letter with strong praise for Vatican II and its reform and renewal of the church's liturgy—something that undoubtedly did not dispose Mother Angelica to like the document, given the direction in which the televised liturgies of her own monastery were heading. Further, Mahony spoke of the gathered assembly as a family "gathered around the Lord's Table," something that the nun might have read as too Protestant—gathered around a table, as opposed to an altar. Mahony likewise sought to replace the older perception that the priest "makes the eucharist" with a more contemporary understanding of the eucharist as a community event. Mahoney argued that "when we say 'eucharist' we mean the whole action of presider and assembly," so that, in real sense, "the [entire] Church makes the Eucharist, and the Eucharist makes the Church" (a theologically unimpeachable position based on a quite orthodox understanding of the mass). Further, Mahoney noted in his letter that, after the consecration, as the presider holds up a large piece of the communion bread, the entire congregation sings the ancient three-fold acclamation, "Lamb of God," a hymn "that will carry us until the bread is all broken, the consecrated wine all poured into communion cups." Mahoney's letter to his diocese was a quite sophisticated theological and moving reflection on the eucharist using the best of post-Vatican II Roman Catholic theology.[21]

But Mother Angelica read Mahony's statements about the "bread and wine" on the altar in a way that seemed to imply a downplaying of transubstantiation. Not for her the post-Vatican II emphasis on Christ's gradually unfolding presence, first in the gathered community, then in the Word proclaimed, and finally in the consecrated bread and wine. The very idea that the entire assembly—priest and people together—"made eucharist" was dubious, at best: for Mother Angelica, the mass was about the transubstantiated consecrated host, now most assuredly *not* bread, but transformed into the very Body of Christ. To even refer to the elements on the altar as "consecrated bread and wine" seemed like something very close to heresy, even if the vast majority of Catholic theologians trained in liturgy and sacraments did so. Mother Angelica knew best. Thus, she announced in one of her more famous pronouncements to millions of viewers watching her show, "in fact, the cardinal of California [*sic*] is teaching that it [the elements of Holy Communion] is bread and wine before the Eucharist and after the Eucharist. I'm afraid my obedience in that diocese would be absolutely zero. And I hope everybody else's in that diocese is zero."[22]

But Mother Angelica's constant appeal to the "doctrine of transubstantiation" in her denunciation of Mahoney also revealed a fragile purchase on Catholic theology: the Catholic Church has no doctrine of transubstantiation. It has a "doctrine of the Real Presence," which asserts that the elements of bread and wine were actually transformed into the body and blood of Christ, a transformation that the Council of Trent in 1551 affirmed "has fittingly and properly been named transubstantiation." Transubstantiation was thus a *theological* explanation for the doctrine of Real Presence of Christ and was not itself a doctrine. Indeed, there were other (valid) theological models for understanding how Christ was really present in the consecrated bread and wine. Further, and equally pertinent, Vatican II's famous "Constitution on the Liturgy" situated that doctrine within a much broader context of how Christ was "really present" during the celebration of the eucharist: in the proclaimed Word of God, in the person of the minister of the sacrament, in the worshiping community itself, and in the consecrated bread and wine in a concentrated way. But that last "real presence" was part of a much richer and broader understanding of Christ's sacramental presence, each depending on the others for the unfolding of Christ's presence in the sacrament. And even after that unfolding, the "elements" of bread and wine remained that—bread and wine—although their "substance" was now transformed into something else. Cardinal Mahoney was therefore on very solid (and orthodox) Catholic teaching regarding the sacrament in his pastoral letter.[23]

Mahony regarded Mother Angelica's comments as just one step short of a heresy charge (on a nationally televised "Catholic" network, no less), and demanded an on-air apology from the nun. After all, an accusation of "heresy"—the accusation that one had departed from believing and teaching correct Catholic doctrine—was one of the most serious changes one could bring against any bishop. Further, her televised implication that the Cardinal Archbishop, who was the ranking ordinary for all of the dioceses of California, was teaching heterodox theology was a shocking violation of

Catholic practice, especially for a member of a religious order, like herself, engaged in public evangelism. Mahony responded immediately:

> For you to call into question my own belief in the Real Presence is without precedent. To compound the matter, your call for my people to offer zero obedience to their Shepherd is unheard of and shocking ...What saddens me the most is that EWTN has such potential for being a positive tool for the new evangelization ... But when a network features programs that attack and criticize its own bishops publicly, how can that build up the body of Christ, the church?[24]

Mahony demanded that the nun read an apology on the air, an apology to be written by the nun's own bishop, David Foley, and that it be read a minimum of four times between December 1 and December 25. But such an abject apology was never offered: Mahony's public denunciation of the nun elicited a "conditional" apology from Mother Angelica, saying that she was sorry if she in fact had misunderstood his meaning in talking about the eucharist in his diocesan letter (what secular historians now often refer to as a "Richard Nixon non-denial denial"). Far more problematic than that, however, was the fact that she continued her denunciation of Mahony and his pastoral letter on her on-air programming after her non-denial denial. But both her accusation and her "apology" simply raised the stakes even further: who was Mother Angelica, with no authorization from any church official—and certainly none from her local bishop, who was the only official teacher of doctrine in the Birmingham diocese—to offer commentary on the orthodoxy of the teaching of a cardinal archbishop? Who was Mother Angelica to question the teaching of one of the Princes of the Church? And Roger Mahony was not buying it, including her non-denial denial. Mahony wrote directly to Rome, asking for fundamental changes in the management style and on-air "tone" of Mother Angelica's media empire. Gregory Coiro, the Capuchin priest who was director of media relations for the Archdiocese of Los Angeles, said that:

> the cardinal wants the Holy See to do something about Mother Angelica's whole attitude that she is not responsible to the National Conference of Catholic Bishops or to any of the individual bishops ... It goes beyond her criticism of the cardinal—it's about how the network operates and to whom it is accountable.[25]

Further, Coiro noted that Mother Angelica's remarks about the pastoral letter constituted "technically, a very serious violation of canon law," specifically Canon 753 in the church's legal code, which states unequivocally that all Catholics were to respect the teaching office of their diocesan bishop, and specifically states that only the pope (or whomever he delegates in the Vatican) can correct a bishop's teaching. Likewise, Canon 1373 in the same code forbids any Catholic from advising disobedience to the pope or the bishops, and states that such activity incurs "just penalties," up to and including the very serious imposition of interdict, which places the offender outside the church, and therefore cut off from participation in any of the sacraments.[26]

But as John Allen, the journalist reporting on the incident for the *National Catholic Reporter* (*NCR*), predicted, Mahony's desire for an official rebuke from Rome (or anywhere else) on the nun would "find rough going." Allen recalled that at the 1996 "Call to Holiness" bishops' meeting in Detroit, Mother Angela told her viewers that there were three or four bishops gathered for that event that she refused to interview for her show. Those "outlawed" bishops demanded to know by whose authority she had refused to interview them, and she simply responded, "I own the network." When one of the bishops reminded her that she wouldn't always be at Our Lady of the Angels Monastery, she quipped, "Well, I'll blow the damn thing up before you get it." And Allen's prediction proved to be infallibly correct: no correction came from Rome or from her local bishop. One might reasonably suppose that, however unlettered and unsophisticated her grasp of Catholic doctrine might be, no church official wanted to take on a figure who was watched daily by millions of viewers.[27]

Just two years later, Mother Angelica was again involved in an episcopal dust-up: in 1999, Foley, the bishop of Birmingham, Alabama—and therefore the "ordinary" in charge of the diocese in which Our Lady of the Angels Monastery resided—issued a decree to all the churches and chapels of his diocese stating that priests were no longer allowed to celebrate the mass with their backs to the congregation. *Inter Oecumenici*, the 1964 "instruction" implementing the Second Vatican Council's decree on the liturgy, had argued that altars in Catholic churches should be free-standing, allowing the priest to face his congregation while presiding at the eucharist, and most Catholic churches in the United States had, in fact, followed that directive. And that practice came with the very highest level of approval: when the pope presided at mass at St. Peter's free-standing high altar, the tradition included the possibility of facing the congregation. Thus, the pope's own practice witnessed to and confirmed the directive issued by the Second Vatican Council, as well as supporting Bishop Foley's letter to his Birmingham diocese. Further (and more to the point), Bishop Foley observed in the letter to his diocese that celebrating mass with the priest's back to the congregation had come to be "layered with other meanings" beyond the liturgical and sacramental; indeed, by the late 1990s in the United States, celebrating the eucharist *ad orientem* "amounts to making a political statement and is dividing the people."[28]

As Allen reported in the *NCR* shortly after the decree was published:

> although Bishop Foley's missive never mentioned either EWTN or Mother Angelica by name, both supporters and critics of Mother Angelica, known for her feisty conservatism in church affairs, told the *NCR* that the decree seemed to be directed at EWTN, since its daily mass often shows the priest with his back to the audience [*sic*].[29]

But whatever the wishes of her own bishop on this liturgical question, Mother consistently argued that celebrating mass *ad orientem* was "more reverent" (although it was never clear how that was the case): for Mother Angelica, "Latin was the perfect language for the mass. It's the language of the Church [*sic*], which allows us to pray a verbal prayer without distraction." In her opinion, "so much is spoiled in the vernacular," so that "the way it is today with the priest facing the people, it is something between the people and the priest. Too often it is just some kind of get-together, and Jesus is all but forgotten." During the Latin Mass, in which the priest faced east, her own experience was that:

> it was almost mystical. It gave you an awareness of heaven, of the awesome humility of God who manifests Himself in the guise of bread and wine. The love that he had for us, the desire to remain with us is simply awesome. You could concentrate on that love because you weren't distracted by your own language. You could go anywhere in the world and you always knew what was going on. It was contemplative because as the Mass was going on you could close your eyes and visualize what really happened. You could feel it. You could look to the east and realize that God had come and was really present.[30]

The article which provided the above quotes by Mother Angelica on the glories of the Latin Mass was posted by Brian Williams on the "liturgy guy" blog-spot, and his posting was followed by twenty-eight comments—all by fans of the nun. The first, from "JohnD," was a question about the *novus ordo*, the revised Latin Mass promulgated by Pope Paul VI: "Why do most American 'Catholic' bishops (quotation marks in the original) hate the ancient Catholic liturgy and want the liturgy offered [*sic*] in the most Protestant, secularist and atheistic way possible?" And the answer (presumably posted by Mr. Williams) was, "Maybe your 'Catholic' bishops aren't Catholic but rather wolves in shepherds' clothing." Another poster ("pearl87") observed "not just American bishops, ALL the bishops and cardinals have been selected [for] the destruction of the mass." "John R" observed that "as the late Fr. Malachi Martin said, 'between you, me, and the Holy Ghost, it's the ONLY mass'" ("it" presumably being the Latin Mass). Somewhat further along in the same discussion chain, someone pointed out that an awareness of the poor was one of the graces of real Catholic liturgy, to which JohnD responded "the 'preferential option for the poor' is simply warmed over communist and socialist propaganda ever since the Vatican, the Papacy, and the hierarchy were all infiltrated by the Communist and Socialist Parties prior to and following Vatican II." And pearl87 agreed: "there is no virtue in poverty. Christ told us to be 'poor in spirit.' You are terribly misinformed and lacking in understanding about the Catholic faith, not unlike Jorge Bergoglio [Pope Francis]."[31]

For those who regularly follow the dark under-belly of the Catholic blogosphere, these comments—while certainly disrespectful and (probably) materially disobedient according to the Church's Code of Canon Law—are hardly shocking. Comments like these (and worse) appear on a daily basis on the Catholic internet, evincing rage, resentment, disappointment, and a sectarian understanding of the Catholic tradition (what one of my students calls the "products of the Institute for Data-Free Analysis"). It would thus be tempting to dismiss these posted statements as humorous products of the theologically illiterate, the cranky, or possibly the mentally ill. But such an easy dismissal would be a mistake. And it would be a mistake because both Mother Angelica and her network proactively abetted such attitudes, and at least some of her regular viewers intuited this. One of the most consistent themes linking the twenty-eight comments on the email chain on the "liturgy guy" blog was the consistent praise voiced for Mother Angelica over against "liberal church officials" advancing an atheistic, communist agenda, including Jorge Bergoglio—now known as Pope Francis.

To many critics it seemed as though Mother Angelica ran her media empire as though it were above accountability to mere human church officials, including accountability to her own bishop. In Catholic-speak, Mother Angelica's "taking on" of Cardinal Mahony and her subsequent refusal to back down from her criticism of his pastoral, as well as her seeming indifference to the directives from her own bishop regarding how mass should be celebrated in her monastery chapel, was disrespectful, and arguably something more serious than that. It almost seemed as though Mother Angelica believed herself to possess and teach the "authentic magisterium" over against bishops and cardinals (and, yes—even, or perhaps especially—the pope). And Michael Sean Winters of the *NCR* years later recognized this, and named it as such:

> Of course, *NCR* has regularly published articles that are critical of popes and members of the hierarchy, but the comparison distorts the reality, at least mostly. In the first place, *NCR* has never represented itself as speaking for the authentic Catholic magisterium. We have published essays saying the magisterium is wrong, and that it should be changed, to be sure. [But] EWTN features, and features regularly, those who claim they possess the authentic magisterium, [over against] those are constitutionally endowed with that authority. Phil Lawler, Fr. Gerald Murray, Robert Royal: they are more Catholic than the pope, at least this pope.[32]

C. "The Work of the Devil"

None of these shenanigans eluded the eye of Rome, which was also informed of the details of EWTN programming and its content by major episcopal players like Los Angeles's own cardinal archbishop. Therefore an "apostolic visitation" (never a cause for rejoicing on the part of those being "visited") was set up in 2000: San Juan's Archbishop Roberto Gonzalez Nieves was tasked by the Vatican with visiting Our Lady of the Angels Monastery to explore in situ the content of the station's programming, the legal and canonical question of who actually owned the station, the exact nature of the relationship of the station to the monastery, and the question of Mother Angelica's authority over both the station and the monastery. Archbishop Gonzalez Nieves duly filed his report with the Vatican, as requested, but the contents of that report were never made public. But the next year Mother

Angelica suffered a debilitating stroke, causing her to cease broadcasting *Mother Angelica Live*. She spent the remainder of her life living the secluded contemplative life of a Poor Clare nun until her death in 2016.[33]

But even after Mother Angelica's retirement into monastic seclusion in 2001, EWTN continued its on-air denunciation of "liberals" in the church, arguably in an even more unnuanced style with Mother Angelica no longer on the scene. Indeed, the network's increasingly strident criticism of the Pope seemed quite consciously presented to undermine the collegiality that Francis was trying to establish in the church. And the figure who emerged as the chief "liberal hunter" in EWTN's programming was Arroyo, who gathered a group around him that he himself labeled "the Papal Posse." That group in fact became, in time, a fairly well-defined group of religious and political far-right conservatives, a group that Winters claimed made the Catholic faith subservient to a political agenda, a "Republican and increasingly Trumpian agenda." Arroyo's news "commentary—much like Mother's—became increasingly critical of what he termed "liberal elements" in the Church, always presented as the viewpoint of a "true Catholic" (presumably meaning Arroyo himself). In a pontificate dedicated to actually implementing the reforms mandated by the Second Vatican Council—a pontificate "that has often prioritized the pastoral and evangelical over the doctrinal"—Mr. Arroyo's antipathy unsurprisingly, centered on Pope Francis himself."[34]

Arroyo's recurrent guests included prominent and quite public critics of the Pope: Cardinal Raymond Burke, who famously co-signed the "*Dubia*" letter, questioning Francis's orthodoxy for being open to allowing divorced and remarried Catholics receiving communion. Cardinal Mueller—the fired Prefect of the Vatican Congregation for the Doctrine of the Faith, who published a "manifesto of faith" at the EWTN-owned Catholic News Agency, similarly questioning Francis's orthodoxy about letting divorced and remarried Catholics receive communion—was praised by Arroyo as an instance of "true" Catholic teaching—over against that, presumably, of the Bishop of Rome. After Archbishop Vigano released a (discredited) document critical of the pope for his handling of the McCarrick case and urging the pope to resign, Vigano (himself "*fugitivus*" from the Vatican) appeared on Arroyo's show shortly after the publication of his public denunciation, during the course of which Arroyo called on the pope to "reconcile" with Vigano. Arroyo interviewed Vigano even after Cardinal Marc Ouellet, Prefect of the Vatican Congregation for Bishops, publicly called on Vigano to "come out of hiding, and repent for your revolt."[35]

And a quick tour through the topsy-turvy world of YouTube videos would seem to give support to Arroyo's designation of the "Papal Posse," made up of political figures as well as conservative church leaders like Burke and Vigano: Arroyo's on-air conversation with a spokesperson for "NumbersUSA," a politically organized anti-immigrant organization that referred to migrants as threats to America, let a number of misstatements go unchallenged. And during Arroyo's twenty-minute interview with then-White House advisor Steve Bannon, the latter defended both the Trump administration and other "populist/nationalist/sovereignty movements" as much better reflecting "genuine Catholic social teaching" than Pope Francis, with Arroyo nodding all the while. And during Arroyo's fifteen-minute interview less than two weeks before the 2016 presidential election in Trump's Miami hotel, Trump responded to Arroyo's questions about the *Access Hollywood* controversy by saying that it was "all made up," comments that Arroyo let pass without comment even though the Trump's comments were recorded on tape and were available for anyone to listen to. "All made up?" Arroyo displayed the same kind of fawning attentiveness several years later in a July 2019 interview with then-vice president Mike Pence at Ave Maria University, during which Pence called Democrats "the party of abortion on demand, even the party of infanticide." The *NCR*, commenting on all of these interviews by a "Catholic" newscaster, labeled EWTN and its programming host a "shill for the far-right wing of the Republican Party," and it is difficult not to agree after viewing the programming.[36]

EWTN's ongoing critique of the pope, as well as its troubling relationship with a number of prominent figures from the right wing of the Republican Party, garnered increasing attention from Rome. It was, then, not exactly a surprise when Pope Francis, meeting with a group of fellow Jesuits in Bratislava (Slovakia) on September 12, 2021, remarked on the network's increasingly partisan programming. As reported by Antonio Spadaro, the Jesuit editor-in-chief of the Rome-based magazine, *La Civilta Cattolica*, Francis was uncharacteristically sharp in answering questions put to him by fellow Jesuits: asked about how he felt about being distrusted, disliked, and denounced by some Catholics, Francis replied:

There is for example, a large Catholic television channel that has no hesitation in continuing speaking ill of the pope. I personally deserve attacks and insults because I am a sinner, but church does not deserve them. They are the work of the devil. I have also said this to some of them.[37]

Clement Lisi, reporting on Francis's Bratislava meeting, immediately observed that almost everyone in the Catholic media knew that the pope was talking about EWTN, and especially about that network's news host Arroyo, who had regularly interviewed figures like the schismatic Vigano. As Lisi pointed out, just one of the problems with Arroyo's repeated invitations to Vigano was that he continued to interview him even after the release of Vatican probe in November 2020, exonerating Francis but placing the blame on two of Mother Angelica and Arroyo's papal heroes: John Paul II and his successor, Benedict XVI. What was going on in Arroyo's willingness to continually listen to Vigano's discredited critiques of Francis was clearly about more than simply "getting to the bottom" of very serious charges publicly questioning the orthodoxy of the Supreme Pontiff.[38]

D. "Give Me That Old-Time Religion"

Mother Angelica and the EWTN fit seamlessly into George Marsden's famous definition of American fundamentalism as "reactive, militant, and deeply sectarian." Indeed, EWTN's reactive, militant stance reached even to denouncing the highest authorities in the Church (including Pope Francis himself) for teaching unorthodox doctrine, and skating (early and often) well over the line of material disobedience to the *official teachers* of Catholic Christianity: telling a seated archbishop to "stick his head in the back toilet," and counseling "zero obedience" to millions of Catholics in the archdiocese of Los Angeles to their cardinal archbishop. In terms of the Catholic list of serious sins, "material disobedience" to bishops and the pope ranks pretty high, especially for a vowed religious sister. But from Mother Angelica's viewpoint (just as for Leonard Feeney and Gommar dePauw) witnessing to the authentic magisterium (that is, *her* understanding of the Catholic Tradition) ranked higher than mere institutional obedience, even though she had, in fact, taken a solemn vow of obedience to obey duly constituted ecclesial authorities. In the Middle Ages, the Church had burnt people alive for considerably less than that.

Just like their Protestant second cousins in the opening decades of the twentieth century, Mother Angelica and Arroyo appear to believe that they alone possessed the "authentic magisterium" in passing on the faith. But just like the "old-time religion" advanced by Protestant fundamentalists a century earlier, the "authentic" Roman Catholicism preached by Mother

Angelica and her acolytes was actually neither ancient nor Roman: it was instead distinctly modern and distinctly American. It was modern because it was reacting to the post-Vatican II context in which American Catholicism found itself after 1965: a model of Church which lowered the drawbridge and left the fortress in order to dialogue with modern culture. EWTN's "traditionalist" piety and worship was reacting to that distinctly *modern* circumstance: in this it was exactly analogous to the twentieth-century Protestant fundamentalist understanding of the written scripture as "verbally inerrant"—a distinctly modern doctrine elucidated in the United States after 1919.

The "old-time religion" advanced by fundamentalists after 1919 was a modern elucidation of the gospel aimed at countering the modern theological worldview of the majority of their Protestant contemporaries. Their very effort to argue for a detailed "verbal inerrancy" understanding of the Bible was palpably modern because nineteenth-century Protestants shared an understanding of the Bible as "inspired" that had no need to be spelled out in more detail because it was so universally taken for granted. The theory of verbal inerrancy—that every word in the Bible was divinely inspired, and so had to be taken in its unvarnished literal sense—so painstakingly elaborated by Protestant Fundamentalists after the end of World War I, revealed therein its twentieth-century roots precisely in its effort to close off all possible alternative understandings of "inspired." There was no need for elaboration before that: the need for that elaboration was created by the threats that only appeared in the twentieth century, especially by the rise of historical criticism of the Bible, which argued that scripture reflected the cultural presuppositions of its place of origin, and so had to be interpreted by scholars familiar with Semitic languages and cultures. Historical criticism argued that Bible did not, in fact, mean what it said or say what it meant—a position that both scandalized and terrified fundamentalist Protestants (and many Catholics as well).[39]

Precisely like the contributors to *The Fundamentals*—that series of essays published between 1910 and 1915 that named the resulting Protestant movement—Mother Angelica believed that genuine religion had to be perspicaciously clear, and set out in simple and easy-to-understand propositions that even she (uneducated in theology and the levels of magisterial teaching) could pass on to her vast (and even more theologically unlettered) viewing audience. In this, her detailed "commentary" on the Church's *Catechism*—sitting squarely in front of the camera and offering an "explication" of dense teaching in simple (simplistic?) ways—was precisely to close off any possible alternative readings of the True Faith, even though many of her explanations of that "old-time religion" lacked scholarly nuance. She was, in fact, the precursor to a media type now quite common on the dark underside of the Catholic internet: those many dozens of bloggers who believe that anyone with an internet connection, a copy of *The Catechism*, and grievances to air could now proclaim themselves to be offering the *real* Catholic magisterium, bishops and theologians be damned.

Also like those Protestant "Bible Believers" a century ago, the teaching "passed on" was both a-historical and committed to an older paradigm of Catholicism in which "faith" was both propositional and unnuanced: *The Catechism* could only be interpreted in one way (just like the Bible for Protestant fundamentalists). "Doctrine"—in reality, a multi-valent term in Catholic theology—was presented as both objective (like gravity) and perspicacious (i.e., self-evidently clear).[40]

Mother Angelica opted for an older paradigm of Catholic belief and practice that sought to "freeze frame" Catholic identity in a profoundly a-historical way that was openly scornful of much of post-Vatican II liturgy and teaching: and it was *that* very militancy, marking so much of her often-crude rhetoric regarding back toilets and zero obedience to cardinal archbishops, that sets her off as a genuine outlier from Catholic identity, despite the traditional wimple and veil of the Poor Clare habit, the regular recitation of the Rosary, the loving camera shots of the statue of the Virgin Mary during her televised liturgies, and the Latin Masses broadcast from the monastery's chapel.

Considerably more problematic was the fact that Mother Angelica and her soldiers at EWTN seem to have missed the central ecclesiological component of Catholic identity: *communio*. That is, at the very core of the Catholic Christian identity was the belief that the faithful were "in communion"— with the Bishop of Rome, with their own bishop (the *only* authorized teacher in a Catholic diocese), and with each other. Over against the Protestant belief elucidated clearly in Martin Luther's "Here I Stand" speech at the Diet of Worms, the Catholic tradition had emphasized the vital necessity of remaining in community and in communion with other believers, most especially with bishops and popes. Luther's example—believing that his individual witness to Gospel truths as he understood them was more important than maintaining relations with the pope—had been roundly rejected in the sixteenth century, as it had consistently been throughout Christian history.

The Church had always pronounced a loud and definitive "No!" to all those groups—the Montanists, the Albigensians, the Cathars, the Jansenists, the Feeneyites—who sought to break away and form a purer, less "mixed" community dedicated to an "authentic tradition" that others had strayed from. And more often than not, the leaders of those breakaway groups allocated the authentic interpretation of saving truths to themselves alone. The group of believers that formed around them were still, arguably, Christian; they were just not Catholic Christians. They were, instead, sectarian Christians, adopting the Niebuhrian "Christ Against Culture" stance of the culture warriors. Thus, one cannot help but perceive EWTN and its programming—for all the "Catholic elements" in its broadcasts—as propagating an understanding of the Christian tradition that was Catholic on the outside but something else on the inside.[41]

And EWTN's loudly proclaimed loyalties to the faith of the "Holy Roman Church" appear deeply problematic, given Mother Angelica and Arroyo's apparent disdain and rejection of the current occupant of the Chair of Peter. Arroyo's often-gleeful interviews with some of Pope Francis's most trenchant critics—Cardinal Burke, Archbishop Vigano, etc.—would seem to presume that Catholics were free to "choose" which popes they were going to be loyal to and obey—a deeply *unCatholic* stance closer to the positions of Feeney and DePauw than that of John Paul II or Benedict XVI. Remaining in communion with the Bishop of Rome (whoever that might be) comes close to the very core of Catholic ecclesiological identity. There are many devout and holy Christians not in communion with the pope; they are just not Catholic Christians. In that sense, the Catholicism presented by Mother Angelica and her network was distinctly American, and not "Roman." And that was because most of energies fueling her message were generated by the culture wars dividing American Catholicism no less than mainstream Americans.

That fact—that the American culture wars also explains Mother Angelica and Arroyo's extremely close fusion of religious traditionalism with political conservatism in an almost seamless way—also helps to explain how EWTN was a distinctly *American* phenomenon. As Marsden had argued, while theology and religious belief were certainly the focus of the "Bible Believers" who produced and published *The Fundamentals*, the cultural experience of living in a post-World War I culture also had a great deal to do with shaping their religious commitments. After 1919, Protestant conservatives expressed genuine alarm about the growing threat of "modernist" ideas in American culture itself: their fears about religious and political liberalism witnessed to

the fact that "American fundamentalism was not simply an expression of theology or concern about false doctrine. In the minds of most fundamentalists,
the theological crisis came to be inextricably wedded to the very survival of
Christian civilization." And that crisis was produced by "liberals" across the
theological, political, and cultural spectrum. Heavens! Liberal Methodists
even allowed dancing after 1919![42]

It was in no way accidental that in addition to the conservative ecclesiastical figures regularly interviewed by Arroyo on *The World Over* with
such unalloyed (and sometimes even gleeful) approval, an array of right-
wing Republican figures also became regular "featured guests." All of them
elucidated the grave threat posed by liberals (mostly in the Democratic
Party) to America's "Christian civilization" (the latter a phrase usually left
vague and non-detailed). Just as their early twentieth-century Protestant
forebears shaped a worldview in which the explicitly theological threats became inextricably tied to specific liberal political and cultural stances, so
the "Catholic Perspective" ostensibly presented by EWTN was defined by
an unabashedly partisan, anti-Francis, libertarian, and alt-right Republican
array of journalists, politicians, and newscasters. And that perspective wove
a seamless connection between "true Catholics" and the conservative wing
of the Republican Party, most especially on the single issue of abortion. But
that seamless connection flew in the face of the regular warnings of the US
Bishops' conference that American Catholics were not supposed to be single-
issue voters.[43]

On its Memorial Day broadcast in 2019, EWTN's *News from a Catholic
Perspective* presented two previously recorded one-on-one interviews by
anchor Lauren Ashburn. The first—a ten-minute interview with then-
Vice President Pence during his visit to Ave Maria University in Florida
during which Pence denounced "media and Hollywood liberals," the entire Democratic Party as the "party of abortion on demand (and even the
"party of infanticide"), and baldly described Donald Trump as the "most
pro-life president in American history." In the second eleven-minute interview, during which the anchor served up "softball" questions to former
White House Press Secretary Sarah Sanders, Ashburn asked her guest about
the ways in which then-President Trump had stood up for religious liberty
against assorted "others" (all of whom, it would turn out, were Democrats),
Ashburn mentioned that a recent poll showed white Catholics giving
President Trump a forty-four percent approval rating, but added "I would
say that 44 percent number would be a lot higher if he came on EWTN's

News Nightly." To which Sanders responded with a laugh, "We'll work on that."[44]

Much of this might be dismissed as broadly played antics acted out in "buffo" style for an uneducated section of a theologically unlettered viewing public if it did not play such an important role in shaping the views of so many Catholics who watch EWTN. But the particular "slice" of Catholicism presented on it does not, in fact, present the magisterial Roman tradition of St. Peter and St. Paul, but rather a simplistic (and often crude) form of American fundamentalism much closer in style to the fundamentalist Protestantism that, after 1919, was dedicated to a similarly anomalous "old-time religion" that was modern and American, not ancient and biblical. Similarly, Mother Angelica's old-time religious "take" on the tradition of the Holy Roman and Apostolic Church is about America in the last half century, and is neither Roman, universal, nor apostolic. (Nor, one might reasonably argue, old.)

5

The "Benedict Option" in Kansas

A. Backward, Christian Soldiers!

In 2017, Rod Dreher, senior editor at the *American Conservative* and a prominent commentator on the political and cultural right, published a New York Times bestseller entitled *The Benedict Option: A Strategy for Christians in a Post-Christian Nation*, a book that had people across the left/right religious spectrum talking (or, actually, arguing). Drawing on the writings of Benedict of Nursia—one of the founders of the western Christian tradition of monasticism in the sixth century—as well as from the writings of one of America's most famous philosophers, Alasdair MacIntyre, Dreher called on the Christian faithful to insulate themselves from a dying culture committed to secular values and a thorough-going materialism. The book's title was based on a an observation made in MacIntyre's most famous book, *After Virtue*:

> If the tradition of the virtues was able to survive of the last dark ages, we are not entirely without hope . . . We are waiting not for a Godot, but for another—doubtless very different—St. Benedict.[1]

St. Benedict—founder of the first western community of monks in Monte Cassino in 529—had recognized that in the dark days after the collapse of the Roman Empire caused by barbarian invasions starting in the fourth century, Christianity's call to discipleship in community needed to be preserved in intentional communities in which the faithful could gather with like-minded believers in a very unsafe world. At Monte Cassino (which eventually became the Mother Community of hundreds of Benedictine monasteries around the world) Benedict founded a new social order of monks—and eventually, nuns as well—committed to "*ora et labora*" (work and prayer). It could be (and has been) argued that Benedictine monasticism, modeled on the Monte Cassino community about eighty miles south of Rome, saved western culture by not only preserving the classical writings of western thinkers like Aristotle and Augustine from the destruction wreaked by the Visigoths and Huns, but also by copying them in new manuscript form in scriptoriums across Europe. Those closed monastic communities also provided a regular cycle of reading, praying, and manual labor that attracted (literally) tens of thousands of men and women fleeing from the encroaching darkness brought on by the collapse of Rome and its culture.[2]

And the dust jacket of Dreher's book made that comparison between sixth century and the twenty-first century quite explicit, tipping off readers as to the book's purpose even before they even started reading it:

Today, a new post-Christian barbarism reigns. Many believers are blind to it, and their churches are too weak to resist. Politics offers little help in this spiritual crisis. What is needed is the Benedict Option, a strategy that draws on the authority of scripture and the wisdom of the ancient church. The goal: to embrace exile from the mainstream culture and construct a resilient counterculture.[3]

The outgoing archbishop of Philadelphia, Charles Chaput, described Dreher's book as a "tough, frank, and true assessment of contemporary American culture," while the *New York Times* columnist David Brooks called it "the most discussed and most important religious book of the decade." But notwithstanding the high praise garnered for the book from a range of voices, Dreher's rhetorical arch so elegantly constructed linking the sixth to the twenty-first centuries nonetheless contained an historical error at its very core: St. Benedict had never intended his call for monastic retreat from the world to be seen as a model for all Christian believers—a vision of a sectarian church made up of networks of monasteries dotting the European countryside. Based on both the Hebrew and Christian scriptures, Catholic Christianity had always viewed God's creation as good, however fallen it may have appeared (as it assuredly did to some in the sixth century). Indeed, the Church of the first four or five centuries of the Christian era had repeatedly condemned those groups which denounced the created world as inescapably evil and fallen, necessitating complete Christian withdrawal from it. Benedict had rather envisioned a monastic family that was very different from Christian families living in the world, most evident in his mandate of celibacy for all who sought inclusion in his monasteries. As Benedict understood the monastic vocation, he did so much to shape in writing his famous "Rule"; then, life in a monastery cut off from "the world" was to be one of many forms of the Christian vocation, but a vocation *not* for the many, but precisely for the few. The *real* Benedict option therefore understood that the vast majority of faithful believers would live out their lives of discipleship in the world—which is where the majority of believers had always lived.[4]

But the small community of St. Marys, Kansas, has taken that option precisely in the direction limned by Dreher, even if it is not one of which Benedict of Nursia ever conceived. Located about thirty minutes away from the much larger city of Topeka, and about one hundred miles from the exact geographic center of the continental United States, "St. Marys Mission" was established in 1824 by Belgian Jesuits as a school for Native American boys, which evolved into a college for Jesuit scholastics (priests in training) by the late nineteenth century. In one of those historical ironies that make the study of the past so interesting, the red-brick buildings of what is now St. Mary's Academy (which, unlike the town, uses the apostrophe in its name) were built to both house and educate Jesuit seminarians in a multi-year (and quite rigorous) immersion in both philosophy and theology—all in Latin! But, by 1967, the Jesuits decided that their mission in the middle of corn fields was perhaps not the most strategic location for training priests who would most likely end up teaching in one of the order's largely urban high schools or universities, and they moved their operation to the order's (very urban) St. Louis University. That move cleared the way for a very different kind of religious order to move onto the property: the Society of St. Pius X (or SSPX). On May 22, 1978, Archbishop Marcel Lefebvre, the founder of SSPX, was taken to St. Marys to inspect the grounds, which had been put up for sale. Lefebvre was very taken by the "magnificent" Immaculata Chapel that had been built on the grounds by the Jesuits—a sign from God that the SSPX should purchase the property, which they subsequently did with the help of a sizable donor.[5]

As Emma Green reported in her article about St. Marys in the *Atlantic Monthly* in 2020, the movement of the SSPX into town began a narrative that ran directly counter to the stories of most small towns in the Midwest. Unlike many small communities in Kansas and in other states adjacent to it, which have steadily lost population in the last half century, St. Marys has doubled in size, thanks in large part to the SSPX's "withdrawal experiment." The six masses celebrated every Sunday are regularly filled to capacity, such that overflow services need to be held in the gym of St. Mary's Academy—a school operated by the group. And the St. Mary's Academy itself is constantly running out of classroom space. The real estate prices for the town's properties are closer to those of Kansas's big cities than to neighboring towns, reflecting

the growing need for even more space to accommodate families that sometimes include eight or nine children (reflecting the order's strict adherence
to *Humanae Vitae*, Pope Paul VI's 1968 encyclical condemning the use of
any form of artificial birth control). The constant stream of young families
moving into town is attracted by the opportunity to live beside like-minded
neighbors committed to the same values. But, as Green was quick to point
out in her *Atlantic* article, "many are pushed here as much as they are pulled":

> When they lived in other places, many SSPX families felt isolated by their
> faith, keenly aware that their theological convictions were out of step
> with America's evolving cultural sensibilities and what they perceive as
> the growing liberalism of the Catholic Church, especially on issues such
> as gay marriage and abortion. They were wary of being labeled bigots by
> coworkers and even friends ... But the environment in St. Marys is "as con-
> ducive as possible for children to save their souls."[6]

And the search for a collective withdrawal on the part of families fleeing to
St. Marys exactly mirrors the experience of those evangelical Protestants
after 1919 (the year of the Great Reversal), who found themselves to be aliens
in their own land. Precisely like those evangelicals, the devout gathering
today in St. Marys are deeply concerned about church teaching seemingly
betraying what they take to be sound doctrine; but, also like their evangelical
cousins of a century ago, most of these pilgrims to the very center of America's
heartland are as concerned about the *cultural* experience of alienation. What
George Marsden observed regarding the early adherents to what would become the Protestant fundamentalist movement after World War I can as
easily be applied to the Catholic Faithful in St. Marys today: "American fundamentalism was not simply an expression of theology or concern about false
doctrines. In the minds of most fundamentalists the theological crisis came
to be inextricably wedded to the very survival of Christian civilization."[7]

And the complex web of theological *and* cultural concerns drawing large
families who perceive themselves to be out of step with both their church and
their culture to St. Marys are exactly fitted to be ministered to by the religious
order that tends to their souls: the SSPX. The SSPX is an international fraternity of traditionalist Catholic priests founded in 1970 by French Archbishop
Lefebvre in protest against the teachings of the Second Vatican Council, a
fraternity that, by 2022, included three bishops, seven hundred priests, and
268 seminarians training to be priests. The SSPX itself is named after Pius X,

pope from 1903 to 1914, whose campaign to stamp out modernism in the church has been likened to a reign of terror, experienced as such especially by those theologians and scholars attempting to mediate between the Catholic tradition and the new science of historical criticism. Taking their cue from Pius X himself, the SSPX retains the Tridentine Mass in Latin and enjoins on its lay followers strict adherence to Paul VI's 1968 encyclical forbidding all forms of birth control. That latter directive—something of an article of faith for many of the 2,658 souls who live in St. Marys—of course partakes of a rather large dose of historical irony, as Paul VI was also the pope who oversaw most of the sessions of Vatican II, and who personally promulgated all of its documents at its close as normative for all Catholic Christians. But that irony appears to elude most of the town's clergy and faithful.[8]

But irony aside, St. Marys embodies the most closely held beliefs of Lefebvre. Even before founding the SSPX in 1970, Lefebvre had already cast a long shadow in the French Catholic world: he had served as the Apostolic Delegate for all of French-speaking Africa, Archbishop of Dakar, as well as Superior General of the Holy Ghost Fathers (a French missionary order of priests), when he was called to the Second Vatican Council. At the Council, Lefebvre quickly emerged as a leading traditionalist voice raising grave concerns about the direction in which the council seemed to be going, especially with Council documents then taking shape on the issues of ecumenism (which the SSPX took to be as a form of the heresy of "indifferentism"), religious liberty (granting heretics the right to believe false doctrine that would lead to their damnation), and collegiality (taking authority way from Christ's vicar on earth, who alone had divine commission to teach authoritatively). Those fears coalesced in September 1970, shortly after his retirement as Superior of the Holy Ghost Fathers, when eleven seminarians at the Pontifical French Seminary in Rome sought the Archbishop's advice about transferring to a conservative seminary where they might complete their studies before ordination. He directed them to the University of Fribourg in Switzerland, but within a year thought better of his advice to the seminarians, and received permission from François Charriere, Bishop of Lausanne (Switzerland) to set up a pious union for priests on a provisional basis ("*ad experimentum*") for six years.[9]

At its inception, Lefebvre's priestly fraternity was established following regular canonical guidelines and with the blessing and encouragement of the local ordinary, the bishop of Lausanne—an amicable relationship with the institutional church that would change dramatically over the next several years. Shortly after receiving the blessing of Bishop Charriere on the new union, several Swiss laymen in Écône offered Lefebvre the local seminary (the International Seminary of St. Pius X), a windfall that produced twenty-four candidates in 1971, followed by a further thirty-two candidates the following year. Given his success in attracting an impressive number of seminarians in short order, Lefebvre quickly became something of a star to those who (like him) had serious issues with the Council. But Lefebvre was by no means universally loved by fellow churchmen, especially by his fellow French bishops, whose theological outlook (and view of the Council) were quite different from his. One episcopal defender of Lefebvre reported back to him that at the 1972 meeting of all the French bishops in Lourdes (France), the seminary in Écône had been widely referred to by the bishops present as *le seminaire sauvage* (the "wildcat seminary")—a title that correctly foretold the decision of the same body two years later when they announced that they would not accept into their own dioceses any priests trained at Écône.[10]

The actions of the French bishops focused concerns already present inside the Vatican, so that, in June 1974, a commission of cardinals was formed to look into the activities of Lefebvre's SSPX, which proceeded to set up a canonical investigation (i.e., a formal inquiry) of Écône by two Belgian priests on November 11–13, 1974. While the report of the canonical visitors was largely favorable, both Écône's staff and seminarians reported being shocked by what they considered to be liberal theological opinions expressed by the two canonical visitors. In response to those concerns expressed by the seminary faculty and students, Lefebvre issued what he thought was an internal document to members of the SSPX, expressing his perception that the two Belgian visitors offered proof positive—if further proof was even needed— that the liberal trends unleashed by the Council had now infected even seminary visitors sent by the Vatican itself. But that supposedly internal document was leaked to the press, and it was published in January 1975 in the (French) Catholic journal *Itineraires*.[11]

The year 1975 was not to be an institutionally happy year for Lefebvre. Shortly after the publication of his internal memo in *Itineraire*, the new bishop of Lausanne, Pierre Mamie, wrote to Rome, stating that, in light of Lefebvre's recent declarations, he intended to withdraw the "pious union" status granted to the SSPX by his predecessor. Just a few weeks later, Lefebvre received word that he was to meet with a commission of cardinals set up by Pope Paul VI to investigate both the Écône Seminary and its founder. Lefebvre would later remark that he was surprised that those meetings—on

February 13 and March 3—were marked by a decidedly hostile tone; indeed, it was even reported that French cardinal Gabriel-Marie Garrone had actually called Lefebvre a "fool" (a remarkable instance of *bruta figura* on the part of one bishop addressing another bishop) during a meeting in the Vatican. But other events now rolled along at a breathtaking pace: on May 6, 1975, Bishop Mamie formally withdrew any canonical status for the SSPX, a decision that Lefebvre appealed to the Holy See's highest court, the Apostolic Signatura, which turned down his appeal. At that point, the SSPX lacked any canonical status whatsoever, in effect making it outside the structure of the Roman Catholic Church. Further, in a consistory of cardinals on May 1976, Paul VI publicly rebuked Lefebvre by name (reportedly the first time in two hundred years that a pope publicly rebuked a bishop) and appealed to him and his followers to return from what was now a *de facto* schism from Holy Mother Church.[12]

These rebukes by Vatican officials and by the Pope himself notwithstanding, Lefebvre made headlines all over the Catholic world a little over a year later when he announced that he intended to ordain a number of Écône seminarians by the end of June 1976, an announcement that produced a "canonical warning" from the Vatican's deputy secretary of state. That official informed Lefebvre that proceeding with any such ordination would be a serious violation of church order because he had failed to get permission for such an ordination from either his local ordinary in Switzerland (Bishop Mamie of Lausanne) or from Rome. But Lefebvre did, in fact, proceed with the ordinations as planned, on June 29, 1976. Three days later—on July 1, 1976—the Vatican's Press Office declared that, in accord with canon 2331 of the (1917) *Code of Canon Law*—a canon specifically addressing the serious charge of obstinate disobedience by a bishop to the Supreme Pontiff—the Vatican expected Lefebvre to publicly repair the scandal caused by the illicit ordinations within ten days of receipt of that letter. But Lefebvre's response to that Vatican directive on July 17 only added fuel to the fire: Lefebvre declared in his answer to Rome that he judged his actions on June 29 to be both legitimate and necessary, given the false teaching that was being spread through the implementation of the Second Vatican Council's documents. Not surprisingly, Paul VI found Lefebvre's answer to be inadequate (at best)—indeed, so inadequate that the Pope felt it necessary to direct the Vatican's Congregation for Bishops to suspend Lefebvre "for an indefinite period" from any exercise of the sacraments (including the celebration of the eucharist and confession) until he repented of his violation of church law. And in terms of church law, that last action (suspension of Lefebvre's faculties as a bishop) can be fairly safely categorized as "very serious stuff."[13]

Thus, the SSPX existed in a kind of ecclesiastical suspended animation for over a decade, no longer recognized either by the local ordinary or by Rome as a religious order in good standing with church authorities, but not excommunicated (yet). From the standpoint of the *Code of Canon Law*, the SSPX was an "irregular pious union," lacking episcopal oversight or ecclesiastical approbation. That suspended state, however, did not proceed from any doubts whatsoever on the Vatican's part that what Lefebvre had done in the 1976 ordinations constituted both material and formal disobedience to the highest authority in the church; it rather proceeded from the hope of both Pope Paul VI and his successor, John Paul II, that Lefebvre would repent of his ways while avoiding the kind of public scandal that a formal excommunication would bring. That suspended state, however, would be brought to dramatic closure in 1988, when Lefebvre and Brazilian bishop Antônio de Castro Mayer ordained four SSPX priests as bishops.

In 1987, Lefebvre realized (at age 81) that, if he should die, the SSPX could ordain new priests only through the cooperation and approbation of non-SSPX bishops (an eventuality that had become increasingly unlikely given the strictures that the Vatican had imposed on him after the 1976 ordinations). And if even such a bishop could be found, Lefebvre and other superiors in the SSPX viewed such bishops to be unorthodox (and possibly worse) through their assent to the reforms of Vatican II. In June 1987, Lefebvre again made front page news in Catholic newspapers around the world by announcing his intention to consecrate bishop successors to himself. And while not explicitly stating such, he implied in his announcement that he intended to proceed with such an episcopal ordination—with or without the approval of the Holy See. This was, of course, a quite serious violation of both church tradition and church law, as any bishop is required to have the explicit permission of the pope himself to consecrate any priest as a bishop. And, as a bishop, Lefebvre must have known that, according to church law, any such consecration of a bishop without papal approval automatically imposes excommunication on both the bishop ordaining and the bishop ordained.[14]

Rome was, of course, deeply concerned by Lefebvre's stated plans, but rather than respond in kind, the Vatican entered into private conversation with him and other leaders within the SSPX, which led to something like a preliminary agreement signed by both Lefebvre and Cardinal Joseph Ratzinger on May 5, 1988. That agreement sought to work toward an understanding between Rome and Écône regarding future bishops for the SSPX. But, on May 30, Ratzinger (then Prefect of the Congregation for the Doctrine of the Faith and the future Pope Benedict XVI) wrote again to remind Lefebvre that should Lefebvre decide on another course of action in violation of that preliminary understanding, the promised authorization for future SSPX episcopal ordinations would be withdrawn. On June 3, Lefebvre responded to Ratzinger, announcing that he intended to proceed with the ordinations as originally planned. Six days later John Paul II wrote a personal letter to Lefebvre, pleading with him to abandon what "would be seen as nothing other than a schismatic act, the theological and canonical consequences of which are known to you." But Lefebvre never replied to the Pope's personal letter, which was made public on June 16. A little over a month later, on June 30, 1988, Lefebvre ordained four SSPX priests to the episcopate, being assisted in the ceremony by the retired bishop of Campos dos Goytacazes, Brazil.[15]

On the day after those illicit ordinations, the Vatican Congregation for Bishops issued a formal decree, declaring that Lefebvre himself, as well as the four newly ordained bishops, had incurred an automatic canonical penalty of excommunication. And four days after the illicit episcopal ordination, John Paul II published the apostolic letter *Ecclesia Dei*, in which he noted that the new (1983) *Code of Canon Law* defined "schism" as "withdrawal of submission from the Supreme Pontiff, or from communion with the members of the Church subject to him" (canon 751); in light of that canonical definition, the pope declared that the ordination ceremony itself had constituted a schismatic act, and that—by virtue of canon 1382 in the new *Code*—Lefebvre himself and all four newly ordained bishops had incurred excommunication, and all those who followed Lefebvre were now in formal schism from the Roman Church. Lefebvre himself later referred to the 1988 ordinations as an *operation survie* (a survival operation), perhaps something of a "Caiphas Statement," as they did help the SSPX survive with a new ecclesial identity, although perhaps not one with which everyone in his order felt completely comfortable. The decade-long state of ecclesiastical suspended animation that had defined the SSPX between 1976 and 1988 was now replaced by an alarmingly *specific* identity after the act of schism on June 30: the SSPX now stood outside of communion, not only with the pope, but with the Catholic Church itself.[16]

After the decree of excommunication and John Paul II's apostolic letter were published, some members of the SSPX dissociated themselves from

Lefebvre's society, forming themselves, with the approval of the Holy See, into a new ecclesial group, the Priestly Confraternity of St. Peter—a group just as committed to the Latin Mass, but with no desire to exist outside communion with Rome. And given John Paul II and Benedict XVI's emphasis on continuity as the interpretive key for understanding the work of the Second Vatican Council's reforms, there were continual efforts on Rome's part in the wake of the 1988 decree of excommunication to reconcile both the SSPX as a whole and Lefebvre himself with the Vatican. Lefebvre had correctly read the pope's sympathy with those conservatives who saw many of the reforms called for by Vatican II as too radical to be easily reconciled with the "continuity" understanding of the Council with previous Church teaching. Thus, it was not exactly a surprise that on January 21, 2009, the Vatican lifted its decree of excommunication on the SSPX's bishops, also voicing the fervent hope that all of its members would respond to this gesture by speedily returning to full communion with Rome and the Roman Catholic Church.[17]

B. The Hometown of the Angelus Press

Just part of the attraction of St. Marys to Catholic traditionalists streaming into town was the "uncompromising theological principles" elucidated by the SSPX and incarnated in various ways in the communal values in evidence in that small Kansas town. But along with the cohesion and unity provided by those uncompromising principles to pilgrims to the town—providing a secure buttress against the "godless culture" of mainstream America—there also existed, to outsiders anyway, what might look like a dark underside of the SSPX strategy for living the Catholic life in the modern world, a dark underside that might very well fuel (if not exactly produce) social pathologies.

Central to Lefebvre's message, of course, had been a dramatic rejection of the reforms of the Second Vatican Council—most especially three of the Council's documents: *Sacrosanctum Concilium* (which had called for the reform of Catholic worship and sacramental life) certainly stood among them, as it had for Gommar DePauw. But, along with that document on liturgy, two other conciliar documents provoked the special wrath of Lefebvre: the Council's "Decree on Ecumenism" ("*Unitatis Redintegratio*") and its epochal "Decree on the Relation of the Church to Non-Christian Religions" ("*Nostra Aetate*"). The former document was addressed specifically to non-Catholic fellow Christians. While asserting that the Roman Church was indeed God's only flock, it nonetheless acknowledged that all who have been "justified by faith in baptism are incorporated into Christ, and:

> they therefore have a *right* to be called Christians, and with good reason are accepted as brothers by the children of the Catholic Church. Moreover, some, even many, of the most significant elements and endowments which together go to build up and give life to the Church itself can exist outside the visible boundaries of the Catholic Church: the written Word of God; the life of grace; faith, hope, and charity, with the other interior gifts of the Holy Spirit. All of these, which come from Christ and lead back to him, belong by right to the one Church of Christ.[18]

Likewise, the Council's elucidation of a new understanding of the Church's relation to non-Christian believers, and especially to Jews, overturned what had been a problematic older tradition of praying for Jewish conversions to Christianity, arguably most famously embodied in the Church's Solemn Prayers for Good Friday, in which Catholics were called to remember the "perfidious Jews," and the role they had purportedly played in the death of Jesus. Over against that tradition, *Nostra Aetate* announced that even though most Jews in Jesus's time did not accept him as the promised Messiah, "the Jews remain very dear to God, for the sake of the patriarchs, since God does not take back the gifts he bestowed or the choice [of Israel] he made."[19]

Lefebvre himself had been scandalized by both *Unitatis Redintegratio* and by *Nostra Aetate*: the former seemed to violate the ancient phrase that had so exercised Leonard Feeney—that outside the church was no salvation—by implying that Catholic identity was simply one form of genuine Christian identity that could exist outside the institutional structure of the Roman Catholic Church. Was that ancient phrase no longer considered true? But in Lefebvre's mind *Nostra Aetate* was *the* theological bridge too far and represented a basic betrayal of the True Faith. That document seemed to betray fundamental articles of the Catholic faith—that the Church was the new Israel of God, replacing the old Israel as God's chosen people (a belief known in the theological trade as "supersessionism"). Further, *Nostra Aetate* seemed to repudiate the long-held belief that the Jews of first-century Palestine were indeed responsible for Jesus's death—precisely the reason for the prayer for the "perfidious Jews" on Good Friday in the first place. Had the Church been mistaken in that belief which had shaped its worship for a millennium? *Nostra Aetate* seemed to question the reliability of the New

Testament narrative of Christ's passion and death: what was one to make of the Jewish crowd's response to Pontius Pilate's famous question during Jesus's trial: "Shall I crucify your king?" St. Matthew, in his gospel account of Jesus's trial, reported that the response of the Jewish crowd witnessing it was "Let his blood be on us and on our children" (Matthew 27:25). From Lefebvre's standpoint, the question was essentially one of biblical reliability: was St. Matthew to be trusted in his account or not? And if his account was reliable, how could *Nostra Aetate* state that the Jews were blameless in Jesus's death?[20]

The SSPX, of course, continued to use the older Solemn Prayers for Good Friday in its Holy Week liturgies. In the reformed rite of Good Friday, now observed in the vast majority of Catholic parishes in the United States and around the world, on the other hand, the Catholic faithful are asked to pray that God keep the Jewish people faithful to the (original) Covenant given to Moses on Mount Sinai, while the phrase "let his blood be on us and on our children" has been stricken entirely from gospel account of St. Matthew always read on that day.

But whatever one makes of St. Matthew's account of the Jewish role in Jesus's trial and death, it was not exactly counterintuitive when, in 1989, a Nazi collaborator convicted of committing war crimes in Vichy, France, during World War II was caught hiding out in an SSPX monastery in Nice (France). As the *New York Times* reported it, Paul Touvier, a 74-year-old fugitive known as the "French Klaus Barbie" who once served as the leader of a pro-Nazi militia in Lyons, was seized in the St. Francis Priory in Nice, a monastery run by the SSPX, which had functioned as a safe house for Touvier and perhaps for others with similar beliefs as well. Touvier had been provided by the monastery with the religious habit worn by SSPX clergy so that he could take walks outside the monastery to get exercise and fresh air. That incident of course produced outrage, if not surprise, in both the secular and religious media: how could it be (the *New York Times* implied) that referring to the People of Israel as the "perfidious Jews" in formal worship—and especially on the most solemn day in the Church's calendar, Good Friday—*not* fuel the kind of impulses that would lead to sheltering Nazi sympathizers?[21]

But far greater American media coverage focused on a bishop of the SSPX, Richard Williamson (one of the four bishops irregularly ordained by Lefebvre in 1988), who was found living in an SSPX community in Dickinson, Texas, which staffed Queen of Angels parish in the town. In January 2009, Dickinson had appeared on Swedish television insisting that the Nazis had never operated gas chambers and asserting that Jews themselves invented the idea of the Holocaust during World War II. Indeed, the Southern Poverty Law Center's *Hate Watch* reported that Williamson confidently asserted that "I believe that the historical evidence is strongly against—hugely against—6 million Jews having been deliberately gassed in gas chambers as a deliberate policy of Adolf Hitler." Thus, Williamson asserted confidently that "I believe there were no gas chambers." It is, in fact, easy to dismiss Williamson as a simple-minded conspiracy theorist (he had already accused the US government itself of engineering the 9/11 attacks on New York's World Trade Center). But his antisemitism seemed to witness to a deep-seated hatred that went considerably beyond simple paranoia. At one point in the Swedish television interview, Williamson announced that "the Jews created the Holocaust so that we [sic] would prostrate ourselves on our knees before them and approve their new state of Israel." As several journalists who watched the interview remarked, there was a ferocity in delivering his remarks that went beyond mere paranoia.[22]

In the wake of Williamson's television interview, the Vatican announced that Williamson (whose excommunication for being an irregularly ordained bishop had just been lifted by Pope Benedict XVI that same month) would be immediately suspended from all clerical duties, including both sacramental activity and his position as rector of an SSPX seminary in La Reja, Argentina. But the Superior General of the SSPX order, Bernard Fellay, issued an ambivalent press release on January 27, 2009, regretting Williamson's inappropriate Holocaust denial and forbidding Williamson from speaking on the historical question of the Holocaust in the future. The Superior General referred to Williamson's remarks as "unhappy" and "unhoped for," but in that same statement he also criticized "progressivists" (unnamed) whose denunciation of Williamson was actually part of a much larger campaign to harm both the Pope and the SSPX's mission: as usual, the secular press was making a great fuss about a misunderstanding. And, in any case (Fellay asserted), Williamson's statements "do not in any way reflect the position of our Society."[23] But *Hate Watch*—undertaking a deep dive into the SSPX's media activities—reported that Superior General Fellay's distancing of the SSPX from Williamson's assertions was not quite borne out from what they found on websites sponsored by the SSPX. Indeed, *Hate Watch* reported that, in February 2009, "SSPX officials rushed to scrub their websites of offending material." For instance, a 1997 article by two SSPX priests that called for a return of the practice of locking Jews into ghettos because "Jews are known to kill Christians" suddenly disappeared. Also strangely erased was a 1989 talk

Williamson had delivered at an SSPX event in Canada in which he passion-ately denounced the alleged persecution of Holocaust denier and neo-Nazi Ernst Zundel by the Canadian government. Williamson told his audience that "there was not one Jew killed in gas chambers. It was all lies, lies, lies." But before Williamson's address disappeared from the SSPX's website, the *Huffington Post* had pasted Williamson's talk onto its own website, making it something of a challenge to completely believe the Superior General's distancing of the order from the views of Williamson, who at the time was serving as the rector of the SSPX's main seminary in North America, located in Winona, Minnesota.[24]

In the wake of the Williamson issue, all kinds of unpleasant facts came to light regarding the antisemitism rampant in SSPX books, pamphlets, and statements on officially sponsored websites. On March 9, 2009, the (Jewish) Anti-Defamation League's (ADL)News Service reported that the SSPX was, in fact, "mired in anti-Semitism, which it disseminates through its Web sites and publications"—so mired that it was difficult for the ADL to choose which among a multitude of publications to offer as examples:

> Jews are described in SSPX documents as being cursed by God for dei-cide. Jews are accused of being in control of world financial and cultural institutions, and of plotting to create a "world empire" or obtain "world dominion." One article on the SSPX's [official North American] Web site goes so far as to accuse Jews of ritual murder of Christians, and charges that "International Judaism" engineered usury and capitalism in order to bilk Christians of their money. SSPX writers also encourage their adherents to avoid "entering into commercial, social, [or] political relations" with Jews, and argues that Jews should not be granted the same civic [sic] rights as Christians.[25]

It is, then, challenging to understand the picture presented to the world of St. Marys, Kansas, as a reclusive, well-ordered, and quiet refuge from the searing ideological battles of a godless mainstream culture in light of the fact that the SSPX's chief publishing organ, Angelus Press—many of whose publications are anything but reclusive and quiet—is located in that very town.

A scroll through the backlist of Angelus Press raises troubling questions about Superior General Fellay's bald statement that Williamson's antisemitic positions "do not in any way reflect the position of our Society." The Press offers a number of troubling titles, works like Hillaire Belloc's (famously antisemitic) *The Jews*, and Monsignor George Dillon's *Freemasonry Unmasked* (the unmasking of the title referring to its uncovering of a centuries-old Jewish/Masonic crusade to destroy the Catholic Church). Likewise, the Angelus Press advertised a pamphlet written by the former superior general of the order, Franz Schmidberger, entitled *The Time Bombs of the Second Vatican Council*, in which the author denounced Third World immigration into Europe and North America as "destroying our [*sic*] national identity and, furthermore, the whole of Christianity." Along the way to making that argument, he devoted some space to accusing the entire Jewish race of deicide.[26]

Likewise, the SSPX's official bi-monthly magazine—*The Angelus* (founded in Dickinson, Texas, where Bishop Williamson had been found living at Queen of Angels rectory)—is a treasure-trove of antisemitic rhetoric: Michael Crowdy and Kenneth Novak argued in their article entitled "Mystery of the Jewish People in History" (published in the April 1997 issue of *The Angelus*) that "Judaism is inimical to all nations in general, and in a special manner to Christian nations. It represents in history the eternal struggle of Lucifer against God, of darkness against the light, of the flesh against the spirit." Likewise, the March 2004 issue of the magazine announced that "this curse" [on the Jewish people] is the punishment of blindness to the things of God and eternity, of deafness to the call of conscience to the love of good and hatred of evil, of spiritual paralysis, of total preoccupation with an earthly kingdom." This kind of disturbingly explicit antisemitism represents what appears to be non-exceptional opinion pieces in a magazine formally sponsored, edited, and advertised by the SSPX, who provide pastoral guidance and religious instruction to the devout of St. Marys, Kansas.[27]

C. Pulled (or Pushed) to St. Marys and St. Mary's

Dreher had, of course, addressed his 2017 bestseller to conservative Christians across the denominational spectrum, and not only—or even especially—to Catholics. Further, his book spoke to a withdrawal impulse that had always been alive and well in American culture, starting with the Puritan settlers of New England in the seventeenth century, and famously incarnated in the network of Shaker communities that dotted New England and the Midwest from the late eighteenth century until well into the nineteenth century. Withdrawal from the mainstream culture was evidenced in the various Transcendentalist communal experiments like those at Fruitlands and Brook Farm in Massachusetts, as well as those at the Ephrata Community in Pennsylvania and at the Zoar community in Ohio. Robert Owen's "New Harmony" experiment in Indiana, and the Oneida community in upstate New York (now arguably more famous for its flat-wear and dishes than communal reform) famously sought to establish an ordered community freed of the fractious energies that fueled the emergent capitalism of the nineteenth century. But Dreher's reformulation of that impulse in the twenty-first century struck an especially responsive chord for some Catholic Christians in the United States who found themselves in an ecclesial and cultural moment in which they felt themselves to be strangers in their own church, as well as in their own land. Thus, places like St. Marys, Kansas, witness to the fact that at least *some* American Catholics resonated deeply with that impulse outlined by Dreher. As Green noted in her *Atlantic* article, many perceived themselves to be pushed to places like St. Marys as much as pulled.[28]

One such couple pushed to join the SSPX community in St. Marys was interviewed by Green at length in her *Atlantic* article. As Green describes them, both had grown up attending Latin Masses in various SSPX chapels, and both therefore wanted to raise their children in a context that would nurture both regular Catholic practice and a strong Catholic faith. But it was only after moving to St. Marys that they realized both how lonely they had been before arriving in St. Marys, and how culturally marginalized they felt when viewing mainstream culture in America; indeed, the wife confessed to Green that she immediately felt at home in a way that had not been true when she and her husband had lived "in the world." She freely confessed that she relies on her neighbors for carpooling and in emergencies, trusting them implicitly. "We're all Catholic. We're all raising our children to get to heaven." If her daughters don't become nuns (something she prayed for) she was preparing them to become wives and mothers as committed as she is to raising devout, practicing Catholic children.[29]

That couple fits seamlessly into the demographics of the town itself as young parents of six children. While the median age of towns of similar size in Kansas is 36.9, the median age for St. Marys is 27.5 years old. Two thousand three hundred and eight-two of the 2,759 souls living in town are white—eighty-seven percent of residents, well above the percentage of other similarly sized towns in the United States nationally. While 28.7 percent of residents claim some college education, only 18.3 percent have a

bachelor's degree, and only 4.6 percent have a graduate or professional degree. St. Marys's total black population is thirty-four only a small percentage
of residents (1.4 percent of the town), while 331 identify as Hispanic, whom
are part of the SSPX community. There are only two churches in town, both
Catholic—Immaculate Conception parish and Assumption Chapel (attached to the St. Mary's Academy)—and the vast majority of residents attend
one of the two.[30]

For the devout living in town, there is only one place to send children for a
safe education: St. Mary's Academy. At school the children are separated by
gender, and the genders are separated into upper and lower campus:

> Little girls wear Mary Janes and jumpers to class on the upper part of the
> campus. The boys, in crew cuts and ties, learn in the buildings of the lower
> campus. Female students can compete in intramural sports, such as vol-
> leyball and archery, but only against other girls. The boys compete against
> sports teams in the area, although the school attracted controversy in 2008
> for forfeiting a basketball game when a woman showed up to referee.[31]

In the classrooms of St. Mary's Academy, students are regularly grilled in
the teaching of the *Catechism of the Catholic Church*, and Latin is the only
foreign language offered. Teachers eschew computers in favor of chalk and
blackboards. Girls all wear head covers—most commonly mantillas—at
mass (which is mandatory for all students in the Academy). All of this, although running in contemporary time, sounds very much like Garry Wills's
bitter-sweet recollection in "Memories of a Catholic Boyhood," of what it
was like to grow up Catholic during the 1950s: "we grew up different," he
observed, "not unlike being Amish in Pennsylvania or Mormon in Utah, but
stretching from coast to coast." While Wills's famous description of children
overseen by nuns in full habit foregrounded the great changes in Catholic
education that the Council helped to put in place, his memoir witnessed to
the fact that the pre-Council Catholic school experience itself was indelibly
printed on his memory. Indeed, Catholic identity for these children in parochial schools was experienced as a "vast set intermeshed habits" that *was* the
world of American religion:

> Heads ducked in unison, crossings, chants, beads, incense; nuns in the
> classroom alternately too sweet and too severe; priests garbed in black on
> the street and brilliant at the altar; confession as intimidation and comfort

(comfort, if nothing else, that the intimidation was survived.) . . . We had odd bits of Latinized English that were not part of other six-year-olds vocabulary—words like "contrition" and "transubstantiation." Surely no teenager but a Catholic ever called an opinion "temerious." The words often came embedded in formulae (perfect and imperfect contrition), and distinctions: mortal sin and venial sin, matter of sin and intention of sin. To know the terms was to know the thing, to solve the problem. So we learned, and used, a vast terminology.[32]

The thing that immediately strikes the reader of Wills's 1971 memoir, ostensibly about the US Catholic experience of the 1940s and 1950s that largely disappeared in the wake of the Second Vatican Council, is how closely it mirrors the American Catholic experience in St. Marys, Kansas, *today*, long after the reforms of Vatican II had remade the US Catholic landscape. And that shock of recognition is not accidental. St. Marys feels, and is—thanks to the efforts of the SSPX—a contemporary form of the Catholic ghetto that defined the church of the immigrants from the 1870s until the 1960s— a nurturing but confining subculture marked by membership in "our" institutions from cradle to grave, safe from what Dreher has called "the barbarism of contemporary American life."

From the viewpoint of those Catholic traditionalists who have found a refuge in St. Marys for themselves and their families, finding such a Catholic ghetto in the heartland of America has been a godsend: crime is almost non-existent and all of one's neighbors attend the same church and send their children to the same school, a school in which behavioral issues are largely absent and where inculcation of religious beliefs is an important part of the daily regimen. Most of the Catholic faithful cared for by SSPX priests there feel spiritually nourished and well cared-for. So, in the light of all that—that is, with so much that feels so right in St. Marys, Kansas—why does that religious experiment in communal living raise such interest and concern, both among Americans generally (warranting a story in the *Atlantic*) and also among ostensibly fellow Catholics? There are obvious, and—more interestingly—not-so-obvious answers to that question.

The obvious answers cluster around the increasingly pluralistic and diverse nature of American society itself. The dramatic rise of pluralism(s) in the United States during the past half-century—ethnic, racial, cultural, and religious pluralisms, among others—casts St. Marys, Kansas, as an anomalous, and perhaps as something even darker than a merely anomalous, social experiment. What does one make of religiously motivated individuals, of obvious good will, fleeing from the (sometimes) disturbing welter of pluralisms and divisions in contemporary American society to form a community largely defined by like-minded families? As Green noted in her article about St. Marys, "townies"—citizens who are not part of the SSPX crowd—feel like distinct outsiders even though many of them have lived in town their whole lives. While newcomers might find St. Marys appealing precisely because it is built around uncompromising theological principles and shared social values, for those who aren't affiliated with the SSPX, the town has become a less welcoming place since the SSPX arrived. Parishioners of St. Marys now presume that one of their own will be mayor (a presumption that is always fulfilled), while every seat on the city commission is now held by one of the devout. Doyle Pearl, a long-time "townie" and the last non-SSPX person to hold a seat on the board of commissioners, tells a somewhat more sobering—and less rosy—story about how it feels to be an outsider in her own town:

> In the early days, he said, Society parishioners disapproved of the town swimming pool, the first concrete-bottomed pool in Kansas and a source of pride for old-timers. [SSPX] members were worried about seeing girls in skimpy bathing suits; their kids would try to swim in jeans, which left behind fibers that taxed the pool's filtration system. Later, Society members on the city commission pulled funding from a chamber-of-commerce event, citing concerns about an allegedly ribald country-and-western band.[33]

Pearl and his wife, Laura, are pleased that St. Marys is now a growing town with a lively main street, and they even confess some envy regarding the vibrant church life and constant baptisms of new children born to the SSPX faithful. But they also confess that the town barely resembles the community in which they had grown up: "Its bright future doesn't necessarily feel like *their* future."[34]

The success of St. Marys, at least viewed from the perspective of townies like Pearl, is predicated *not* on inclusion and a shared civic vision, but rather on its opposite—a sectarian vision of one group dominating social life to the de-facto exclusion of other groups. From the standpoint of the challenging issues presented by the cultural, racial, and religious pluralisms facing the United States in the twenty-first century, the model of St. Marys—a model dedicated to successfully incarnating Dreher's vision of a Christian withdrawal experiment—is a non-starter. Its very success in setting up a civic culture in which only the insiders are allowed a seat at the table (literally, in the case, on the town board of commissioners), and outsiders (even those native to the place) are marginalized represents a model of community that mainstream culture seeks to move away from, not toward.

But the not-so-obvious answers to the unease that St. Marys engenders as a model of community are actually theological in nature, and more specifically Catholic in origin. The very sectarian nature of the community sponsored and nurtured by the SSPX in St. Marys represents an impulse that stands as the polar opposite of what the word Catholic means. The Catholic Christian tradition has largely been a resolutely public and inclusive tradition, a tradition that has condemned elitist models of Christian discipleship as profoundly unCatholic, as witnessed by the Church's condemnation of the Montanists in the second century, the Albigensians in medieval Europe, the Jansenists in seventeenth-century France, and of Feeney himself in the twentieth century. In Catholic Christianity, the faithful who sought a more rigorous and purified model of Catholic identity were channeled into the monastic tradition or into religious orders for both men and women.

But Catholic ecclesiology has always emphasized that the Church itself is open to the world and its needs—thus the vast portals of the medieval cathedrals, open to the town square and inviting all to enter. All who entered were sinners, of course (some more than others), but all were welcome to enter the sacred space and take up the sacramental life it offered. All were called, on some level, to be *in communio* with other believers, the pure with the not-so-pure, the converted with the not-so-converted: all were members of the faithful—a mixed lot, to be sure. As James Joyce correctly remarked (himself not exactly a devout Catholic) "Catholicism means here comes everybody." But Joyce's quip (however flippant) is borne out in serious theological reflection: the opposite of Catholic is not Protestant, in fact, but sectarian. And the Catholic community residing in St. Marys, Kansas, has a distinctly sectarian feel to it.

And the uncanny feel of St. Mary's Academy as an institution in real time implementing the style of Catholic education of the 1950s described by Wills in his memoir *Bare Ruined Choirs* ("heads ducked in unison," etc.) witnesses to yet another impulse that seems to pervade the place: the SSPX has resolutely set its face against models of Catholic education and faith formation that have shaped post-Conciliar Catholicism. And while the phrase "you can't put the toothpaste back in the tube" was not originally offered as a theological maxim, it applies to the world of religion as well as to anywhere else.

The older paradigm of Catholic education certainly shaped its students in an institutional identity in which belief was propositional, intellectual, and objective: almost every student produced by that parochial world could explain, using highly technical scholastic terms, the difference between the Corporal and Spiritual Works of Mercy, and parse the distinction between mortal and venial sin, or perfect versus imperfect contrition. As Wills remembered his educational experience in a parochial school, "to know the terms was to know the thing, to solve the problem. So we learned, and used, a vast terminology." That paradigm was focused with laser-like attention on the avoidance of individual sin (especially sexual sins), but was less successful in instilling the social, economic, and political duties of Catholic Christians in a pluralistic world.

From the standpoint of post-Council teaching, the gold standard of Catholic catechesis (the *Baltimore Catechism*, which reigned supreme in parochial schools from the late-nineteenth century until 1965), had gotten it only half right: it had taught that feeding the poor was one of the corporal works of mercy, an act of charity enjoined on faithful Catholics. But in the years after 1965, Catholic moral theologians taught a markedly different version of that duty: feeding the poor was not an act of charity, but a *duty* of basic justice. We *owe* the poor basic goods; we do not just give to them out of charity. Working for economic and racial justice was not an add-on for the faithful, but a basic component of Catholic identity. Christian discipleship after the Council was about considerably more than avoiding personal sin: the object of Catholic identity was no longer about presenting oneself unsullied to St. Peter at the gates of heaven at the end of one's life, free from the depredations of individual sin. In a word, after the Council Catholic educators believed that the older paradigm of Catholic educational formation no longer effectively prepared its students for living in a complex and highly pluralistic society like that in the United States, in which the faithful would—by and large—*not* be living in a Catholic ghetto, surrounded by people largely like themselves (save for places like St. Marys, Kansas). And "The Faith" was no longer just intellectual and propositional items to be memorized in a classroom, focused on being good citizens of an institution that was the earthly incarnation of the Kingdom of God itself. Faith now also included personal witness and distinct social and political duties fighting the corporate structures of sin, which were just as real—indeed, arguably more real—than individual sin. In the newer paradigm of Catholic education, to know the term was *not* necessarily to know the thing; memorizing the vast terminology of the Catechism was *not* necessarily to solve the problem. This, admittedly, made for a far messier and more complex set of goals for structuring Catholic schools, but one probably better fitted to living in a complex and pluriform modern world.

St. Marys's embrace of an a-historical understanding of Catholic Christianity, derived in large part from the SSPX's ongoing rejection of the teachings of the Second Vatican Council, is exactly analogous to the vision that had lured both Feeney and DePauw to embrace a changeless model of Catholic Truth. But the price of that embrace, which provided such a secure bulwark against the unsettling relativist values of the surrounding culture, was exceedingly high—indeed so high that most Catholic Christians today would sense something very wrong in its articulation of the tradition.

Just as in the case of their Protestant second cousins from the early twentieth century, the principles that motivated and shaped both St. Marys and St. Mary's were profoundly theological in origin; but, also like those Protestant distant relations, those theological concerns included distinctly cultural and social concerns that included education, social relations, and the structuring of civic life. As Marsden had observed about the emergence of Protestant fundamentalism after 1919, "[Protestant] fundamentalism was not simply an expression of theology or concern about false doctrines. In the minds of most fundamentalists the theological crisis came to be inextricably wedded to the very survival of Christian civilization." Thus, in St. Marys, the town board of commissioners, the Academy, and the public swimming pool were inextricably wedded to a distinct theological vision abetted by the SSPX. As is the case for fundamentalism in all of its expressions. How could it be otherwise?

This sense of being in a primitivist time warp of the 1950s is not accidental when visiting St. Marys and St. Mary's: that sense of witnessing an a-historical Catholic ghetto, based on a paradigm of Catholic Christianity long since jettisoned by the mainstream community of believers, is not incidental to that community's identity. It is, rather, part-and-parcel of what the town and its Catholic institutions are about at their very core. It is a paradigm of the Catholic past that—if it ever actually existed in the form the SSPX envisioned, which is open to serious historical doubt—had long since been replaced by another paradigm. But, then again, the past isn't what it used to be.

PART III
"CHRIST THE TRANSFORMER OF CULTURE"

Part III of this book examines those Catholic sectarian movements that seek to actively transform mainstream Catholic and American culture rather than just withdraw from it for the sake of group purity.

6

Dreaming of Christendom in the Blue Ridge Mountains

A. A Society in Which Christ Reigns

These were the years America passed through a-near revolution (1968–1970) and ceased to be a Christian nation, becoming secular and neopagan. Surveying the destruction of those years, Carroll opted for the Benedict Option and founded Christendom College. And while . . . the spiritual revival of the papacy of St. John Paul II may have masked for a time the further descent of Western Civilization into madness, there can be little doubt that if Carroll was ahead of his time, he was only slightly so.[1]

Thus was Warren Carroll lauded in a review of his biography in the *Catholic World Report*, a reliably right-of-center journal published online. Carroll was, by any standard, an impressive character, whatever one's church politics: degrees from Bates College and Columbia University, author of a massive six-volume series entitled *A History of Christendom* (a narrative account of both western civilization and the Catholic Church from antiquity to 2010), and the winner of numerous honors and awards. But the accomplishment, amidst all these others, that stood out and made him something like an uncanonized saint among Catholic traditionalists was his founding of Christendom College in Front Royal, Virginia, in 1977.[2]

A coeducational liberal arts college with about 540 students, Christendom finds itself snugly situated between the Blue Ridge Mountain Range to the east and the Massanutten Range to the west. It is also snugly situated in the Roman Catholic diocese of Arlington (Virginia), a diocese famous for its fierce devotion to the hardline church politics of both Pope John Paul II and Benedict XVI. Like its home diocese, Christendom is unapologetic in its fidelity to what it takes to be Catholic magisterial teaching and in its loudly proclaimed loyalty to its own bishop. One cannot read any published account of the institution without quickly encountering those Catholic institutional loyalties proudly announced early on. Thus, even before reaching the bottom of the first page of its history of "The First 35 Years (1977–2012)" one finds a testimonial stating that each year the entire faculty of the College makes "a voluntary oath of fidelity to the Magisterium and a profession of faith before our Lord in the Chapel of Christ the King."[3]

Those Catholic loyalties, announced on the first page of the institution's history, are noteworthy but hardly arresting to the casual reader. What is considerably more arresting (to both the casual and the careful reader) is the quote from Carroll found on the second page of that same history, in which he elucidates the College's mission. That mission, Carroll announced, was not only to provide a truly Catholic liberal arts education of the highest quality (a mission shared with a number of other small Catholic liberal arts institutions in the United States):

> but to maintain the idea of "Christendom" and to show how "Christendom" works in action, even on a small college campus . . . Our college takes its name from the word which *embodies the Christian social and political ideal*: a society, a culture, a government in which Christ the King reigns. The mission to contribute to the building of a Christian society—the re-Christianizing of the temporal order—gives Christendom College its name.[4]

That Christian social and political ideal is either inspirational or chilling, depending on the reader's position on the question of whether the entire temporal order (government, education, economic policies, and civil rights) should be placed under the immediate authority of the Roman Catholic Church. And those various reactions—aspirational, chilling, or something even more disturbing—testify in an illuminative way to the conflicted heritage of both the term and the social reality toward which the name Christendom witnesses.

"*Cristendom*" is an Anglo-Saxon term thought to have been invented in the ninth century by a scribe (possibly in the court of King Alfred the Great) translating Paulus Orosius's *History of the Pagans*, written in the early fifth century. That busy scribe was seeking a term (non-existent before his efforts) to express the idea of a universal culture in which Christ (and Christ's Church) held direct sway over every human creature. Thus Diarmaid MacCulloch, in his magisterial *History of Christianity*, defined the term as the immediate "union between Christianity and secular power" in which religious, political, and cultural pluralism were nonexistent, because dissent in all of its forms (by definition) had to be eradicated as a rebellion against Christ's rule. That notion of all of Europe as *one* holy religious space inhabited solely by Catholic Christians, ruled by Christ through the Church, and blessed by God, flourished for fourteen centuries and even survived the Reformations of the sixteenth century. Thus, as Thomas Curry noted in his study of the term, in Christendom as it was embodied in medieval Europe:

> full membership in society and adherence to Christianity became synon-ymous. To abandon Christianity or to practice a form of it not sanctioned by the civil authority put one outside the pale of society and often involved forfeiting life itself. Even after the Protestant Reformation begun by Martin Luther in 1517 precipitated a major division within Christianity, both the worlds of Catholicism and Protestantism continued the traditions of Christendom inherited from the past.[5]

The idea itself only entered a prolonged death agony with the rise of the modern secular state that emerged after the Enlightenments of the seven-teenth and eighteenth centuries, when governments started refusing to up-hold the teachings and practice of Christianity as in any sense a concern of a now-secular state. And however traumatic the resulting slow death and final demise of Christendom must have appeared to religious leaders accustomed by centuries of obedience to unquestioned authority over the secular sphere, it could only have appeared as a release from persecution and an invitation to genuine liberation to Jews, other non-Christians, and those hundreds of other Christians who were lumped together by Holy Mother Church as "heretics and infidels," all of whom were (by definition) well on their way to hell-fire. Far from being the fall from grace (both literally and figuratively) that many—including Carroll—perceived the break-up of Christendom to be, many devout devotees of the Enlightenment in both the Old and the New World resonated deeply with Thomas Jefferson's perception that making a go of a society without an established church or religion was a fair experiment in ordered freedom—an experiment that came close to defining the United States as "the first new nation." And it was perceived as the *first* "new nation" because the separation between church and state (thus making religion a purely *voluntary* affair) became the norm and model for almost every other industrialized country on earth by the mid-twentieth century.[6]

The insight so central to the American understanding of the public sphere—that making religion a purely voluntary affair was, finally, in the best interests of both the government and of religious groups—and was embraced by almost all Protestant groups in the years after the American Revolution. In those decades spanning the late eighteenth century and the first few decades of the nineteenth century, Christendom as an ideal was replaced in the United States by a new form of ecclesiastical organization unknown to European Christians: the denomination. In place of the unified field theory of Christendom—an understanding of culture that *necessarily* included a formally established church to uphold cultural values—denominationalism became the normative form of religious organization in the United States. "Denominations" in the American sense eluded both categories offered by Ernst Troeltsch to explain European Christianity in his classic work on the subject, *The Social Teaching of the Christian Churches*. Denominations were *neither* sects (groups like the Mennonites and the Amish, opposed to a nation's established church) *nor* churches (religious organizations like the Church of England, established by law to provide the *official* religious sanction for political and cultural values). In that specific, Troeltschian, sociological sense, then, there are no churches in the United States: unlike nations like Great Britain, Denmark, or Sweden (all of which have religious establishments supported by public taxes), all religious groups in the United States are defined by the voluntary principle, which means that, in the eyes of the government, all churches were equal and free to evangelize (or not). It also means that religious affiliation is a *voluntary* personal decision, a decision in which the government had no duty or right to interfere. And if the result is a "naked public square" (naked, at least, regarding religion), most advocates of denominationalism argued that *that* was a very good thing indeed: religious values could (and, most denominational leaders argued, probably *should*) be brought into that square. But religious *institutions* had no place in it.[7]

It is, in fact, difficult to overstate how important that displacement of the idea of Christendom by denominationalism was in the history of Christianity. Arguably the scholar who most lucidly contextualized that displacement within the two millennia history of Christianity was Sidney Mead. In a series of brilliant essays of breathtaking range, Mead—sometime student of Alfred North Whitehead and an historian of American religion still revered many decades after his death—contextualized the import of the First Amendment to the US Constitution within the broad sweep of two thousand years of western Christianity:

> In Christendom from the fourth century to the end of the eighteenth, Christianity was organized in an established church or churches . . . [reaching] its peak in expression and power during the twelfth and thirteenth centuries. At that time it actually possessed and wielded tremendous tangible, overt power in the affairs of men [sic], and more subtly, tremendous and formative cultural power in the souls of men. It claimed inclusiveness and universality as the one true Church of Christ on earth.[8]

As Mead argued, there were really only two hinges for understanding the two thousand-year bureaucratic history of Christianity: the first hinge (which established Christendom as the administrative norm for western Christianity for fourteen centuries) was first elucidated in the Edict of Thessalonica in 380 CE by the Emperor Theodosius I, which made the Catholicism of the Nicene Creed the official state church of the Roman Empire. The very idea that such a model of church–state relations was in any way problematic eluded most western Christians for almost a millennium and a half after that edict—until the Treaty of Westphalia of 1648, which finally brought to an end the exceptionally long and bloody Thirty Years War. With that treaty, religion became territorial (i.e., dependent on the religion of a region's ruler), thus implementing the Treaty's principle of *cujus regio, ejius religio*. But that Treaty also overlapped with an international religious and philosophical movement known as the Enlightenment (sometimes put in the plural form—Enlightenments—as it took various forms in different countries). And it was in the midst of what are usually termed the English and Scottish Enlightenments of John Locke and Francis Hutchinson that the thirteen British colonies of North America became the United States.[9]

Thus, the second hinge—replacing the church–state arrangement established by the Edict of Thessalonica in 380 CE—came in the wake of both the Treaty of Westphalia and the Enlightenment; and much like the Edict of Thessalonica, it can be dated very specifically: it occurred in December 1791, when the US Congress formally voted to accept the Bill of Rights as having the same authority as the Constitution itself. The First Amendment of that Bill declared that "Congress shall make no law respecting an establishment of religion, or prohibiting the free exercise thereof." That's it. The tradition of fourteen centuries was simply replaced within a relatively brief time span of

several dozen years, establishing the voluntary principle as the norm to replace Christendom, which had served as the administrative norm for mainstream Christianity since the Roman Empire. As Mead himself observed:

> The importance of this change can hardly be overestimated. Professor W. E.
> Garrison has rightly called it "one of the two most profound revolutions
> which have occurred in the entire history of the church on the administra-
> tive side." And so it was.[10]

"And so it was"—sort of. For while the vast majority of Protestant groups accepted this new model of church organization called "denominationalism"
as the normative organizational framework for their religious communities
within a generation of the publication of the Bill of Rights, the Catholic community in the United States took somewhat longer to come to terms with the
idea that their church—at least from a Troeltschian standpoint—was not a
church at all sociologically, but rather a denomination.

And much of the explanation for that longer period of acceptance within
the American Catholic community was based on a theory imported from
European Christendom. For most of the nineteenth and for the first half of
the twentieth centuries, US Catholicism operated under a theory usually referred to as the "thesis/hypothesis" proposition first elucidated by the French
bishop Felix Duplanloup in the early nineteenth century. According to that
proposition, religious pluralism (like that found in the United States) was
an unfortunate reality that the Church had to reluctantly accept in the wake
of the collapse of Christendom. But only for the sake of peaceful social relations in cultures in which Catholics were a minority population would
the Church (again, reluctantly) allow its faithful to participate in a culture
in which the Catholic Church was not the only legally established form of
Christianity: this was the thesis part of the proposition. And an important
part of this reluctant permission for Catholics finding themselves in cultures
like that of the United States was the then-dominant Catholic principle that
"error has no rights." That is, theologians elucidating Catholic theology
after Christendom's disappearance had argued that it is the responsibility of
governments in cultures wherein Catholic Christians made up the majority
of the population to suppress non-Catholic religions, as governments did
not have the right to publicly express any religion other than Catholicism.
"Error has no rights" was based on a belief central to the idea (and the reality)
of Christendom itself that there was only one True Church, presided over by

the Bishop of Rome. Those in religious error (e.g., Protestant Christians), who failed to recognize that truth, had to be corrected and brought into the true fold: they had no right to proselytize or enjoy any kind of legal sanction for their erroneous beliefs, although they could practice their false religion privately.[11]

But if and when Catholics became the majority of citizens, they had a *moral obligation* to establish the Catholic Church as the only legally recognized religious community enjoying complete freedom and a central role in discussing (and judging) political, economic, and moral questions: this was the hypothesis part of Bishop Duplanloup's thesis. The moral error of Christians belonging to Protestant groups (which were denied the title of churches in Catholic theology in any case) would then be corrected legally, allowing only Catholic churches to be built. Thus, in Rome's eyes, US Catholics could give provisional assent to the First Amendment's separation of church and state and freedom of conscience—*for now*, until they achieved majority status in the United States, at which time they were under a serious moral obligation to establish Catholicism as the state church. Thus, American Catholics were perceived by many Protestant leaders throughout the nineteenth century and well into the twentieth century as only *provisionally* on board with Jefferson's Fair Experiment in religious freedom and voluntary religion, and that perception was at least partially correct ("partially" only because the vast majority of American Catholics, then and now, had and have never heard of the thesis/hypothesis proposition).[12]

By the mid-twentieth century, the thesis/hypothesis heritage of Christendom was already wearing thin among Catholic intellectuals and theologians in the United States, most especially with the American Jesuit John Courtney Murray. Murray was arguably the most brilliant public intellectual in the American Catholic community in the twentieth century, trained in Rome and teaching on his Order's most distinguished theological faculty in Woodstock, Maryland, all while serving as editor-in-chief of what would come to be called the Cadillac of American theological journals, *Theological Studies*. Several years before Vatican II was even called, Murray had published what is generally conceded to be one of the most important Catholic texts of the mid-twentieth century on precisely this question.[13]

We Hold These Truths: Catholic Reflections on the American Proposition, published in 1960—the year of John F. Kennedy's campaign for the White House—represented the fruits of Murray's wrestling with Duplanloup's thesis/hypothesis theory over the course of several decades, and the result was generally considered an epochal replacement of that proposition with an entirely different model of Catholic church–state relations. In a famous series of articles published in the 1950s in *Theological Studies* (collectively referred to as the "Leonine articles"), Murray had attempted to situate Pope Leo XIII's strong support for Duplanloup's theory within a larger historical context. By the time he finished that series, Murray had come to the conclusion that Duplanloup's theory rested on false premises: the French bishop had asked the wrong question, resulting in a deeply flawed resolution to that question. Murray proposed that the most basic question was *not* whether the Church was legally established or not, but whether the Church was left free to accomplish its mission of preaching the Gospel and evangelizing culture. In Murray's view, the American circumstance set up by the First Amendment offered a far better answer to that question than the thesis/hypothesis proposition: the American-style separation of church and state left the Church free to undertake its mission of evangelizing culture while also leaving the Church free from messy political entanglements with governments. And while the church–state arrangements in Italy, Spain, and Portugal were never mentioned by name, they could clearly be discerned in the background as the wrong answers in Murray's argument, made by good-intentioned but misguided Catholic countries to incarnate Duplanloup's deeply problematic ideal of church–state relations. As Murray persuasively argued it, the American answer to church–state relations was not only equal to Duplanloup's model, but decidedly superior to it, as it left the Church free to accomplish its mission without governmental interference.[14]

By 1955, when Murray wrote the last of those articles studying the context in which Leo XIII had supported Duplanloup's theory as part of the official magisterium of the church, Rome stepped in and blocked the publication of his last article: someone—or more likely, a group of people, most probably European bureaucrats—in the Vatican saw Murray's historical scholarship as undermining papal teaching and ordered him to leave the topic. Thus, "Leo XIII and Pius XII: Government and the Order of Religion," was not published in 1955 as planned, but only saw the light of published day thirty-eight years later, in 1993, when it was included in a collection of Murray's published and unpublished work.[15]

But as historian Will Durant once famously observed, at the Reformation the Catholics opted for an infallible pope and the Protestants opted for an infallible Bible, and over the centuries it has proven easier to change popes. And, by 1959, Durant's observation proved to be infallibly correct: a new pope, "Good Pope John" (XXII) was already contemplating a call for a new ecumenical council of the world's bishops (the first in a century); the very next year saw a Roman Catholic running for the presidency of the United States. Murray's book, *We Hold These Truths* changed the field of play, both in the United States and in Rome. So it was that, when John XXIII finally did announce the gathering of the Second Vatican Council a year later, Murray's ideas were not only exonerated, but Murray himself was actually called to Rome as a *peritus* to the Council, advising the bishops present there on how best to replace the thesis/hypothesis proposition with something decidedly more twentieth century (and American).[16]

But Murray's exoneration went considerably further than even that. Murray himself penned the initial draft of the document that would become *Dignitatis humanae*, the Second Vatican Council's epochal "Declaration on Religious Liberty," passed by a large majority of bishops present in December 1965. That document overturned Catholic Christianity's fifteen-hundred-year-old support for the idea of Christendom by announcing, rather matter-of-factly, in the very first sentence in Chapter One, that:

> the Vatican Council declares that the human person has a right to religious freedom . . . The Council further declares that the right to religious freedom is based on the very dignity of the human person as known through the revealed word of God and by reason itself. That right of the human person to religious freedom must be given such recognition in the constitutional order of society as will make it a civil right.[17]

Thus, the first hinge was slammed shut in 1965 by over two thousand bishops of the Roman Catholic Church, and the second hinge was flung open. Holy Mother Church had simply shut the door of the church–state arrangement, elaborated in the idea and the reality of Christendom, that had served as its primary model for fifteen hundred years, and had replaced it with a model of church and state dedicated to freedom of conscience and religious liberty. It also made the American model of church–state separation (at one time just "permissible") the normative model for the world church by the end of the twentieth century. Murray's "American" solution to the seemingly intractable problem of reconciling the thesis/hypothesis proposition to modern, pluralistic democracies itself became the model held up by the Church for understanding its relationship to pluralistic, secular cultures like those in the United States, and increasingly in western Europe as well.

The point of this long sidebar dive into the Edict of Thessalonica, Bishop Duplanloup, the British and Scottish Enlightenments, the Bill of Rights, and Mead and Murray (the latter two individuals being deceased by the time Christendom College was founded) is simply to highlight how singular Carroll's description of Christendom's mission really was in the context of American Catholicism in the late twentieth century. By the time of Christendom College's founding in 1977, both American Protestantism and Roman Catholicism had moved considerably beyond the belief that Christendom was a model of church–state relations that was desirable, or even possible. After the adoption of the Bill of Rights, religious groups in the United States either embraced or made peace with the idea that older "throne and altar" models of church–state relations that sought the institutional melding of Christianity with the state was no longer sustainable in modern democratic societies. And with the promulgation of *Dignitatis humanae* in 1965, the Catholic Church (itself the primary beneficiary of the idea of Christendom for over a millennium and a half) had formally declared itself in favor of freedom of conscience and the institutional independence of the Church from a secular state. Thus, to present the model of a "society, a culture, a *government* in which Christ the King reigns" as something actually desirable for a Catholic institution's mission in twentieth century America is singular in the extreme, and arguably something considerably darker than singular.

What, exactly, then was the founding of Christendom College in the last quarter of the twentieth century really about, given its formal dedication to that Christian social and political ideal? A good place to start in answering that question would seem to be the review of Carroll's biography, which noted that Carroll, "viewing the destruction" of American culture in the 1960s and 1970s, "opted for the Benedict Option" and founded the institution in Front Royal, Virginia. Much like the Catholic community in St. Marys, Kansas, Carroll sought to use the vision adumbrated by Rod Dreher in *The Benedict Option* as an ideological blueprint for an educational institution that would turn its back on the previous half-century of American Catholic higher education and return to a more parochial model of Catholic education that eschewed even the attempt to converse with a "secular and neo-pagan" culture. Baked into the very fabric of that institution's mission was the goal of "maintain[ing] the idea of 'Christendom,' and to show how 'Christendom' works in action, even on a small college campus."

But also baked into that mission was a call to return to a much older paradigm of what Catholic education was about—a paradigm that had been reshaped and transformed after the Second Vatican Council, which had elucidated a very different paradigm for Catholic higher education in its relation to culture. The primitivism that marks the Catholic community in St. Marys, Kansas, was replicated in the Blue Ridge Mountains. That commitment to "live ancient lives," modeled on a supposedly purer primitive moment when the Catholic intellectual project had more solid boundaries between the "safe inside" and the contaminated outside has always been— and still is—one of the chief attractions of sectarianism. But it is based on profoundly a-historical understanding of the Catholic past (and of the Catholic present, as well). And like the fundamentalist stories narrated in preceding chapters, there was a conscious reaching out for political monikers in defending the founding of Christendom: over against a liberal secular culture that Carroll described as neo-pagan, Christendom would stand as a kind of conservative "No!" to a progressive ("woke") culture run amok. Reaching back to an earlier time (i.e., when Christendom as both ideal and reality provided western Europe with a safe model of a "culture and government in which Christ the king reigned"), the small college in the Blue Ridge Mountains would function as something like a traditionalist city on a hill, a model for others to see and to emulate.[18]

Such was the hope, anyway. And while the effort to build a traditionalist city on a hill might be viewed as courageous ("courageous" depending on one's viewpoint, of course) the attempt to reconfigure the Catholic intellectual life from the Blue Ridge might equally be considered quixotic, because Catholic genies (like all genies) never go back into the bottle.

B. The Faithful Community of (and at) Christendom

Roughly forty years before Rod Dreher would raise awareness of just how Christians might respond to a culture for which an extreme conception of liberty serves as the lodestar for a descent into decadence, Carroll grappled with the descent just as it was picking up steam.[19]

The narratives regarding the success of the college founded by Carroll would seem to bear witness to his confidence in its future. The *Northern Virginia*

Daily, in a story entitled "Christendom College Ranked Sixth for Best Value," reported the most recent college rankings released by *Kiplinger's Magazine*. In the Kiplinger category of "Best Values in Private Colleges Under $20,000," Christendom ranked right after Berea College, Brigham Young, Principia College, Yale, and Amherst, but ahead of Harvard and other bigger, better-known institutions. And being thus highly ranked in Kiplinger's "Top 10 Schools," was not anomalous: *The Arlington Catholic Herald*—the official church weekly for the diocese of Arlington, Virginia—announced in its September 28, 2022 issue that incoming Christendom freshmen hailed from thirty-two states and from the United Kingdom, and included multiple high school valedictorians, a Cardinal Newman Society Essay Contest-winner, and five National Merit scholarship winners. It also noted that seventy-two percent of the entering freshman class were on academic scholarships.[20]

Those reports fit seamlessly into other college rankings as well: Christendom was ranked in the "Top Ten Most Radical Colleges" in the *Huffington Post*, in the "Top 50 All-American Colleges" by the *Intercollegiate Studies Institute*, as the "Top Conservative College" by the Young America's Foundation, as being "Joyfully Catholic" [*sic*] by the Cardinal Newman Society, in the "Top College for American Values" by Newsmax.com., and as "One of the Top 20 Christian Colleges in the Nation for Student Success and Satisfaction" by FaithOnView.com.[21]

The *Huffington Post* arguably offered the most reliable ranking in naming the College among the top ten "Most Radical Colleges" in the nation. For Christendom unapologetically asserts that its unique general education set of requirements is indeed radical by contemporary educational standards—a fact that "sets us apart and is what allows us to be the gold standard for Catholic liberal arts education today." Further, in its evaluation of Christendom, the Cardinal Newman Society focused on the radically Catholic nature of its core curriculum as its greatest strength in serving as "an alternative to [the] secular trends in Catholic higher education," marking it as "a national model of *faithful* liberal arts education and Catholic formation" (adding that "the medieval-style Christ the King Chapel will be a great addition in spring 2023"). The Newman Society further noted approvingly that "class time is set aside daily for Mass, which is celebrated with great reverence," and that there is a nighttime curfew observed across the campus, by which time all students are required to be in their single-sex residence halls. Further, every Christendom student was required to attend the March for

Life in Washington, DC, to protest the *Roe* decision which had guaranteed abortion rights. Christendom consciously fostered religious vocations among its student body, so that more than one hundred of its alumni are now priests. The statistic that is not mentioned in any of these accolades is that the school currently has a ninety-one percent acceptance rate—a statistic more common to community colleges than to places like Yale, Amherst, or even Brigham Young.[22]

And the assertion of being radically set apart from other Catholic liberal arts institutions is certainly borne out by the required courses that every Christendom student takes over the course of their four years there. The six required courses in theology are spelled out quite explicitly and are all taught by professors who are required to receive a *Mandatum* from the bishop of the Arlington (Virginia) diocese. All freshmen take "Fundamentals of Catholic Theology I" and "Fundamentals of Catholic Theology II" during the fall/ spring semesters of their first year, while all sophomores take "Introduction to the Old Testament" and "Introduction to the New Testament" in their fall/ spring semesters (respectively). Every junior is expected to enroll in "Moral Theology," and all seniors take "Catholic Apologetics."[23] Four history courses are likewise required to graduate, but the specific courses that meet that re-quirement all seem to focus on the rise, flourishing, and fall of Christendom itself in western culture: all freshmen spend their fall and spring semesters (respectively) in "The Ancient and Biblical World" and "The Formation of Christendom," while every sophomore enrolls in the two-semester sequence of "The Division of Christendom" (presumably a course studying what most other liberal arts institutions term the Reformation Era) and "Church and World in the Modern Age." Likewise, the required political science course required for all sophomores has an ecclesiastical cast ("Social Teachings of the Church"), while the set course taken in the spring of sophomore year is "Metaphysics." And the fall course required in junior year is (unsurprisingly) "History of Medieval Philosophy."[24]

This heavily Catholic core curriculum reflects the ideological commitments of the faculty and trustees (one hundred percent of whom are Catholic) and of the student body as well, upward of ninety-five per-cent of whom self-identify as Catholic. Eight of the forty-two full-time faculty members themselves graduated from Christendom, while thirteen received their doctorates from the Catholic University of America, and five from the University of Notre Dame. Three faculty received their terminal degrees from the John Paul II Institute for Marriage and the Family in Rome, while a further two received pontifical degrees from the Angelicum (the Pontifical University of St. Thomas Aquinas, run by the Dominican order in Rome). Professors from every department, as well as the College president, are required to make public profession of the Oath of Fidelity to the Catholic tradition, and to make Profession of Faith in the presence of their bishop. All of this, at least in the eyes of the Cardinal Newman Society, evinces the College's "extraordinary commitment to faithful education and formation, refusing to compromise on things like opposite-sex visitation in residences and accepting government aid."[25]

What immediately strikes the reader is that the College's Core Curriculum witnesses to the institution's name. Christendom as a medieval ideal in fact forms the central focus for the required history courses in the Core, and all four required English courses in the Core are labeled "The Literature of Western Civilization (I, II, III, IV)." There is, then, a resolute and laser-like focus on the literary products of western Christianity during its supposed heyday—Augustine, Chaucer, Thomas Aquinas, and the like—as though Catholicism were simply a western, European tradition; the entire sense of the Church as a truly global institution with ancient roots in Africa, Turkey, Armenia, and Syria (areas that do not fit seamlessly into the historical construct of "Christendom") would seem to be ignored or downplayed. From the point of view of twenty-first century pedagogical theory, then, students are indeed deeply immersed in the classics of western culture; but their understanding of Catholicism as *katholikos*—that is, as truly universal—is dramatically fore-shortened.[26]

Likewise, in its explanation for the College's requirement of two years of college-level work in a single foreign language, either classical or modern, the Core Curriculum document explains that:

> The study of a foreign language, particularly of an inflected language such as Latin or Greek . . . enhances linguistic skills and enables the student to gain a fuller appreciation of the European roots of American culture, a purpose which is also served by four courses each in the great heritage of Western literature and the history of Western civilization . . . The transformation of all history by the Incarnation makes a truly Christ-centered study of the past an indispensable hallmark of a Christendom education. Without this focus, it is nearly impossible to truly understand the present and shape the future.[27]

But the very insularity from the outside ("neo-pagan") world that Christendom seeks has its dark side as well, a dark side that has played out in various ways. Like sectarianism in all of its forms, creating a tightly disciplined inside over against a polluted outside comes at a price, as Adele Smith (Christendom Class of 2012) herself discovered. Well before she even arrived on campus, she admitted that she knew that both the College's classes and its social life would be conservative. But she confessed to being bemused by the strict segregation of genders she encountered once she got there. For instance, she noted that while all the residence halls on campus were segregated by gender, once a semester every student residence would sponsor an open house at which male students could visit female halls and vice versa. As she tells the story:

> The girls would get baked goods and candy, and the guys would come into the dorm and take a tour. It was very much like a museum, like an exhibit. It was the same with the guys' open house, except they'd have TVs and video games. "This is how the native people on the men's side of campus live!" This is not how young people engage in a normal way. It felt like a human zoo.[28]

But with the benefit of hindsight, Smith recognized that the rigid guidelines governing male–female campus interactions were not just odd but could end up being dangerous as well. Indeed, she eventually argued that the very rules in place prohibiting any public displays of affection on campus were so restrictive that it drove couples off-campus. And off-campus meant the woods, fields, or the Skyline Drive National Park, given the College's remote location. As she later argued, "just to hold hands, they'd go off campus for a date. It's just a natural human need to connect with someone you're in a relationship with," even if that connection was just holding hands. But connecting in the isolated areas that students were forced to find could easily get out of hand. And that is precisely what she claimed happened on October 2, 2009, when she claimed that she was raped by her then-boyfriend (a fellow Christendom student) in Skyline Drive National Park.[29]

A sophomore at the time, Smith borrowed a friend's car so that she and her boyfriend could find a quiet place to chat and—yes—even hold hands. But when her boyfriend's advances crossed the line into what most college students would describe as date rape, Smith confessed that she was so naïve that she didn't realize what had actually occurred. "He had sex with me, and I didn't want to" was how she put it to her friends back on campus. Self-recriminations would occur years later ("In retrospect I can say 'you're a dummy,' but back then I was 19. He was my friend. I knew him, I knew his sister").[30]

As Smith recounts the narrative, the former boyfriend apparently did not appear remorseful after the Skyline Drive incident: he began approaching Adele on campus and provoking her. One day he sat down beside her and put his hand on her leg; on another he approached her and began to insist that she slap him: "He kept saying 'Hit me.' He kept grabbing my hand and trying to make me slap him." He also spread the rumor among his friends that Adele had pulled a knife out in the car on Skyline Drive and forced him into sexual acts.[31]

In July 2011, well over a year after the reported rape incident, the school explained to Adele and to the Smith family that the former boyfriend would be charged with harassment but the charges failed to mention rape. And at the disciplinary hearing following that letter on July 28, 2011, the school determined that the accused assailant was responsible for the "violation of harassment," and received the punishment of not being allowed to live on campus for one year, as well as being forbidden to contact Adele Smith. Smith and her family were aghast (and said so). But Christendom based its disciplinary decision on two facts: there was, in 2011, no clause in the student handbook prohibiting sexual assault, a policy not put into the handbook until 2013 (i.e., two years after Smith's reported incident). Further, and equally pertinent in its estimation, Christendom pointed out that Smith had not formally reported the incident until well after the event itself, which in any case had occurred off-campus, so that the application of the College's *in loco parentis* policy (designed, the school said, to regulate on-campus interactions) seemed inapplicable.[32]

But as Smith recounted to Simcha Fisher in the latter's two-part blog articles on the incident, "Are Women Safe in Christendom's Bubble?" students were, in fact, regularly punished for coming back to campus drunk after drinking off-campus, which to Smith seemed like the College was saying "we care if you drink off campus, but not if you rape off campus."[33] Whatever the failings of Christendom's administration in handling Smith's case (and there appeared to be several big ones) it turned out that Smith herself was not unique in her unfortunate experience. Indeed, the Catholic News Agency reported in a 2018 online article that the vice president of the Christendom Advocacy and Support Coalition (CASC), Donna Provencher, reported that Smith's case was not the first such case of rape reported at Christendom. Despite its name, CASC is unaffiliated with the College, which accounts in part for its raising pointed questions about the purportedly safe bubble in the Blue Ridge Mountains: Provencher reported that it had "spoken to 12 victims whom the [Christendom] administration personally failed, and is aware of six more potential victims." In total, Provencher reported that her group had found that "18 known rapes and sexual assaults [occurred] between the 1980s and 2016, 16 of those between 1998 and 2016 under [current Christendom president] Timothy O'Donnell." On January 24, 2018, President O'Donnell acknowledged the school's failings in handling cases like these: "To those students who have been harmed, I am deeply sorry. We will do better."[34]

To understate the case by half, those unreported numbers are unsettling, even allowing for the fact that Christendom's Student Handbook failed to explicitly list sexual assault (as opposed to the prohibition of physical assault, which the Handbook did list) as a disciplinary offense until 2013. But as unsettling as those numbers are, one could argue that equally unsettling was the response to both Smith's allegations and Fisher's articles by *some* (but by no means all) Christendom students and alumni to the critiques aimed at the school. "Stacey" (an alumna of the school), posting on February 7, 2018, observed on Fisher's website:

> so many allegations, so little evidence . . . I find these allegations of Christendom "mishandling" the alleged rape laughable. The school did not "force" her to go off campus. The alleged victim seems hell bent blaming everyone but herself . . . for putting herself in that situation, for not reporting it, for wanting to stay at the school in his presence . . . I am for women which is why I find blaming the school for her poor judgment reprehensible.[35]

Stacey's comments reflected a heated online exchange that had been going on for several weeks, primarily among Christendom alumni/ae, many of whom found Fisher's two-part blog coverage of the school generally unfair, and specifically anti-Catholic. Thus "Steve J," posting on January 18, 2018, had argued that:

> I strongly suggest that the real story here is that the Fishers . . . can't stand a truly Catholic college,—or rather, I should say that you were fed that poison

by your previous *false Catholic formation that deprived you of truth*. What you can't stand is that Christendom is not "progressive," "inclusive," etc. and does not place a priority on liberal "social justice" issues . . . The general belittling of the college ("a bubble") and its many traditional Catholic policies tell me that the sexual abuse incidents are mere fodder for being crassly exploited for a wider agenda of assaulting the very existence of such a thoroughly orthodox Catholic faith-centered college.[36]

Similarly, "Maryann," on January 19, 2018, posted:

Can't help wondering, why Christendom? The place is teeming with kids from lovely, big Catholic families. I'll go out on a limb and say it's political. In its way Christendom did create a kind of bubble, where students can transition to the world while getting a great education in the faith. So know what, Fishers? About that bubble? Not your business. And next time you want to get all save-the-worldley [*sic*] try not to use your generous platform to make all Catholics look bad, but especially try not to scar the reputation of a pretty defenseless little school that's trying really, really hard to do something good, limping along without taking tax money.[37]

What the back-and-forth on Fisher's blog site (running to well over forty pages) exemplifies—besides a disturbing obtuseness on the part of some students and alumni regarding the best way to respond to rape claims—is the relative success of Carroll's founding vision for Christendom College: at least *some* students and alumni of that institution have clearly internalized Carroll's passionate commitment to a word which embodies the Christian social and political *ideal*: "a society, a culture, a government in which Christ the King reigns." That privileged institutional ideal of witnessing to (and being) Christendom—set apart from the secular and neo-pagan American mainstream culture—was called to be the safe (or maybe better, orthodox) inside, which had to be defended against the assaults of a corrupt (and maybe even demonic) outside. And battles involving issues of sexuality (and sensuality) represented core issues for those perceiving themselves to be on the side of the angels. From that vantage point, the surprise is *not* that the denunciation of those spewing poison caused by previous "false Catholic formation" is marked by such vituperation; the surprise, rather, is that it is not even more trenchant.

C. "To Live Ancient Lives": Integralism on the Blue Ridge?

As Theodore Dwight Bozeman argued so brilliantly in his study of the primitivist dimension of American Puritanism, there has always been a marked tendency in certain religious reformist movements to return to a purportedly purer primitive moment, when Christians ostensibly got it right. Indeed, for certain kinds of sectarian believers, true reform has always been about going back, not moving forward.[38]

For the British Puritans who landed in New England in the seventeenth century, that purer moment was the primitive Christian community of Jerusalem, described in the fifth book of the New Testament, "the Acts of the Apostles." That New Testament account of the first Christian community in Jerusalem made no mention whatsoever of bishops, set prayers in liturgy, priests, or kneeling to receive communion (all components of the worship and governance of the Church of England, in which the Puritans were nominal members). It was precisely those elements of the corrupt Anglican Church (elements singularly absent in the narrative of the primitive Church described in Acts) that had to be purified and replaced with godly traditions. And it was that vision—of replacing modern inventions with the pure (primitive) traditions of Jesus's first disciples—that largely defined the efforts of first two generations of Puritans in New England.[39]

For Carroll and his avid supporters in the founding of Christendom College, the primitive moment they sought to replicate in the last quarter of the twentieth century occurred considerably after the first-century Jerusalem community described in Acts. Their eyes were rather fixed on the high medieval centuries when the Catholic Church and western civilization were ostensibly melded into a unified historical reality known as Christendom— "a society, a culture, a government in which Christ the King reigns." It was *that* social and political ideal that constituted the primitive, perfect fusion of religious, political, and cultural identities into a unified identity, and it was that ideal which Christendom College sought to embody. No matter that Christendom as a medieval social ideal was, in fact, a social imaginary imposed on fractious centuries far less unified, cohesive, or orthodox than Carroll presented them in his scholarship and public discourse. Many parts of "Christian Europe" fought (both literally and figuratively) against popes who themselves had their own armies—genuine armies, not just metaphorical ones. And many devout Catholic Christians in the twelfth, thirteenth, and fourteenth centuries lived well outside the confines of that social imaginary, hardly aware of themselves as part of any larger synthetic whole. Part and parcel of Carroll's social imaginary of Christendom was his devotion to primitivist impulses as well: those impulses seemed to presume that one could stop history, rewind it, and freeze-frame time itself to establish the supposedly perfect society within an historical process. His vision for (and of) Christendom thus implied that one could exist outside of history—that one could, in fact, live ancient lives in defiance of the implacable, forward-moving historical process.[40]

Carroll believed that he could establish, as Mircea Eliade limned in laying out the worldview of those who sought to implement the profoundly *unCatholic* impulse of sectarianism:

> a precinct of righteousness, within and over against the unredeemed world of sin, pronouncing judgment upon it and calling it to repentance, but never entering into dialogue with it, much less collaboration on matters of common social, political, or religious concern. For the sectarian, dialogue and collaboration are [simply] invitations to compromise.[41]

Carroll's vision in founding Christendom College likewise would seem to embody a number of shared assumptions and goals with the integralist impulse pressed by some contemporary conservative Catholic intellectuals. As elucidated by scholars like Patrick Dineen at Notre Dame, Gladden Pappin at the University of Dallas, and Adrian Vermeule at Harvard, Catholic integralism can be understood as the effort to re-integrate religious authority and political power in an about-face rejection of modern liberalism. For Dineen (in *Why Liberalism Failed*) the "L" word encompasses the entire modern political project since the Enlightenment: his argument is with the *entire* "political philosophy conceived some 500 years ago, and put into effect at the birth of the United States 250 years later." Dineen argued that the entire constellation of beliefs that most Americans (until recently, anyway) took for granted was mistaken from the very beginning. Separation of church and state, freedom of conscience, denominationalism as the preferred form of religious organization, religious pluralism as a positive value, and so forth, had to be jettisoned in favor of a return to a strong government in which individuals would not be free to choose their religious affiliation nor able to propagate false religious ideas. That strong government, overseen and directed by the Church, would be composed of orthodox believers who should use the considerable political power at their disposal to ensure that the common good explicitly elucidated by the Church be the law of the land.[42]

William Galston, a senior fellow at the Brookings Institution, has portrayed Catholic integralism as a form of American conservatism that believes (like Dineen) that the political principles on which the United States was founded were flawed from the start, so that something like a quite conscious counter-revolution is necessary to put things back on track:

> The focus on individual rights comes at the expense of community and the common good, and the claim that government exists to preserve individual liberty creates an inexorable move toward moral anarchy. These tendencies have moved us so far from traditional decency and public order that there is little of worth to "conserve." Our current situation represents a revolution against the forces—religion, strong families, local moral communities—that once limited the worst implications of our founding mistakes.[43]

Integralists therefore believe that the only remedy for this revolution launched by the Enlightenment against religious and family values basic to the Christian message is a counter-revolution: instead of limited government, the United States needs a strong government which will *enforce* the common good by defending moral common sense against an array of "woke" threats posed by unelected elites. So understood, integralism seeks not to correct the flaws in the founding documents and ideas of the Republic, but to *replace them.* As argued by advocates like Vermeule and Dineen, integral Catholicism existed long before the Enlightenment drove modern culture off the tracks. In their reading of the past, integralism began with the Emperor Constantine and was classically embodied in the Edict of Thessalonica of 380 CE by Emperor Theodosius I—that first hinge of church–state relations purportedly replaced after the American Revolution with the second hinge of the First Amendment. Among many other things, a culture-wide return to the implementation of that first hinge would preclude most notions of religious liberty as now understood. Thus, Pater Edmund Waldstein wrote in his terse "Integralism in Three Sentences":

> Catholic Integralism is a tradition of thought that, rejecting the liberal separation of politics with the end [i.e., the ultimate purpose] of human life, that political rule must order man [*sic*] to his ultimate goal. Since, however,

man has both a temporal and an eternal end, integralism holds that there are two powers that rule him—a temporal power and a spiritual power. And since man's temporal end is subordinated to his eternal end, the temporal power must be subordinated to the spiritual power.[44]

Vermeule, of Harvard Law School (himself a convert to Catholicism), and one of the most eloquent advocates of what has been termed the "common good constitutionalist" version of integralism, has argued that the government needs to direct individuals, associations, and society as a whole toward what Catholics term the common good, and (more disturbingly) that strong rule to achieve that goal is entirely legitimate. This means (in practice) "a powerful presidency ruling over a powerful bureaucracy." In contrast to traditional American conservative principles, Vermeule presents his version of integralism as an *illiberal legalism* quite consciously willing to legislate morality for everyone, regardless of their own beliefs regarding the issues being enforced.[45]

One might very well conceive of Carroll's vision, and of the college he founded, as the small, advance guard of the kind of integralist society Dineen and Vermeule envision—in their case, not for 450 students, but for the United States itself. At the very least, one can legitimately conceive of Carroll as a prophetic voice witnessing to a vision that would emerge as a more robustly political movement in the generation after Carroll founded Christendom College. But there are distinct tensions, as well, in fitting Carroll and Catholic integralists like Dineen and Vermeule into the same ideological box without remainder. Carroll espoused a distinctively sectarian vision of Christendom that stood in tension with the *national* integralist vision espoused by Dineen and Vermeule. Carroll's ideal was sectarian in a literal sociological sense: it *presupposed* an outside culture hostile to, and distrustful of, his institution's religious, pedagogical, and social protocols. Indeed, the very essence of Christendom College's identity as a prophetic witness to ideals and values *not shared* by the vast majority of higher education institutions in the United States provided a significant part of its identity. That *frisson*— that very tension between the godly inside and the corrupt outside—was central to his institution's identity, and indeed to its success. Any lowering of the wall of separation between inside and outside would *not* contribute to the College's success; indeed, it might very well undercut the prospects of its valiant efforts to eschew governmental funding and "gender and inclusion" oversight by state officials. It was *precisely* its refusal to cooperate with governmental agencies that lent energy and identity to its witness. And Catholic integralists like Dineen and Vermeule lacked Carroll's primitivist loyalties. Both of them sought the kind of close cooperation achieved (or, at least, putatively achieved) in the glory days of Christendom, but neither thought it possible (or desirable) to "live ancient lives" in the twenty-first century. Too much had changed in both society and in the church for that to happen, and the United States (even with its many problems) was not the Roman Empire nor even the Holy Roman Empire. A new model of union— or of united purposes, anyway—was necessary to implement the illiberal legalism that Vermeule sought. The very idea that the strong president that Vermeule sought could be the Holy Roman Emperor *redivivus* was risible: in that sense, anyway, one might allow that Dineen and Vermeule were better historians than Carroll.

But Carroll *did* illustrate—just like the integralists in the generation after him—the cultural utility of using the political monikers of "left/right" in delineating his own stance over against the neo-pagan society he denounced as corrupt. The complex point to note in this is that, like the Protestant fundamentalists of over a century earlier, Carroll's crusade really *was* what he claimed it was: a quite specific set of *theological* loyalties elucidating what a truly faithful Catholic education looked like. It was, as a result, no surprise that his school drew praise from a spectrum of Catholic *religious* leaders and thinkers one can safely describe as "right of center" in the Catholic theological subculture: Cardinals Francis Arinze, Francis George, and Raymond Burke, as well as American figures like Benedict Groeschel, who had founded a late-twentieth-century traditionalist reform movement within his Franciscan order.[46]

But it was equally unsurprising that Christendom drew forth praise from political and cultural conservatives as well. As Marsden had also noted in his study of Protestant fundamentalists in the first three decades of the twentieth century, the explicitly theological crisis that so exorcised them was inextricably wedded to profound fears about the very survival of Christian civilization in America, so that those on the *religious* right found common cause with *political* and *cultural* conservatives who shared their profound worries. It is, therefore, not to deny the profoundly religious and theological concerns that led to Carroll's founding of Christendom to note as well the number of strong *political* supporters on the "right" who saw in the small Virginia college the embodiment of precisely the same principles they sought to implement in their own careers: Supreme Court Justice Clarence Thomas, Vice President Mike Pence, journalist George Weigel, among others.[47]

Further, as Margaret Bendroth noted in explaining the militancy of the Protestant fundamentalist denunciation of liberals in their churches, a significant element of that militancy was "generated by the masculine persona that fundamentalists identified as the true hallmark of the Christian *warrior*"—a gendered subtext in the denunciations of liberals across the board that perhaps can help to explain several puzzling incidents that have occurred at the small Virginia college, among them the rape reported by Adele Smith. Those who eschewed that warrior persona—liberal Catholics variously described as unfaithful, soft, ideologically polluted by a corrupt liberal Catholic culture, or even "feminized"—were somehow suspect in their refusal to embrace the hard line that Jesus enjoined on his disciples. Any deviation from that hard line generated results that the supposed victim probably deserved. This would, in part, explain the hostile reactions online to both Smith's rape charges and Fisher's reporting of that incident: "the school did not 'force' her to go off campus. The alleged victim seems hell bent on blaming everyone but herself" and "You were fed by poison by your false Catholic formation that deprived you of truth. What you can't stand is that Christendom is not 'progressive' or 'inclusive,' and does not place a priority on liberal 'social justice' issues."

Christendom as a medieval social imaginary, of course, unraveled in the early sixteenth century as a result of the theological protests voiced by Martin Luther, John Calvin, and even by Catholic humanists like Erasmus, all of whom reissued the famous theological call uttered by Catholic theologians in the late medieval period: *ecclesia semper reformanda* ("the church must always be reformed"). And part of that reformation was that the very idea of Christendom had to be jettisoned for other social imaginaries that have largely defined the modern period. Christendom, the social imaginary that seemed so unchanging (and unchangeable) in fact dissolved in the early modern period into what would become, in time, nation-states, eventually committed to secular governments separate from the religious institutions existing in their territories. The modern religion/culture/politics social imaginary centers more on denominational structures independent of the secular state, which—quite counterintuitively—has made religion more successful in terms of both practice and numbers than it had been in the Middle Ages. But that is a different study to be considered at a different time.

It is a risky historical game to base predictions for the future on what appears to be the purportedly unchanging nature of modern church–state relations. But if one were a betting historian, I think the safe bet would be that the chances of resurrecting Christendom as the normative political/cultural/ religious vision for our post-modern era of history are remote, at best, and unlikely to become more likely any time soon.

7

"The Violent Bear It Away"

ChurchMilitant.com

A. The Crusade Against the "Covid Reich"

Michael Voris, the founder of the (appropriately named) ChurchMilitant.com website is a complicated person, even by the rough-and-tumble standards of the Catholic blogosphere. A graduate of the University of Notre Dame with a degree in communications and a "license" in theology (a church degree normally awarded to scholars who plan to teach in Catholic seminaries), Voris claims to have decided to found a media outlet after seeing the lies told about the Catholic Church in both the book and the Hollywood movie version of *The DaVinci Code*. Voris's reaction to that largely fictional work (ostensibly offering a "glimpse behind the veil" of a corrupt Catholic Church teeming with plots and counterplots—on the intellectual level of the "Spy v. Spy" section of the old *Mad* magazine) was of course, completely understandable, and perhaps even praiseworthy. And he cites the death of his brother from a heart attack in 2003, and the death of his mother from stomach cancer in 2004, as moving him from being "a lukewarm Catholic, someone who just went through the motions at Church" to being a crusading Catholic media personality. That conversion from lukewarm to super-Catholic was a dramatic one on several levels, for Voris freely admits to having lived an "extremely sinful" life earlier in his career:

> For most of my years in my thirties, confused about my own sexuality, I lived a life of live-in relationships with homosexual men. From the outside, I lived a lifestyle and contributed to scandal in addition to my sexual sins. On the inside, I was deeply conflicted about all of it. In a large portion of my twenties, I also had frequent sexual liaisons with both adult men and adult women . . . That was before my reversion to the Faith. Since my reversion, I abhor all these sins.[1]

Indeed, that conversion led him in a dramatically different direction, leading him (and John Mola) in 1997 to found St. Michael's Media, a media outlet that produces catechetical and news videos on the website ChurchMilitant.com (originally named "Real Catholic TV"). Voris founded St. Michael's Media after a highly successful media career as a television anchor, producer, and reporter for various CBS affiliates in New York and the Midwest: in 1989, he became a news reporter and producer for the Fox affiliate in Detroit, where he won four Regional Emmy Awards for production between 1992 and 1996. And St. Michael's Media (and especially its website ChurchMilitant. com) would appear to be both a vocation and an avocation for Voris, as he confesses to working "up to 18 hours a day, seven days a week." That conversion also transformed him from being lukewarm Catholic to a self-described "aggressive global advocate for conservative Catholics, on a burning mission to save Catholicism and America by trying to warn the public about what is a decline of morality in society"—a burning mission that, by 2018, had an annual budget of $2.8 million per year.[2]

And an important part of that "burning mission" was his decision to inform both Catholics and others of the dangerous gay subculture in the United States. Indeed, his regular posts regarding that dangerous subculture led the independent Catholic news site Crux to label him "one of the Catholic Church's most vocal opponents of LGBT causes." Since founding St. Michael's Media, Voris has attracted a considerable base of supporters (180,000 Facebook followers, thirty thousand YouTube subscribers, twelve thousand Twitter fans); but he has, as well, produced a number of vociferous critics, who charge that his postings—especially about the gay subculture in the United States and in the Catholic Church—tend to "promote division and extremism." Among the evidence produced to back up that latter accusation was an article posted on January 26, 2018, on the Facebook page of Churchmilitant.com, announcing that his alma mater, the University of Notre Dame, was "once again aligning itself with the pro-homosexual agenda while claiming to be a faithful Catholic institution." The article reported on a Notre Dame on-campus retreat for its LGBT students co-sponsored by the Gender Relations Center (GRC) and by the Office of Campus Ministry which ostensibly promoted their gay identity as a grace, and the way "God wants them to love." That retreat was scheduled less than three months after a lecture by Jesuit James Martin, also co-sponsored by the GRC and Campus Ministry, on his book *Building a Bridge: How the Catholic Church and the LGBT Community Can Enter into a Relationship of Respect, Compassion, and Sensitivity.* His Facebook piece about Notre Dame, along with a number of other pieces published earlier, led the Southern Poverty Law Center in 2018 to include Voris and Church Militant on its annual list of LGBTQ hate groups.[3]

But Voris has argued that his fight has been an up-hill battle because the American Catholic hierarchy has seen fit to align itself to the "LGBT Agenda"—an alignment that led Voris to identify a number of the American Catholic hierarchy as members of the "the lavender mafia." Further, in a podcast entitled "Weak Men Suck," posted on Church Militant's podcast site, *The Vortex*, on August 10, 2022, Voris vociferously denounced the weak episcopal leadership of the American Church: "there is certainly no shortage of weak men in the Church"—most especially the "emasculated gang" who form the "sissies in charge of large parts of the Church these days." Those ostensible leaders have been infected with the idea that all masculinity is toxic by the woke anti-fa left in charge of the media, in the process adopting "a feminine cadence." In dramatic contrast to the Church *Fathers* ("who understood the concept of evil and spiritual war and fully embraced it") the current crop of "fathers" in charge of Christ's Church are an embarrassment: if American bishops ever actually read the works of the Fathers of the Church (who luxuriated in the idea of "warfare," spiritual and other), that encounter:

> would cause today's hypersensitive bishops to hike up their skirts, kick off their pumps and run over a cliff—that is if most of them could get their out-of-shape bodies to actually run.[4]

In Voris's view, "bishops and their wealthy enabling class have a lot to answer for": they who have hitched the fortunes of the Church itself to the "phony man-made climate change narrative," or who have made the Catholic Church complicit in "destroying a nation's borders" by claiming "social justice" for illegal immigrants. And that particular *The Vortex* podcast generated considerable positive energy among its readers: "Charging Charlie" posted that "these guys are duds . . . I'm sorry, but they are. They are feminized duds," while "John Joseph" posted that Voris hadn't even mentioned Pope Francis, "and isn't Francis the biggest antagonist to masculinity? He's constantly saying something nasty about strong-willed men. He's been trying to feminize the church since he got into power!" "Br. Christopher" addressed the bishops directly, stating "for God's sake, why do you damnable sodomites pursue the heights of ecclesiastical dignity with such fiery ambition?" while

"Baseballmomof8" added that "many of those bishops have a, shall we say, 'close' relationship with those perps."[5]

The most dramatic and public event focused on that particular Church Militant hobbyhorse—that American Catholic bishops have conspired to cover up sex abuse by clergy (or were even involved themselves in that abuse, or at least were sympathetic with the perpetrators)—involved a proposed prayer rally on Pier 6 of Baltimore's Inner Harbor on November 16, 2021. That event, advertised as "Bishops: Enough Is Enough Prayer Rally," was to feature Voris himself, as well as former Donald Trump adviser Steve Bannon, and reportedly had twenty-one hundred attendees who had already purchased tickets. But the prayer rally was canceled by Baltimore's City Solicitor James Shea, because of its "potential for significant disruption." Church Militant's attorney, Mark Randazza of Las Vegas, filed a formal complaint in Baltimore's US District Court against that cancelation, arguing that Shea did not, in fact, "have any factual basis whatsoever to believe the rally would pose a risk of violence to anyone or anything."[6]

But that event on Pier 6 had been carefully timed to coincide with the annual fall meeting of the US Conference of Catholic Bishops (USCCB) in Baltimore—a meeting to be held at the Baltimore Marriott, literally facing Pier 6 across Baltimore's Inner Harbor. Voris complained that Baltimore's reaction, and the cancellation of his proposed prayer rally, was grossly unfair, as well as being a product of mainstream media bias: "you're all down with the whole homosexual agenda. Are we a hate group because we are telling them, 'You're not living according to your vows?'"[7]

But Church Militant's regular (and vociferous) denunciation of the "LGBT agenda" was by no means the only target of its reporting. Indeed, after his visit to the Marian shrine in Fatima, Portugal, Voris's headquarters—a nondescript plain two-story brick building in the Detroit suburb of Ferndale—became what the *Detroit Free Press* called the nerve center for "an anti-gay, anti-feminist, Islam-fearing, human-caused-climate-change-denying," reporting that publicly advertised its hope that the forces that elected Donald Trump as president would "tear down the wall between church and state." Indeed, Voris compared Trump to Constantine, the Roman Emperor who (seemingly like Trump) was a "power-hungry egomaniac" but who nonetheless ended the persecution of Christians and became the "human vessel who elevated Catholicism to the state religion." With Trump's election "the entire established order has been thrown up in the air." Now, Voris announced, "we're allowed into the discussion."[8]

Voris's hope that Trump would "tear down the wall between church and state" sounds very much like the integralist vision propounded by Patrick Dineen and Adrien Vermuele, and institutionalized in the founding of Christendom College, although Voris himself has never used that word in any of his public statements or podcasts. While certainly not the only American Catholic advocating that integralist vision of a church and state united in a single social reality, Voris brings to that discussion an entirely new element: the reminder that the Catholic Church has never taken an absolute pacifist stance and has, in fact, advocated the use of coercion in certain circumstances, most famously embodied in the medieval crusades, but also in the "high Catholic theological tradition of just war theory. Thus, for Voris, "violence must always be an option."[9]

From the videos filmed inside the TV station, viewers immediately pick up the "Catholic vibe" prominently featured inside the building: crucifixes everywhere, a sign over a door that reads "Mother Angelica's Studio," a photo of (one-time) media star Archbishop Fulton Sheen hung in one of the work cubicles, and so on. But while those icons of an unapologetic Catholic identity are proudly displayed, Church Militant is not afraid of attacking other, more recent, icons of the Church. One of the station's favorite targets is the American Catholic hierarchy. One Church Militant video posted on *The Vortex* raises questions about Chicago Archbishop Blasé Cupich's teaching regarding "the consistent ethic of life" approach to ethical issues. That ethic, first elucidated by Cupich's saintly predecessor, Cardinal Joseph Bernardine, taught that "life issues" were broader than just abortion, and included cradle-to-grave issues, such as attention to prenatal care and the condemnation of the death penalty, as profoundly anti-Christian. Such a focus on "life issues," avers Church Militant, in fact represents a liberal "distraction" from the culture war that "real Catholics" are called to wage in the godless, secular culture that is America: and there is only one predominant issue in that culture war: abortion. The COVID mandates supported by the majority of US bishops represent the "Covid Reich," while the Black Lives Matter (BLM) movement is termed a "terrorist, Marxist, pro-LGBT, pro-abortion organization."[10]

But Church Militant's followers are treated to a fairly broad array of denunciations, powered by Voris's own theory that "news is a door to theology," That theory has led Voris to declare that America has been living in what amounts to a "secular dictatorship," a dictatorship that needs to be answered in kind:

The only way to run a country is by benevolent dictatorship, a Catholic monarch who protects his people from themselves, and bestows on them what they need, not necessarily what they want.[11]

And life under that proposed "benevolent" Catholic dictator would offer a difficult row to hoe, especially for Jewish Americans. For Mark Weitzman, director of the Simon Wiesenthal Center (a Jewish human rights group based in New York), "it's worth knowing that these people are out there, because any threat to the democratic system is worth paying attention to." Especially concerning is the network's espousal of "supersessionism," the belief that God's promises to the People of Israel are no longer operative as the Church has become the "New Israel of God."

Such a belief usually results in what is de-facto *theological*—if not racial—antisemitism. In Weitzman's estimation, Church Militant was therefore worthy of close monitoring—a small group "with some influence and the ability to make a lot of noise."[12]

Church Militant's thirty-five full-time employees publish ten stories and post three videos every weekday, many of whose headlines resemble those posted on *Breitbart News*, the news organization previously run by White House Chief Strategist Bannon. Thus, the three headlined stories posted by Church Militant on the day that the *Detroit Free Press* published its story about the Ferndale operation were "Bombshell: Priest at Forefront of Pushing Birth Control in Canada Admits Gay Lifestyle," Dismantling Obama's Legacy," and "72 Terrorists Come to U.S. From Seven Banned Muslim-Majority Countries."[13]

While this daily round of stories aired by the station are unsettling, arguably even more disturbing is Church Militant's regular insistence on the necessity of violence—even physical violence—in advancing the "Catholic agenda" in what it perceives to be an extremely hostile cultural environment. In November 2022, Voris described Election Day in the United States as "a day of reckoning for the communists who have seized so much control of the country and wreaked so much havoc on America"—an unsettling statement for many in the wake of January 6, 2020. Equally unsettling was a video editorial posted on Church Militant TV, in which Voris warned that in the ongoing "all-out war going on between the forces of darkness who have complete control of one political party and partial control over the other," Catholics (and other true conservatives) might have "no choice but to fight back—violently if need be." As Kathryn Joyce reported on the *Salon* website,

Voris warned that Catholics who failed to vote for Trump because he was too vulgar shouldn't complain when they found themselves "herded onto trains headed for the camps" [sic] or "gunned down in the streets." And it was precisely because of that possibility of finding oneself on a train heading for the camps that violence (including political violence) must always on the table as one of the "true" Catholic options in fighting a corrupt political and media culture.[14]

As Voris laid out the apocalyptic future he saw confronting America on the video posted at ChurchMilitant.com, Catholics who recognized what was going on were at Kierkegaardian moment of decision:

> Now we are in a pitched battle in the political arena—the last remaining line before all-out civil war. The idea that violence must always, at all times, always be avoided is not Catholic. Remember the Crusades? Sometimes violence must be unleashed to protect the innocent. But lethal violence—because of its drastic you-can-never-come-back-from-its-consequences—must never be the first resort. In fact it must always be the last resort ... But violence does—must always be an option. Welcome to a fallen world.[15]

And the fact that the episcopal leadership of the Church in the United States has remained mum on the Catholic option of violence in the face of the "all-out civil war" that Voris saw just over the horizon led him to label American Catholic bishops as part of the "international crime syndicate" quietly abetting violence for their own purposes.[16]

Furthermore, Voris's advocacy of violence would appear to be more than simply empty rhetoric: Church Militant appears to have ties to the "Groyper" movement, led by live-stream media personality Nick Fuentes. That movement itself is a loose network of groups and individuals whose goal is to "normalize" white nationalist ideas within mainstream conservativism, and especially within the Republican Party. Gathered around *America First* podcast host Fuentes, one of whose goals is to capture members of Generation Z by presenting American Christian nationalism as the only genuine set of values for true patriots, Groyper's message is a simple one: shifting racial and cultural demographics present a genuinely existential threat to both white European Americans, and to the "Christian values" on which American culture was built. Groypers are, thus, fixated on US borders and immigration politics. Two days before the January 6 Capital Hill riot, Fuentes raised the issue of killing state lawmakers, although he quickly backtracked his comment on his *America First* show. Fuentes was himself present at the January 6 "protest," and while he did not enter the Capital building, he described the riot as "awesome." And a number of rioters, both at the rally on the steps of the building and inside the Capital, were seen wearing *America First* merchandise.[17]

Salon.com's two-part investigation, in November 2022, reported on a number of direct lines of support between Church Militant and the "Groyper" movement: Voris's staff in Ferndale regularly praised Groyper events and "interventions" during interviews with various alt-right figures, and likewise regularly published ads that encouraged Groyper followers to join forces with its own supporters to counter pro-choice and gay rights demonstrations. Indeed, Church Militant made far-right live streamer John Doyle—himself a Groyper-aligned activist—into something like a cultural hero: Doyle led an especially ugly protest outside a LGBTQ bar in Dallas, Texas, during a drag show taking place inside, during which—as Church Militant approvingly reported on its own site—Doyle called on Texas law enforcement to enter the bar and "put bullets in all their heads. They'd be rewarded for it. That's what the badge is for." As Salon.com reporters Joyce and Ben Lorber reported on the story, "the Dallas incident rapidly worked its way up the right-wing food chain, from the Daily Caller to Alex Jones to Steve Bannon and then, inevitably, Tucker Carlson," who introduced his segment on the Dallas event on Fox News by quipping "Just another day in Weimar."[18]

B. "A Disgrace to the Chair of Peter"

But even given Church Militant's regular denunciation of the episcopal leadership of a corrupt Church aligned with the woke Democratic Party, Pope Francis himself holds pride of place among hierarchy as the special object of the website's disdain and distrust. A podcast posted on *The Vortex* on February 23, 2016, entitled "A Disgrace to the Chair of Peter," was ostensibly about what John Henry Newman feared in 1870 about the promulgation of the dogma of papal infallibility: "common infallibility." What Newman meant by that latter phrase was the idea that might take hold among the faithful that papal infallibility might "bleed" into other areas of papal teaching, so that Catholics might assign an authority to all of a pope's pronouncements that they did not actually possess. In commenting on Newman's worry, Voris observed in his podcast that:

a potential[ly] dangerous mix could now form in the minds of the regular faithful. The mix was that everything any pope said was held as infallible . . . We have arrived at that point in the Church's history. Too many
Catholics, as well as enemies of the Church, have in their minds that
whatever issues from the mouth of the Pope enjoys an air of infallibility,
or near infallibility. The fact that a Pope could say something wrong or be
misinformed simply doesn't occur to them.[19]

In the course of the podcast, Voris offers a list of popes who have lived lives of
public sin or scandal: Benedict IX, elected in 1032 (whom the 1913 *Catholic
Encyclopedia* called a "disgrace to the chair of Peter," thus providing the name
for this podcast); John XI; and John XII (himself fathered by another pope),
among others. Voris's point in recounting these pontiffs is simple and correct: "men in the office of Pope can be wrong. That shouldn't be a headline
for Catholics." Until modern times few Catholics ever heard from the Bishop
of Rome, "but now it's nonstop. Catholics have gone from hearing their
popes to hearing too much. Men in the office of pope can be wrong."[20]

Up to that point, no theologian (traditionist or progressive) would take
any issue with Voris's remarks in the podcast. But shortly after that remark
the mood of the podcast changes, and the real subtext reveals itself: the
changed atmosphere of the podcast commences with Pope Francis's famous response to then-presidential candidate Trump's announcement in
2016 that he would build a wall along the US/Mexico border to keep people
from crossing illegally into the United States. Francis's response to Trump's
announcement (as reported in the Associated Press) was: "I'd just say that
this man is not Christian if he said it in this way. A person who thinks only
about building walls, wherever they may be, and not building bridges, is not
Christian."[21]

What becomes considerably clearer after that point is that the "disgrace"
referred to in the podcast's title was aimed at the current occupant of the
Fisherman's office (Pope Francis), and not the popes of the eleventh and
twelfth centuries who had lived such scandalous lives. "Did you hear what
the pope said?" Voris asked in the podcast: "Referring to Donald Trump as
not Christian has no magisterial weight. Jorge Bergoglio can easily misspeak."
The "disgrace" was that Jorge Bergoglio (known to Catholic Christians as
Pope Francis) had no business using a media event ("a press conference has
no magisterial weight") to make weighty statement that Catholics might
easily take for official teaching:

Why should reporters even be allowed to pop questions at the Pope? Any pope? Always a bad idea. What a pope says about climate change has no magisterial weight. What a pope says about economic systems has no magisterial weight. What he says about immigration has no magisterial weight.[22]

Voris was, of course, correct: Francis's off-the-cuff remarks about Trump during a press conference with reporters had no magisterial weight in terms of official church teaching. Francis was offering a personal opinion—a private observation by someone who also happened to be Bishop of Rome. But it could be argued that Voris over-stated his position a tad: while only a private, non-magisterial comment, it nonetheless embodied the sense of someone who was, by his office, what canon law called "the universal ordinary," and therefore whose statements were worthy of at least thoughtful consideration, if not the "due submission of will" that Catholics were expected to show to magisterial papal teaching, even non-infallible teaching. But far more important than Voris's quite correct reading of the "authoritative weight" of Francis's comment of February 2016, was the trajectory it limned. Two years later Voris released a considerably more denunciatory statement about the Supreme Pontiff.[23]

On August 27, 2018, Voris posted, on *The Vortex*, the "Church Militant Statement on the Pope" that represented the closing coda to the overture he had played in 2016. One gets the overall sense of the apocalyptic tone that suffused this *The Vortex* posting from its opening sentences: "Given the horror that has increasingly seized hold of the Church these past 50 years—and which has climbed to unimaginable heights under the pontificate of Pope Francis," Voris and Church Militant now felt compelled to speak out against a pope who was now himself the cause of public scandal, given his central role in the coverup surrounding the clerical abuse scandal:

Pope Francis, Holy Father, for the salvation of your own soul, you must now step down from the Chair of Peter [*sic*] and do so immediately. You have treated too many of the faithful with coldness and callowness, abusing the power of your office in regard to their sufferings over this horrendous unconscionable evil which you have facilitated . . . Given the revelations over the weekend from Abp. Vigano's testimony—a testimony you do not deny—it is now clear that you yourself are one of the cover-up bishops.[24]

And the apocalyptic rhetoric becomes more overt and dramatic as the video goes on: "you have drawn into the temple of God, the most holy of sanctuaries, wicked men who have both raped and covered up the rape of innocents"; "your hypocritical and shameless parade of empty words of sorrow and pleading for forgiveness are an egregious front to those who believe in God"; "the men you have surrounded yourself with have no supernatural faith"; "a man who aids, abets, protects and promotes such wicked, sexually perverse and predatory men is not fit for the Chair of Peter—he is fit for far worse."[25]

"Given the horror that has increasingly seized hold of the Church these past 50 years, which has climbed to unimaginable heights under the pontificate of Pope Francis," now was the time, Voris announced, for the faithful laity to publicly decry the wickedness in high places that has stained God's holy tabernacle. And apparently without a hint of self-irony, Voris stated that "this is the danger of a media-driven papacy":

> It can be manipulated by those who control the media and those in the Church who want to exploit it. They want the impression to exist that everything a pope says is Catholic dogmas [sic] so that when the man who is Pope misspeaks or is wrong, they can pounce on it and capitalize on it.[26]

Voris's call for Francis's resignation was based on the accusations of Archbishop Carlo Maria Vigano, Apostolic Nuncio to the United States from 2009 to 2011 and someone who had been a high-flyer within the Vatican bureaucracy long before that: he was consecrated as a bishop by John Paul II in 1992, who had subsequently sent Vigano on a number of diplomatic missions in which Vigano performed with some distinction. Vigano was appointed Secretary General of the Vatican City Government in 2009, in which position he reformed the finances of Vatican City and turned a budget deficit into a surplus. But in cleaning out that particular Vatican swamp, he also complained directly to then-Pope Benedict XVI about the financial corruption inside the Curia that led that pontiff to form an investigation into financial practices inside the Vatican.[27]

But Vigano is now most famous (or infamous) for an eleven-page public letter that he posted on August 25, 2018, in which he accused Pope Francis himself and his "cronies" inside the church hierarchy—both in Rome and in the United States—of concealing shocking accusations of sexual abuse against then-cardinal Theodore McCarrick. Vigano stated (without any material evidence, as it would turn out) that Pope Benedict XVI had imposed serious canonical sanctions against McCarrick which Pope Francis had subsequently refused to enforce; indeed, Vigano stated in his letter that—far from disciplining McCarrick—Francis had actually made McCarrick into an important advisor on church matters in the United States. According to Vigano, Francis knew from information that Vigano himself had delivered to him as early as June 2013 that McCarrick was a serial predator: "He [Pope Francis] knew he was a corrupt man, [but] he covered for him to the bitter end." Thus, in his public letter Vigano declared that:

> In this extremely dramatic moment for the universal church, he [Pope Francis] must acknowledge his mistakes, and, in keeping with the proclaimed policy of zero tolerance, Pope Francis must be the first to set a good example to cardinals and bishops . . . and resign along with them. We must tear down the conspiracy of silence with which bishops and priests have protected themselves at the expense of their faithful, a conspiracy of silence that in the eyes of the world risks making the church look like a sect, a conspiracy of silence not so dissimilar from the one that prevails in the mafia.[28]

In that same letter Vigano accused three consecutive Vatican secretaries of state (again, without evidence) of knowing about McCarrick's behavior but doing nothing about it; further, and more damning, Vigano baldly stated that McCarrick had orchestrated the appointments of three major American cardinals (Cupich of Chicago, Joseph Tobin of Newark, and Robert McElroy of San Diego), precisely to "buy their silence" on his misdeeds. But the truth of those accusations was immediately questioned in the secular media: the *New York Times* stated that Vigano's letter was in fact full of "unsubstantiated allegations and personal attacks," and declared the missive to be "an extraordinary public declaration of war against Francis' papacy." And the role Vigano gave to Pope Benedict was likewise perceived as being deeply problematic: McCarrick continued his regular public appearances at the Vatican all during Benedict's papacy, meeting with Benedict himself a number of times, including the scheduled *ad limina* visit to the Vatican in which he entertained both the pope and other American cardinals. During those highly public receptions Pope Benedict showed no hesitation whatsoever about meeting and publicly chatting with McCarrick. And if indeed Vigano was correct in reporting Pope Benedict's stern disciplining of the American cardinal, "Why Was [McCarrick] Allowed at the Gala Events?" (as Laurie Goodstein of the *New York Times* entitled her investigative article on Vigano's accusations). Why indeed.[29]

Further, the release of the letter itself stating Vigano's very public accusations against the pope and three "major players" in the American Catholic hierarchy (Cupich, Tobin, and McElroy) raised significant questions about the former nuncio's real purpose in launching such an unprecedented open attack on the Pope: Vigano's letter was initially made available only to news outlets in both the United States and Italy, both known for their opposition to both Francis and his ecclesial program of moving the Church more resolutely in the direction of being a "field hospital for the wounded" and away from being a "Perfect Society" situated above history's battlefields. Further, the timing of its release raised even further questions: Vigano released the letter to a very specific set of news outlets during Pope Francis's two-day visit to Ireland to attend the World Meeting of Families and on the eve of his flight back to Rome, thus seemingly designed to blindside the pontiff with questions from reporters during his customary in-flight press conference. Could that timing be purely serendipitous?

At least one news reporter found the "serendipitous explanation" for Vigano's release of his letter to be highly unlikely: Michael O'Loughlin, writing in *America* magazine on August 26, 2018, allowed that Vigano might indeed be frustrated at Francis's seeming lack of urgency in addressing the issue of clergy sexual abuse; but he also noted other factors that might have played a more decisive role in Vigano's intentions. O'Loughlin noted Francis's decision to remove the Archbishop from his Washington diplomatic position in 2016 because he had "become too enmeshed in U.S. culture wars, particularly involving same-sex marriage." And the public event that galvanized the sense that Vigano was indeed deeply enmeshed in the American culture wars (Catholic and otherwise) occurred during Francis's visit to the United States in 2015, when Vigano had arranged for the pope to meet Kim Daniels, the former Kentucky county clerk who refused to sign a marriage certificate for a same-sex couple: at the time of that event with Daniels, Francis was apparently unaware of the fierce political overtones that the meeting itself embodied. But Vatican officials were furious at the media coverage that short encounter generated, seemingly situating Francis in the culture wars over gay marriage without his knowledge or consent. Vigano's days as nuncio after that fateful meeting were most assuredly numbered.[30]

But a series of investigations both inside and outside the Vatican revealed that—much like the reports of Mark Twain's death—Archbishop Vigano's accusations against Francis were not only exaggerated but lacked any substance. Cardinal Marc Ouellet, the then-Prefect of the Vatican Congregation for Bishops, released a public, scathing letter to Vigano on October 7, 2018, stating that a careful investigation undertaken independently of the Pope revealed that there were no records whatsoever backing Vigano's claim that Francis had lifted or rolled back sanctions on McCarrick supposedly imposed by Pope Benedict. Indeed, Ouellet reported that there was no paper trail whatsoever of Pope Benedict "disciplining" McCarrick, making Vigano's accusations "incredible and unlikely from all points of view." Further:

> Your current position seems to me incomprehensible and extremely reprehensible, not only because of the confusion that sows in the people of God, but because your public accusations seriously damage the reputation of the Successor of the Apostles . . . After reviewing the archives, I note that there are no documents in this regard signed by either Pope [ordering] McCarrick to silence and a private life, with the rigor of canonical penalties.[31]

Indeed, the cardinal prefect called on Vigano to "repent of your revolt and return to better feelings toward the Holy Father." Ouellet confessed that he understood "how bitterness and disappointment have marked your path in service to the Holy See. But you cannot end your priestly life in this way, in an open and scandalous rebellion." And Ouellet's stern rebuke was echoed in the secular press as well, as in CNN's religion reporter Daniel Burke's story, entitled "The 'Coup' Against Pope Francis." Burke reported that fellow CNN analyst John Allen had uncovered a 2014 memo documenting how Vigano himself had demanded that evidence be destroyed in an attempt to end an investigation against a former archbishop of St. Paul, Minneapolis, Minnesota. Likewise, a story in the *New York Times* similarly cast Vigano's accusations as part of a conservative coup whose larger agenda was based on ideology, and not on scandalous behavior.[32]

Vigano's quite bizarre "disappearance" after the carefully controlled release of the eleven-page letter raised still further questions as to what was actually going on. As the *Washington Post* announced in its story about the former Vatican nuncio to the United States on June 10, 2019:

The retired Vatican ambassador to Washington wrote a bombshell letter calling on Pope Francis to resign on the grounds that he had tolerated a known sexual abuser. As that letter was published, Vigano turned off his phone, told friends he was disappearing, and let the church sort through the fallout.[33]

Almost a year later, Vigano did finally agree to an interview with two reporters from the *Washington Post*, but he still refused to disclose his location or to say anything about the reasons for his self-imposed exile. But he nonetheless continued his vociferous denunciations of Pope Francis without offering any further proof of the truth of his charges: "it is immensely sad," Vigano told the *Washington Post* reporters, "that the pope is blatantly lying to the whole world to cover up his wicked deeds."[34]

The complete lack of any proof grounding Vigano's shocking accusations of papal support in covering up clerical abuse at the very highest levels of church government does raise troubling questions as to why Voris wanted to position *The Vortex* in the middle of a battle over scandalous documents that never appeared to exist. Indeed, Vigano's accusations seemed analogous to Trump's regular references to a hidden "Deep State" pulling the strings of the "real power" in Washington (similarly without material evidence). *The Vortex* seemed to offer its readers the *real* inside story, albeit a story lacking evidence of any kind, apart from the prophetic denunciations by Vigano. And the continued support offered to Vigano—in the face of an almost complete absence of anything resembling a paper trail on either side of the Atlantic—raises troubling questions about the *kind* of Catholicism pressed by St. Michael's Media, even with its ubiquitous crucifixes and pictures of Catholic personalities.

C. "St. Michael the Archangel, Defend Us in Battle"

Years before Voris's public call on the pope to resign in 2018, the Catholic Archdiocese of Detroit had sought to distance itself from the activities of what the *Detroit Free Press* called the "right-wing Ferndale fringe group." In 2011, the Archdiocese had contacted Voris to say that "it did not regard [Voris] as being authorized to use the word 'Catholic' to identify or promote [his] public activities." Citing canon 216 of the (revised) *1983 Code of Canon Law*, it pointed out that Voris had never requested (nor received) permission from Detroit's archbishop to use the word "Catholic" in its website title. Thus, in 2011—that is, seven years before the Vigano imbroglio and Voris's public call for the pope's resignation—the Catholic Church in Detroit insisted that "Real Catholic TV" change its name, which it did, in 2012, switching to "ChurchMilitant.tv" (and shortly after that to "Church Militant.com"). That distancing, in fact, witnessed to an awareness early on that—whatever Voris's understanding of his website as launching a Catholic crusade against a corrupt culture both inside and outside the Holy Roman Church—St. Michael's Media constituted something of a problem if conceived as a "Catholic"—as opposed to a Catholic's—undertaking. Voris himself took some umbrage at the diocese's directive: "to this day," he argued, "the archdiocese of Detroit has never specified any programming or content . . . that it has found heterodox or problematic. It has issued no censure or delict against this apostolate which remains in good standing with the Church." The Archdiocese never responded to those complaints but St. Michael's Media dropped the name "Catholic" from its website, opting instead for "Church Militant"—a technical theological term that Voris has defined in his own way.[35,36]

Indeed, Voris's statements in the *Detroit Free Press* article about the theology that constituted the heart of his work probably did little to calm the fears of archdiocesan officials worried about public scandal:

> The problem with America is America never sat down and had the right discussion about which religion is the right religion . . . The only way to run a country is by benevolent dictatorship, a Catholic monarch who protects his people from themselves and bestows on them what they need, not necessarily what they want.[37]

Much like other fundamentalist movements across the denominational spectrum (and especially like other American Catholic fundamentalists), Church Militant undertook its crusade for a complex mix of cultural, political, and ideological reasons by crafting a profoundly sectarian understanding of Catholicism itself—a Catholicism perceived to be under attack, not only from outside the Church by "woke" secularists, but even more alarmingly by archbishops (and even popes) inside what Voris referred to as "the holy temple." As religion scholar Mircea Eliade had adumbrated in sketching groups at the opposite pole of Christian identity from Catholicism, sectarian believers always created a movement:

that holds that the [true] church is a community of true believers, a precinct of righteousness within and over against the unredeemed world of sin, pronouncing judgment upon it and calling it to repentance, but never entering into dialogue with it, much less collaboration on matters of common social, political, or religious concern.[38]

Voris's very efforts to draw a tight circle around the "elect" who took part in the crusades advanced by St. Michael's Media pointed to the fact that Voris had a distinct (and distinctive) understanding of Catholic Christianity, an understanding from which the Roman Catholic Archdiocese of Detroit sought to distance itself. Likewise, Voris's fusion of political and theological issues in his cultural crusade evinced yet another sign that his undertaking was a distinct form of fundamentalism. As George Marsden argued, the Protestant conservatives he studied really were (just as they claimed) focused on theology; but the *cultural* experience of living in post-World War I America shaped their religious message in profound and lasting ways: the theological loyalties of the first several generations of Protestant fundamentalists became fused with political loyalties in an almost seamless way. Therefore, Marsden noted that:

> they expressed alarm not only about modernism and evolution, but also about the spread of communism. Occasionally even anti-Jewish sentiments were incorporated. At the same time *unqualified fundamentalist patriotism* was growing rapidly . . . In minds of most fundamentalists, the theological crisis came to be inextricably wedded to the very survival of Christian civilization.[39]

And in Voris's perception, the "Christian civilization," once securely established in the United States, was now under attack from a number of sources that had to be battled in a political and cultural crusade he sought to initiate from Ferndale, Michigan, especially "the LGBTQ agenda" pressed by woke politicians no less than by the "lavender mafia" of Catholic bishops (who themselves "broke their vows" by taking part in a gay lifestyle). Indeed, Voris's regular denunciations of that agenda led the Southern Poverty Law Center in 2018 to include both Voris himself and Church Militant on its annual list of "LGBTQ Hate Groups."[40]

The targets of Voris's cultural crusade also included a much broader spectrum of groups threatening the survival of the Christian civilization of the

United States: Muslim terrorists; illegal aliens sneaking into the United States, whose morally despicable efforts to break immigration laws were defended by the lavender mafia under the specious umbrella of "social justice"; the "Covid Reich" spreading false stories about the necessity of vaccination; and those woke liberals opposed to former President Trump's courageous efforts to "tear down the wall between church and state" so that Catholicism might, at last, become the official state religion of the United States. Indeed, as previously discussed, Voris regularly and vociferously defended Trump as being exactly analogous to the Emperor Constantine (admittedly a "power-hungry egomaniac") who nonetheless became the "human vessel who elevated Catholicism to the state religion" of Rome.[41]

Equally important in understanding the continued wariness of the Detroit Archdiocese regarding Voris's media crusade, even after he replaced the name "Real Catholic TV" with that of "Church Militant," was his singular understanding of the latter term. In Catholic theology, "church militant" does not refer to the physical or political violence necessary to battle the evil forces of secular society—an understanding that Voris advances in light of the Church's support for the medieval crusades against the "infidels" in the Holy Land. In Catholic theology, "church militant" is much more commonly used as a component of the Catholic belief in the *communio sanctorum*— the communion of saints—which is confessed whenever believers recite the Apostles' Creed. The "militant" in the phrase "church militant" referred to St. Paul's famous observation in his Epistle to the Romans: "But I see another law at work in me, waging war against the law of my mind, and making me a prisoner of the law of sin at work within me." St. Paul therefore admonished the early Christians in the first century church in Rome to "battle" the personal sins of pride, avarice, sloth, envy, and so on, in their effort to live out the life of Christian discipleship. "Militant" in this (Pauline) sense did not refer to political or physical violence, but rather to the "battle" against the world, the flesh, and the devil that all Christians were obliged to wage.[42]

"Church militant," then, referred quite explicitly to the "inner combat" that living Christians were called to undertake, uniting them in a profound spiritual undertaking, as distinct from the "church suffering" (the spiritual union of Christians with fellow believers in purgatory) and the "church triumphant" (the spiritual union that Christians have with believers in heaven). What Catholic Christians mean when they state during worship that they believe "in the communion of saints" is that all those gifted with the Holy Spirit at baptism become part of the "Mystical Body of Christ": *all* of the faithful—on earth, in purgatory, and in heaven—share in the common life and striving for holiness "against the law of sin at work within me." And while the groups (militant, suffering, triumphant) are distinct, they are nonetheless united by a common bond of charity and hope: they are, in a word, alive and united to each other, praying for the faithful in other states of discipleship. Far from being a divisive and highly politicized term advanced to sponsor political and moral positions in the culture wars of North America, "church militant" referred to the mystical *union* that Christians had with one another—the living with the dead, the perfect in heaven with those still being perfected on earth and in purgatory.[43]

But it was the very opposite of lightning in a cloudless sky when Voris posted a video editorial in November 2022, arguing that, on the next presidential election day, *real* believers had to remember that "violence is not immoral . . . it must always be an option." Indeed, the election day two years later was to be "a day of reckoning for the communists who have seized so much control of the country and wreaked so much havoc on America." And he warned that, in the "all-out war going on between the forces of darkness who have complete control of one political party and partial control over the other," conservatives might have "no choice but to fight back violently if needs be." And in an all-out war, "violence must always be an option."

And while the "hyper-masculinity" of Voris's advocacy of violence might shock some Catholics, it is salutary to remember Margaret Bendroth's penetrating study of the role of women in Protestant fundamentalism at the beginning of the twentieth century. In light of Bendroth's insightful scholarship, Voris's very unapologetic militancy, like the militancy of his Protestant fundamentalist forebears, "was generated by the masculine persona that [all] fundamentalists identified as the true hallmark of the Christian *warrior*."[44]

For the Protestant fundamentalists a century earlier, the church had been seen as an institution whose membership was primarily female: thus, *masculine* language and a conscious advocacy of violence was a revered way of taking back control of a corrupt (i.e., "feminized") institution. And Voris's use of that same trope of "liberalism as effeminate weakness" likewise has a long (and predictable) history in both Protestant and Catholic fundamentalism: Leonard Feeney had denounced the liberals in his own Jesuit order as well as the liberal Archbishop of Boston as weak men betraying the strong meat of orthodoxy, no less than Gommar DePauw had decried the liberals at the Second Vatican Council who undermined the "changeless" mass of the 1570 Roman Missal to curry favor with the degenerate culture of the Modern

West. All of this was seen long before Voris arrived on the scene, lauding violence as the option that "strong men" would not shrink from choosing in witnessing to a manly faith, as opposed to the "milquetoast wimps" now in charge of the Temple.

The Protestant fundamentalists' literal reading of the Bible ("biblical inerrancy") was an approach to scripture that the vast majority of American Protestants in 1870 had accepted without a second thought, based on a "Baconian Realist" understanding of both science and the Bible. In Thomas Kuhn's language, the American Protestant mainstream had undergone a "paradigm revolution" after World War I, so that Fundamentalist Protestants operated out of the older paradigm of Baconian realism, while (modernist) mainstream Protestants operated out of another. And while both groups used exactly the same words and phrases (the Bible as God's revealed truth, "building a Christian civilization in the U.S.," etc.), they meant completely different things by them.[45]

Voris and Church Militant similarly operated out of an older (and now discarded) paradigm of Catholicism in which "error had no rights," so that Catholics were morally bound to establish Catholicism as the official religion of the state when they were in a position to do so; a paradigm in which Catholics were obliged to (literally) fight against infidels to win back the Holy Places in Palestine, and the only legitimate authority was focused on male hierarchs. Almost every part of that older paradigm had been supplanted by a newer paradigm of Catholic Christianity during the last two centuries in which "violence" (with a few exceptions) referred to spiritual exertion; in which official church teaching celebrated the rights of conscience and religious freedom; in which non-clerics—and even women—could serve as chief administrators for parishes, or as official canonists for entire dioceses.

But Voris's singular leadership of St. Michael's Media ended suddenly, and seemingly independently of his vociferous campaigns against the "LGBTQ Agenda" and the "lavender mafia" of bishops who betrayed the Church, and of his political effort to raise awareness of the "communists who have taken over so much of our culture." On November 21, 2023, Church Militant simply posted an announcement that "Voris has been asked to resign for breaching the Church Militant morality clause. The board has accepted his resignation." The board noted that this was understandably a shock to Church Militant's regular followers, "but our founder and former CEO is stepping aside focusing on his personal health."[46]

In the fourteen-minute video posted later that evening on the same web-site, Voris failed to specify what exactly had led the media outlet's board to ask for his resignation, but he alluded to some personal problems that he faced, and that he was going on a retreat to address challenges that he described as "spiritual terror":

> There are things I have to go away and address and work on. They are again, horrible ugly things, not going to share them. Nobody else's business but mine . . . . Sometimes it takes very horrible events, even at your own hand, in your life to surface things that need to be faced. There are some very, very ugly truths from my past that I have for essentially 62 years have avoided facing.[47]

But Mile Lewis, at the website "Where Peter Is," noted that the Church Militant board's call for prayers and understanding for Voris during what was undoubtedly a very difficult time, both for him and for the media outlet he founded, stood in marked contrast to how Voris himself had treated many Catholics whom he viewed as the "enemy within." Lewis stated that Voris's "over-the-top attacks against LGBT people and his absolute intolerance of even the mildest sign of welcoming or accepting them" stood in dramatic contrast to the call for forgiveness and prayer in the wake of Voris's forced resignation:

> He regularly and indiscriminately tossed around rumors about the sexu-ality of bishops and priests without proof. He encouraged his viewers to harass Fr. James Martin, calling speaking venues to get his talks cancelled, and cause bishops to mistrust him . . . We certainly have to pray for Michael Voris. We also have to understand the immense harm he did to so many and to the Church. Voris's rhetoric has undoubtedly led many Catholics to fear LGBT people and fostered an unwillingness to even consider ways the Church can act with basic human decency towards members of the LGBT community. The old adage "hurt people hurt people" seems to apply here.[48]

The paradigm of the Church as "Militant" in Voris's over-heated rhetoric quite overtly pointed to a distant medieval past in which Christian "warriors" had battled infidels to win back the Holy Places of Palestine. Whatever its ap-propriateness centuries ago, Catholic theology—even in the Middle Ages—had always maintained a certain ambivalence about that violence, fencing it with concerns about "just war" and "commensurate force" that produced trenchant critiques of the crusader's behavior. Even then, physical violence on behalf of "righteousness" was viewed with concern and close scrutiny. But that past, in any case, was now separated from contemporary American culture by many centuries.

And in the event, that violent language did not serve Voris well when his own fall from grace occurred at St. Michael's Media. Voris's primitivist and sectarian understanding of the Catholic tradition of Christianity—focused on almost-palpable anger and even violence against those whom he saw as traitors *within* the Household of Faith—failed him as a resource in navigating his own time of trial. Perhaps a purchase truer to the genuine Catholic understanding of "church militant," in which the faithful were encouraged to struggle with their failings in working out their salvation before joining the "church suffering," and eventually the "church triumphant," might have contextualized that difficult time within an ancient and revered Catholic trope of discipleship. *All* the faithful (even those pressing the "LGBT agenda" in the Church) were called to wrestle with the dark side of their lives: all of them belonged to the church militant, and not just those who visited Voris's website in Ferndale, Michigan.

As Lewis so correctly observed, all Catholics should pray for Voris. But they should also "understand the immense harm he did to so many, and to the Church" in the course of his Catholic fundamentalist crusade.

8

On the Dangers of Swimming the Tiber

Crisis Magazine and the Premillennialist Embrace of Catholicism

A. "Conservatism's Inevitable Conversion to Catholicism"

In one of the more provocative essays published in *Crisis* magazine in the past few years, Jessica Kramer argued that it was all but inevitable that American political conservatives would find their way to the Roman Church. And to some extent her prediction reflected the contours of her own autobiography:

> The Left has entirely abandoned Christianity and fully embraced secular liberalism. I believe the right, though still deeply influenced by liberalism—especially classical liberalism—will more and more find its way toward the Tiber. This is at least what I have observed in the last three years since my own conversion to Catholicism and in the witness of conversion among my peers. My friends, including fellow graduates of Liberty University (the epicenter of American evangelicalism) and other Washington, D.C. conservatives, have either returned to the Catholic Church after going through a Protestant phase or are seriously flirting with the idea of converting to Catholicism themselves.[1]

Indeed, Kramer offered a considerably more specific prediction than that: American political conservatism as a whole, "post-Trump, will eventually convert to Catholicism and be deeply influenced by Catholic integralists." However singular such a prediction might seem at first glance, there were some weighty historical examples from the last three to four decades to back up her prognostication of political conservatives who perceived the Roman faith as their true spiritual home: Russell Kirk, one of the most influential architects of the American conservative movement; Robert Bork, a conservative judge refused an appointment to the US Supreme Court after bruising congressional hearings; Robert Novak, an influential political commentator; Richard John Neuhaus, the sometime progressive Lutheran pastor who founded the reliably center-right periodical *First Things*; J. D. Vance, author of the best-selling *Hillbilly Elegy* before becoming a Republican senator from Ohio; Methodist convert Rod Dreher, columnist for *The American Conservative* and author of the best-selling *The Benedict Option*; Deal Hudson, the Southern Baptist minister who edited the journal that published Kramer's article; as well as the current editor of *Crisis* magazine, Eric Sammons. All these men have been among the American political conservatives who have embraced Catholicism.[2]

US Catholicism, of course, has always celebrated high-profile Protestants (and Jews) who "swam the Tiber" (Catholic-speak for conversion to Roman Catholicism), oftentimes holding them up as trophy converts to the True Church, despite the fact that Protestant converts have never made up more than a few percent of the American Catholic community. In narrative histories of US Catholicism, those "trophy converts" take up considerable space given the paucity of their numbers: Dorothy Day, one of the founders of the Catholic Worker Movement; Thomas Merton, a Trappist monk and most visible Catholic advocate of Catholic spirituality in the twentieth century; Elizabeth Ann Seaton, the mother foundress of one of the most important communities of religious women in the American Church, the US branch of the Sisters of Charity; Avery Dulles, the son of Eisenhower's Secretary of State who became a cardinal and famed theologian; Clare Booth Luce, the spouse of the publisher of *Time*, *Life*, and *Fortune* magazines who herself served in a major ambassadorial post and as a member of the US House of Representatives; Mortimer Adler, an American philosopher and educator who became a major voice in the American neo-Thomist movement. All of these (among a number of others) are presented as signal exemplars of Catholicism's attractions to Protestants in the Land of the Pilgrims: "see," their stories would seem to proclaim, "American Catholicism might be a community composed primarily of immigrants and their children, but its attractions are such as to attract the Great and the Good among the WASP ascendency."[3]

Scholars of the stature of Anne C. Rose, Patrick Allitt, and Jenny Franchot have produced penetrating and persuasive studies of converts to the institution that their Protestant forebears had once termed the "Whore of Babylon" earlier in the nineteenth century. Thus, Rose followed the career of eleven converts—seven men and four women—who entered the Catholic

Church between 1836 and 1869: six had been raised as Episcopalians and five were reared as either Unitarians or Transcendentalists. Many were part of the Romantic reaction to the "reasonable tradition" that had emerged as the Unitarian movement in New England or were seeking a tradition that offered richer access to the mystical and aesthetic elements in religion. Many came from the ranks of "High Church" Anglicanism who were dissatisfied with the evangelicalism that defined the mainstream Protestant Episcopal Church or sought a more aesthetically fulfilling spiritual tradition that stood over against what Ralph Waldo Emerson had termed the "corpse cold Unitarianism" of New England. But what Rose's diverse group shared was a common effort to escape either the evangelical (and to some extent, anti-aesthetic) religion of the Second Great Awakening, or a "culture religion" too invested in the political and social status quo of the Boston Federalist aristocracy. The very fact that Roman Catholicism was most assuredly *not* on the cultural or political "inside," and lacked access to any kind of political power, were among its chief attractions to those nineteenth-century converts.[4]

But Kramer's prediction of the broad appeal of Catholic Christianity to a spectrum of twenty-first-century American evangelicals presumes a somewhat different range of denominational attractions than those appealing to the converts studied by Rose, Allitt, and Franchot. In place of the aesthetic attractions of Roman Catholic ritual, music, and architecture to High Church Anglicans, or Catholicism's very "outsider" status to the centers of American political and cultural influence for Unitarian Brahmins in the nineteenth century, Kramer's prediction seems to presume that Catholicism promised to provide the best ideological launching pad for former evangelicals to undertake their political crusades in America's ongoing culture wars. Indeed, the contemporary efforts of Catholic integralists like Patrick Dineen and Adrian Vermeule to resurrect the medieval Catholic ideal of "Christendom" appeared to Kramer like a providential signal for evangelical swimmers to start gathering on the shore of the Tiber.[5]

Far from seeking a Christian tradition eschewing political or cultural power, Kramer sought to celebrate a tradition that had lured the likes of Robert Bork, Russell Kirk, Richard John Neuhaus, and Rod Dreher to the "safe" side of the Tiber from which to launch their conservative political crusades. As Kramer put it, "a political philosophy and ideology needs an intrinsic telos. What then is conservatism but a commitment to *conserving* tradition? And what is western tradition? Christianity." And, she adds, what Christian tradition has done the most to preserve the best insights of the western tradition? For Kramer there was only one logical answer: "the Holy Catholic and Apostolic Church."[6]

And while Kramer allows that "integralism will certainly not be the Republican Party Platform for 2024," it will, nonetheless, be the:

> new libertarianism of the present-day Right, the thorn in the side of non-purists. But rather than champion a hyper-individualism, their focus will be on facilitating the common good and establishing a society ordered toward objective Truth. Truth that aids in human flourishing.[7]

But Kramer's rhapsodic paean to the political delights of the Roman Church as offering a fortress-like bulwark from which evangelicals might launch more secure forays into America's culture wars, from an historical perspective anyway, represented a radical break from what the founders of *Crisis* magazine envisioned as its purpose. Founded in a small office on the campus of the University of Notre Dame in 1982 as "Catholicism in Crisis" by Ralph McInerny (a philosophy professor there) and Michael Novak (a public intellectual and academic famous for his book *The Spirit of Democratic Capitalism*), it was, from its inception, a magazine that has been described as a "place where Catholic neo-conservatives have tried to shape debate both within [their own] Church, and within the public square, and [it] has met with some success on both fronts." It moved quickly from that small office in South Bend to K Street in Washington, DC, a move that has been described as attitudinal as well as geographical (in part because "on K Street, you don't do battle, you do lunch"). Both McInerny and Novak were cradle Catholics, and while both were most certainly card-carrying neo-conservatives, neither could hardly be described as cultural warriors in the twenty-first-century sense of the term. Both possessed wide-ranging intellectual interests whose carefully argued articles on behalf of a conservative view of American politics and economics were marked by thoughtful argument and a charitable (if deeply critical) view of their political adversaries. After their years of editing the magazine, *Crisis* entered a "sleeper" mode, posting a listing of recent posts—mostly from right-wing Catholic blogs. But in May 2011, its then-editor, Brian Saint-Paul, announced its "rebirth":

> The American Catholic Church in 2011 is in better shape—and is better led—than the one Ralph and Michael contended with in 1982. Theological sanity returned through the pontificates of Blessed John Paul II and

Benedict XVI, and the temporal assertions of the Church are no longer reliably leftward.[8]

When Hudson took over as editor in October 1994, *Crisis* had six thousand active subscribers, but—in Hudson's own words—"it was still a
'journal.'" Under Hudson's editorial hand, it became a full-colored magazine with robust coverage of the arts, especially music and film, in addition to the magazine's monthly fare of theology, spirituality, politics, and
the Church, and it reached a pinnacle of thirty-three thousand subscribers
in 2003. Unlike cradle-Catholics McInerny and Novak, Hudson had been
a Southern Baptist minister who converted to Catholicism in 1984. But in
many ways Hudson brought his pre-conversion commitments with him into
the Roman Church: he had studied the history of Christian doctrine under
Karlfried Froelich at Princeton Theological Seminary, and he had earned a
doctorate in philosophy at Emory University. The intellectual lineaments of
Reformed Protestantism he had learned at Princeton Seminary continued
to manifest themselves throughout his career as a Catholic academic and
editor, both at *Crisis* and beyond. And those lineaments are revealed both
in his editorial career at *Crisis* and in his subsequent monographs: *Onward
Christian Soldiers: The Growing Political Power of Catholics and Evangelicals
in the United States* (Simon &Schuster); *How to Keep from Losing Your
Mind: Educating Yourself Classically to Resist Cultural Indoctrination*
(TAN Books); and *The Desecrators: Defeating the Cancel Culture Mob and
Reclaiming One Nation Under God* (TAN Books). It was, therefore, hardly
a surprise when presidential advisor Karl Rove asked Hudson to create a
Catholic advisory group to then-President George W. Bush. Hudson's bona-
fides as a respected political conservative who claimed friends on both sides
of the Catholic-evangelical divide made him something of a logical choice to
organize such an advisory group.[9]

Hudson, like the magazine's founders, was a smart neo-conservative, but,
unlike them, he was a convert. The current editor of *Crisis*, like Hudson, is
also a convert to the Roman Church; but the similarities with Hudson end
there. Sammons was named editor-in-chief of the magazine in December
2020, and has led it in a decidedly different direction, with a different set
of editorial strategies. Sammons was received into the Catholic Church in
1993, and he holds an MA in Theology from the Franciscan University of
Steubenville. So, unlike previous editors, he was not trained in academic theology or philosophy. And before coming to *Crisis* he had served as a diocesan

director of education, as well as the "head of evangelization" for a Catholic parish for a decade. And under his editorial hand, *Crisis* has come to embody impulses foreign to both the style and the content of *Crisis* before his arrival.[10]

Indeed, despite the "hyper-Catholic" rhetoric that marks most of Sammons's online editorials—consistently calling for Church leaders (especially Pope Francis) to return to "orthodox" Catholic belief and practice from their heterodox positions—what immediately strikes a reader who doesn't share Sammons's apocalyptic worldview or foreshortened historical perspective is that most of the articles and editorials published in the magazine seem somehow decidedly *unCatholic*. And they seem unCatholic because they lack the kind of theological grounding that undergirds Catholic identity.

There is also a decidedly "come-outer" feel to many of Sammons's postings, named of course for the Protestant fundamentalist usage of the apocalyptic call in the Book of Revelation to early Christians to "come out of Babylon" to flee from its coming destruction by the Armies of the Lamb (more anon). "Come-outerism," in fact, came to define the movement in the United States as a spectrum of fundamentalist leaders called upon their hearers to reject the leadership of mainstream Protestant churches and form themselves into purer, more focused ecclesial groups to stand over against the corrupt teaching of mainstream churches which had fallen into modernist heresy. The giveaway phrase that Sammons and his devoted readers always use is "faithful Catholics": *we're* the faithful Catholics, Sammons regularly asserts, and all those other supposed Catholics—the ones who champion the efforts of Jorge Bergoglio (otherwise known as Pope Francis) to move the Church in a different direction—they are not faithful Catholics. And because of that ecclesial fact, *Crisis* has set up something like a "counter church," led not by the current Bishop of Rome, but by the likes of Cardinal Raymond Burke and Archbishop Carlo Maria Vigano, who have accused the current of occupant of the Chair of Peter of heresy, or of something very close to it.

"Come out from her, and flee the wrath that is to come" was the famous call in the Book of Revelation, and Sammons seems eager to heed that call, and advises his readers to do the same. But in the Catholic imagination, there is nothing to "come out" into. Protestant Christians, especially Protestant fundamentalist Christians, assert that the true church is the Invisible Church, whose members are known to God alone. Institutional affiliation for such fundamentalist believers is, then, a second-order question because no single historical body of believers can claim that title. But Catholic Christianity has always asserted that the True Church on earth subsists in the Roman Catholic Church and is made up of those who are in union with the Bishop of Rome. Many other believers who are not Catholics are certainly true Christians, and their ecclesial bodies share in the life of grace unleashed by Christ's death and resurrection. But in terms of *institutional* identity, there is only one true church of Christ, the Holy and Apostolic Church of Rome. A "Catholic" not in communion with the Bishop of Rome is a contradiction in terms, and believers who have "come out" of the Church in communion with the pope may be many things; they are just not Catholic Christians. It is, then, difficult to discern how Sammons understands himself as a Catholic.[11]

There is also a consistent argument in Sammons's postings at *Crisis* that seems to presume that Catholic doctrine rests on an unchanging and propositional "deposit of faith" almost exactly analogous to how Protestant fundamentalists understand the King James Bible. For those "Bible Believers" (a giveaway phrase exactly analogous to "faithful Catholics") every word of the Bible is literally true (a theory called "literal inerrancy") and must be understood at face value. Thus, if the Book of Genesis states that God created the world in seven days, then that is how creation came into being. And if the Book of Joshua announces that Joshua made the sun stand still so that he and his armies could kill more of Israel's enemies, then that is what happened. And even though the Book of Genesis has two opposing creation accounts, and we now know that if the sun literally stood still, the earth would be hurled into it, those biblical accounts mean what they say, and say what they mean, and must be accepted as literal fact because there cannot be any kind of "development" in our biblical interpretation.

In an almost eerily analogous way, Sammons discusses Catholic doctrine as though it were static and unchangeable, and decidedly *not* marked by development and evolution—sometimes radical development. As Cardinal Newman famously argued over a century ago, there has been a "development of doctrine" within the Catholic tradition over the course of many centuries, and both Newman's famous phrase and his understanding of doctrinal history that it witnessed to most decidedly "won" at the Second Vatican Council, and that belief in development is itself now considered to be something like "settled doctrine." But as Sammons seems to understand it, the "deposit of faith" is a metaphor that itself shapes the content of his argument: doctrine is almost like a buried treasure that cannot "develop" any more than buried gold or silver can.

Reading through the articles and blog postings on the *Crisis* magazine website, then, can give the careful Catholic reader the unsettling sense that its editor is a non-Catholic writing for other non-Catholics—that indeed its editor is a Protestant fundamentalist who is stuffing Catholic belief and practice into casings manufactured outside Holy Mother Church, and who is unequal to the task of actually containing the Catholic Christian tradition. The result is the sense that Sammons may have indeed swum the Tiber, but he did so in a Protestant wetsuit that left him untouched by Catholic holy water. And the resulting product of that swim is—to mix metaphors—an online journal presenting Protestant fundamentalist mutton dressed up like Catholic lamb.

B. "How the Church Lost Her Mission, and How We Can Reclaim It"

Sammons's editorials posted on the *Crisis* website offer a glimpse into the ideological edge and apocalyptic urgency that informs his editing of the online journal, especially regarding the Bishop of Rome. For instance, in an editorial from December 15, 2022, entitled "The Rebranding of the Latin Mass Movement," Sammons regrets that a significant reason why less than two percent of American Catholics attend the traditional Latin Mass is that regular attendees of that rite are unfairly portrayed as "mean," "unwelcoming," or have an insular attitude to Catholic worship—a perception actively abetted by Pope Francis himself. Indeed, Francis:

> supports and endorses this negative perception of traditional [*sic*] Catholics every time he talks about them. In fact, he gave this perception as the reason he was restricting the Latin Mass in his motu proprio *Traditionis Custodies*... But, to be blunt, this is gaslighting. First [it has been demonstrated] that the bishops do not oppose the Latin Mass as Francis claimed. Second, it's hard to believe that a pope would think contradicting his predecessor and causing massive headaches for bishops around the world would be the proper response to a few mean trad tweeters.[12]

Sammons holds Pope Francis, who "sees Catholicism through a modern post-Vatican II lens" (as though there could be another after 1965), as being responsible for propagating the erroneous belief among the world's bishops that "the *Novus Ordo* is the Mass of the Church, and the Latin Mass, for all its beauty and grandeur, is simply a relic that a few Catholics still cling to." But Sammons's targeting of Francis on this is, at best, deeply problematic, as the *Novus Ordo* is, in fact, now the normative form for the celebration of the eucharist in the Western (Roman) Church. Sammons's key point in the editorial—that Francis has somehow misled the universal episcopate on the issue of the normative rite to be used by western Catholic Christians for celebrating the eucharist—was mistaken at its very core: Francis's predecessor in the Chair of Peter, Benedict XVI, never implied that his allowance of the Latin Mass "for pastoral need" in any way displaced the post-Vatican II mass in the vernacular as the normative liturgy for Catholic believers. The editorial question of who was gaslighting whom on this issue is, then, more tangled than would at first appear.[13]

For Sammons, Pope Francis is himself largely responsible for the disrespect accorded to the Latin Mass. But Sammons's fixation on the pope as the chief reason why the Church had lost its way finds expression in editorials that are considerably sharper and more recriminatory than such comparatively mild pieces like the December 15, 2022 article on the Latin Mass. For instance, on July 8, 2023, Sammons posted an editorial entitled "Be Angry," in which he focused on recent papal appointments: the editorial opened with the rather astonishing observation that "this past week has not been a good one for the cause of orthodoxy in the Church." Pope Francis's appointment of Archbishop Victor Fernandez as head of the Dicastery for the Doctrine of the Faith "was a blow to anyone who cares about souls." Likewise, the papal selection for attendance at the Synod to be held in Rome the following October—among whom were American Cardinals Blasé Cupich, Joseph Tobin, and Robert McElroy—were "confirmed progressives who have shown a willingness to jettison Church teaching for their own ideologies, as well as a disdain for traditional Catholic teaching and piety." The exact nature of the Church teaching these three were supposedly so willing to "jettison" was left unnamed, although Sammons felt free to identify them as "card-carrying members of the McCarrick wing [*sic*] of the American hierarchy." But in Sammons's view, these three ecclesiastics in the McCarrick wing "aren't even the worst papal selections. No, that honor belongs to Fr. James Martin . . . the most infamous priest in America, the priest who has done more to promote "homoheresy" [*sic*] in this country than anyone else." In Sammons's opinion, the situation in the Church is dire, as the pope himself is undermining true Catholic belief and practice:

We now have religious leaders—up to and most definitely including Pope Francis—who are actively working to undermine the Catholic Faith handed on by our [*sic*] ancestors. They are sowing confusions among poor souls who often know no better and thus will go down a path that leads to eternal destruction . . . So let us be angry, and in that anger work against the machinations of unholy men who seek the destruction of souls . . . Like I said, you should be angry, at least if you care about souls.[14]

Among the noteworthy issues that the "Be Angry!" piece reveals is the sense that Sammons's controlling metaphor of Catholic doctrine as the "Deposit" of Faith seems to imply an unchanging (and unchangeable) list of positivist propositions that cannot develop or "unfold" over time. Further, he seems to presume that doctrine and our purchase on it are the same thing, so that the very possibility of anything like the "Development of Doctrine" that Cardinal Newman proposed—an understanding of Catholic doctrine that largely won the day at the Second Vatican Council by the vast majority of (presumably orthodox) Catholic bishops attending that Council—is disallowed from the start. One is, therefore, left wondering what, exactly, he means when he refers to princes of the Church jettisoning traditional Catholic teaching and piety.

Equally disturbing in Sammons's call for believers to "be angry" is his inclusion of Pope Francis himself among the "unholy men who seek the destruction of souls," actively sowing heresy among the faithful, whose resulting moral confusion would inevitably lead to their going "down a path that leads to eternal destruction." This would seem to be, at the very least, calumny, as Sammons implies that he knows the *intentions* of both the pope and the other "card-carrying members of the McCarrick wing of the American hierarchy" to lead helpless souls astray. Such apocalyptic rhetoric had, of course, always been one of the telltale signs of American Catholic fundamentalism, marking the career of Leonard Feeney (among others), in his case leading to eventual excommunication and exclaustration from the Jesuit order. Feeney, of course, had been a theological *naif*, so one can easily dismiss his fragile purchase on the Catholic theological tradition as the result of ignorance, resentment, and/or paranoia. It would appear that Sammons is a comparative theological *naif* as well, so the surprise in his editorials is less in his own contorted arguments than in the fact that such a respected Catholic journal of ideas as *Crisis* magazine, founded by such intellectual heavyweights as McInerny and Novak, should end up in such hands.

Sammons's editorials seem to have functioned as warm-up exercises for an editorial entitled "10 Years of Confusion, Political Ideology, and Scandal," posted on the *Crisis* website on May 13, 2023. That very day, Sammons announced, was the "10th anniversary of the election of Jorge Bergoglio to the papacy." But Sammons decided to ignore the advice of his mother ("if [you] can't say anything nice, say nothing at all"), confessing at the outset, "I guess I'll ignore mom" (as well as the path of prudence, it would seem). He opens by stating that the:

> blunt reality is that the papacy of Francis, by any Catholic measure, has been a disaster. It's not that he hasn't at times done some good acts or spoken some good words: it's that the overall thrust of his pontificate has been one of confusion, political ideology, and scandal.[15]

It's not exactly clear what Sammons means by noting the Pope's "political ideology," although it would seem that Francis's openness to reconsidering how, pastorally, the Church should address the climate crisis caused by global warming, or how it might welcome LGBTQ and divorced and remarried people into the Church, play significant roles in his use of that phrase (as it does among the majority of contemporary Catholic fundamentalists). Discerning how pastoral practice might be used in a more welcoming way hardly constitutes the stuff of heresy; and Francis has never implied by word (or even implication) that he seeks to change Catholic magisterial teaching regarding marriage and divorce. One might call to mind the practice of the eastern, Orthodox Church (the validity of whose orders the Roman Church has always recognized) which teaches that Jesus condemned divorce, but which also believes that Jesus gave the Church the power to forgive that sin and welcome divorced and remarried believers back to the life of the sacraments. For Orthodox Christians, Jesus's teaching regarding divorce remains firmly in place; the Church's pastoral practice of dealing with divorced and remarried believers is something else again.

It is, then, not surprising that very near the beginning of the May 13 editorial Sammons references the famous moment when, "in the first year of his papacy, Francis uttered the *infamous* words, 'Who am I to judge?' and ever since then he has done far more to confuse the faithful than confirm them." But Sammons also argues that Catholics should presume that the pontiff means what he says in such statements, "even when what he says makes little sense." But how, exactly, the pope's statement of "who am I to judge?"

constitutes an infamous statement, or how it purportedly makes little sense, is never explained as such. In countering Sammons's perplexing judgment of the universal ordinary, one might easily point to the ancient Catholic moral precept that reminded confessors that they were to "hate the sin but love the sinner," or to the revered teaching of St. Alphonsus Liguori, the patron saint (literally) and model of all who hear confessions, who famously warned priests to make a clear distinction between (absolute) moral teaching and the gravity of moral acts actually performed by those confessing their sins. Perhaps a long weekend reading St. Alphonsus might help Sammons to come a reconsideration of the sense of Francis's statements.[16]

All of this, not surprisingly, becomes grist for the mill: in Sammons's estimation, Pope Francis "has turned the Vatican essentially into political NGO." For while every pope had a right to comment on politics, the office of the papacy was solely to proclaim the saving gospel of Christ as found in the Catholic Church:

> Yet Francis seems to use his moral authority not to urge people to convert to the Catholic Church (in fact, he appears to abhor conversions) but to push the latest globalist political agenda, such as combating climate change or immigration reform. By associating himself—and thus the Catholic Church—with these worldly [sic] goals, he diminishes the ability of the Church to rise above political differences to point to a spiritual path to salvation.[17]

Sammons fails to offer any kind of proof that the pope "abhors" conversions: indeed, the reader is hard-pressed to imagine what such evidence might look like. Further (and far more disturbing if the accusations were true), Francis's ten years in the Chair of Peter "has been rife with scandal." Quite apart from the scandal of Francis's own words ("Who am I to judge?"), Sammons asserts that there have been dozens of scandals about abusive priests and bishops who have supposedly received preferential treatment simply because they are "ideologically aligned" with Francis's political agenda. Indeed, the public revelation of former Cardinal of Theodore McCarrick of Newark "as a monster" seriously undermined Francis's stated goal to clean up the church:

> Here was a man who was known as a predator by many high-ranking Catholics—including the pope himself—yet he was placed in the "inner

circle" by Francis early in his pontificate. Countless other scandals have littered the past ten years . . . Confusion, political ideology, and scandal have been our continual companions the past 10 years . . . Pope Francis will have to answer for [all of this] on his day of particular judgement.[18]

The surprising—or perhaps not so surprising—fact about these unsubstantiated assertions is that they are a mish-mash of discredited accusations made by the *fugitivus* Archbishop Vigano (who was publicly rebuked and denounced by the Cardinal Prefect of the Vatican Dicastery for Bishops), confused and vague questions about Francis's doctrinal orthodoxy put forward in *dubia* published by Cardinal Burke (who had been removed from his Vatican office by Francis himself for serious insubordination), and the fragile purchase on Catholic theology and church teaching of Sammons himself. What is going on in these inflated rhetorical denunciations of the Universal Ordinary, a figure whom Sammons often likes to identify as Jorge Bergoglio (as though using his family surname rather than his papal title somehow robs Francis of the authority he actually possesses, with or without the approval of Sammons)?[19]

Yet again, one might question *whose* ideology is sticking out in these accusations, as when Sammons accuses Francis of seeing Catholicism "through a post-Vatican II lens." Yes, Francis does indeed see contemporary Catholicism through that lens. But what other lens could a faithful Catholic use to understand Catholicism but through the most recent universal council of the Church, whose final documents were formally promulgated by Pope Paul VI? If indeed "the Church lost its mission" under Pope Francis because of his insistence that the *only* legitimate way to understand contemporary Catholic issues was in light of the teachings of the Second Vatican Council, then the pesky question of ecclesiology rears its head: what is Sammons's understanding of the Church in these editorials? After 1965, what other ecclesiology is possible to understand the Church except as "the People of God," the Council's preferred ecclesial metaphor in its most authoritative document, *Lumen Gentium*, "The Dogmatic Constitution on the Church"? Its very name explains its authority—it is a "dogmatic constitution"—that is, it has the status of official dogma (than which there is no higher authority).

One would be on very safe ground, I think, in asserting that what is going on in these editorial denunciations of "Jorge Bergoglio" and the scandalous chaos of his papacy is a radically sectarian, a-historical, primitivist, and premillennialist understanding of the tradition of Catholic Christianity.

Over against the deep Catholic instinct for "communion," Sammons seems to think that believers can pick and choose which popes and bishops one can be in communion with, a hallmark of evangelical Protestantism, which asserts that because no historical institution can legitimately claim to be the "true church," individual believers were free to choose which religious authorities they would obey. And in an analogously primitivist way, Sammons would appear to believe that the pinnacle of Catholic worship had been achieved in the *Missale Romanun* of 1570, so that Catholic believers were encouraged to see that older rite as in some way "truer" and more faithful to the tradition, a position (correctly) distrusted by Pope Francis, who "insists on seeing Catholicism through a post-Vatican II lens."

Equally unsettling is Sammons's quite overt linking of the cause of genuine Catholic Christianity with the right wing of the Republican Party in the United States. Somehow concern over global warming, pastoral concern for LGBTQ persons, and the issue of who should be welcomed at the eucharist appear to be proof positive for Sammons of Pope Francis's efforts to turn the Vatican into an NGO and pressing a quite specific political ideology over against the pope's real brief—the salvation of souls. In reading many of Sammons's editorial in *Crisis*, one is struck by how similar they are to Republican denunciations of "liberal Democrats" as undermining America's experiment in ordered liberty.

That "liberal/conservative" binary had emerged, of course, with Feeney in the Boston Heresy Case: for Feeney, it had been the "Liberals" (usually identified with a capitol "L") who were the real enemies of The Faith, both in Boston and in Rome. Feeney's usage of those political monikers had been singular, as before him most Catholics held a quite different binary: faithful Catholics and lapsed Catholics. Lapsed Catholics had not been conceived as "liberal" in any meaningful political or cultural sense, any more than faithful Catholics were considered to be conservative (the vast majority of whom identified with the "progressive" Democratic Party). With Feeney, the idea that one could use an American political label to describe a group undermining the True Church was a startlingly new and noteworthy phenomenon. The possible historical exception might have been "Americanists," like Archbishop John Ireland during the 1880s and 1890s, who had been denounced by Rome in the apostolic letter *Testem Benevolentiae* for pressing for greater acculturation of Catholicism to the American context. Most historians now argue that Rome's worries elucidated in that letter constituted a "phantom heresy" that ever really existed. And, in any case, Rome's missive never identified the supposed culprits as liberals in any meaningful political sense. It had been Feeney himself who had forged that link. And in that sense Sammons was the quite legitimate ideological great grandson of Feeney himself.

But in addition to Jorge Bergoglio, Father James Martin, S.J. also serves as a regular presence in Sammons's editorials (perhaps linked together by their shared Jesuit identity). Thus, in an editorial entitled "The Devilishly Heretical Fr. James Martin," Sammons opens his piece by confessing that he is under Twitter suspension again, this time for "offending Big Gay," or more specifically for offending "the chaplain to Big Gay, Fr. James Martin." Martin, it would seem, had been "at it again" in January 2023, responding to the Catholic League for Religious and Civil Rights's statement regarding the same-sex marriage of Pete Buttigieg, President Joe Biden's Secretary of Transportation. The Catholic League had tweeted that "it is true that Pete Buttegieg [*sic*] is married, but that is a legal fiction." In response to the League's statement about Buttigieg's marriage being a legal fiction (at best, a confusing designation, as it was, in fact, *legally* performed in the Episcopal Cathedral of South Bend, Indiana), Martin had simply responded that "Pete Buttigieg is married." The *legality* of Buttigieg's marriage is (and was) never in question in the state of Indiana, which constitutionally allows marriage between same-sex partners. The question of the sacramental *validity* of that marriage is something else again. Either Sammons doesn't understand this very important distinction, or he is being coy: "This is typical Martin fare" Sammons announced to his *Crisis* magazine readers. Martin's "fare," it would seem, "was to make a statement that he clearly wants to be interpreted in a heretical way" but is written so that he has plausible deniability if by some miracle a Church hierarch should challenge it:

So when Martin says that Buttigieg is "married," without any qualifier, the most plain meaning (and the one that Martin wants you to have) is that Buttigieg's gay "marriage" is a true marriage, not just a legal one. In making such weaselly statements, Martin imitates that master liar, Satan . . . So as we can see, Martin's playbook is as old as mankind itself. His ambiguous, partially-true statement is far more effective than an outright lie: it allows those who want to be deceived to claim a Catholic covering for their deception, and it fools the naïve into letting Martin off the hook.[20]

But Sammons went on to warn his readers that "when dealing with the devil (or his minions), Catholics need to oppose half-truths ambiguities with clear, direct, and fully-true statements." The reader is left with the presumption that Father Martin—a priest in canonical good standing in both the Catholic Archdiocese of New York as well as in the Society of Jesus—himself holds some kind of leadership role among those "minions":

> In this situation, we need to state directly that Fr. James Martin is a heretic who should not be allowed to continue his public ministry as a priest. If we mitigate that truth [*sic*] in any way, trying to defend Martin or giving him the "benefit of the doubt," we simply fall into the trap designed by the devil himself and practiced to perfection by Martin.[21]

It is, of course, unclear how Sammons himself—lacking both ecclesiastical credentials like a Licentiate in Sacred Theology and hierarchical office—believed he possessed the authority to publicly declare anyone a heretic (a very serious ecclesiastical charge that carries canonical penalties for anyone so accused—as well as for anyone who falsely makes such charges). If he had been delegated by an ordinary to undertake such a formal investigation, Sammons never reveals what actual hierarchical figure had in fact vested him with the authority to undertake such serious business. And the all-important canonical distinction between "legal" and "valid" likewise seems to elude his grasp. There are many things that are quite legal in American law (i.e., capital punishment) which the Church condemns as profoundly immoral. The Catholic Church's condemnation of the death penalty in no way questions its legality (it has no constitutional authority to do so) but rather questions its moral status as an action Christians can take part in.

C. "We're in the Era of the Great Apostasy"

But more unsettling than any of these features of Sammons's editorial policy at *Crisis* (at least from a Catholic theological perspective) is his use of Protestant fundamentalist premillennialist theories and biblical categories for bemoaning (and explaining) the crisis currently gripping Catholic Christians in the United States. Premillennialism had emerged among proto-fundamentalist Protestant sects like the Plymouth Brethren in the United Kingdom in the late nineteenth century, embodying a literal approach to reading scripture—especially the "prophetic books" of the Bible like Daniel and the Book of Revelation. In that approach to biblical interpretation (which took as axiomatic the truth of the literal inerrancy of every word of scripture), the Bible represented something like a "blueprint" for God's action in history, especially God's action in bringing history to an apocalyptic end. In that end, the vast majority of humankind would be damned while the small number of the "Elect" would be raptured into heaven before the final, dreadful battle of Armageddon. And knowing how to interpret scripture as a blueprint for the fearsome end times was *the* key to escaping the fiery end that awaited most of the fallen mass of humanity.[22]

A classic instance of that quite bizarre blending of premillennialist theory with Catholic theology can be found in a fifty-minute podcast interview with Joshua Charles that Sammons posted on the *Crisis* website on July 20, 2023. Charles (like Sammons himself) was a Catholic convert, and co-author (with Glenn Beck) of the *New York Times* bestseller *The Original Argument: The Federalists' Case for the Constitution.* More recently than that latter work, Charles had edited a book entitled *The War of the Antichrist with the Church and Christian Civilization.* The entire conversation between Sammons and Charles is a kind of "out of body" dialogue, more redolent of a dispensationalist and premillennialist lecture at a fundamentalist Bible study summer camp than a theological conversation between Catholics. Catholic Christians, of course, are neither dispensationalists (believing that God divided up history into "dispensations") nor premillennialists (believers in Christ's sudden appearance to smite evil doers and deliver true believers from the terrible judgments which God will inflict on the world by "rapturing" them into heaven). Just part of the out-of-body sense of listening to the July 20th podcast is the fact that neither Sammons nor Charles ever alludes to the fact that both dispensationalism and premillennialism are totally foreign to Catholic discussions of the "Four Last Things," and constitute a different theological language than that used by Catholic theologians. Indeed, premillennialist language itself is a hallmark of those Protestant sectarian movements who "came out" of mainstream denominations after the "Great Reversal" of 1919 to prepare for God's judgment on a sinful world.[23]

But be that as it may, Sammons opened the July 20th conversation by observing that there were definite "signs" in contemporary culture of the terrible "End Times" foretold in the Book of Revelation and extensively written about by Protestant fundamentalists. Commenting on the signs of the

End Times in contemporary culture, Sammons observed that one of those signs was:

> the undermining of the Eucharistic sacrifice, the Mass, in our own time, so you don't have to say "Oh look, the Antichrist is coming." But it's not even sensationalist to say this is a spirit of Antichrist [because] anything that leads to 30% or less Catholics actually [believing] in the real presence is a spirit of Antichrist . . . We are living in the era of Antichrist. And it's kind of funny, because the progressives love dropping the definite articles. Instead of saying "the Eucharist," they say "Eucharist." But in this case, there's a reason.[24]

And the "reason" why dropping the definite article is a sign of the presence of Antichrist can only be discovered by wading into the quite long and convoluted conversation that follows that statement—a conversation marked by the kind of premillennialist language and logic that most American Catholics would find bewildering (and also probably profoundly disturbing). Premillennialism is a decidedly fundamentalist Protestant reading of the Bible which reads biblical prophecy as offering "hidden clues" to recognizing the "good guys" and the "bad guys" for those who know how to correctly read those prophecies. Classically embodied in the *Scofield Reference Bible*—the key reference work for understanding Protestant fundamentalist biblical interpretations—premillennialism is structured around a series of "dispensations," in each of which God works through chosen vessels (both persons and groups) which provide the only safe places for God's chosen ones to gather in an increasingly evil and idolatrous world. And it is important to be safely "inside" that small gathering of the Elect as things end very badly indeed—in the last great battle of Armageddon, at which the "Armies of the Beast" (Satan, the Antichrist, and all their legions) will be cast into the bottomless pit, while the Armies of the Lamb (Jesus) will inherit a new heaven and a new earth. And the conversation between Sammons and Charles seems to presume both knowledge of the *Scofield Reference Bible* and that their listeners (presumably mostly Catholics) share Sammons's and Charles's belief that the Bible itself is somehow literally true and can be read as a blueprint for understanding history and history's end.[25]

But things get considerably more confusing for the hapless Catholic reader of the transcription of that conversation between Sammons and Charles: Sammons remarks near the beginning of the exchange that he's reading John's Gospel, and references verse 6 of the 10th chapter in that gospel, in which Jesus refers to himself as the sole doorkeeper to the sheepfold. Immediately after Jesus's statement, John's Gospel states that "this [is the] figure Jesus used, but they did not understand." To which Sammons then observes that:

> I feel today that we are in a situation in which we cannot fully understand. Everyone on Twitter will tell we can, but we cannot understand exactly what's going on today, with Pope Francis, with having the church, with the loss of faith we see, with doctrinal confusion, all of that. We can't fully understand it.[26]

But in the midst of that apocalyptic confusion (which we can't fully understand, or at least this reader can't) there are clues to be found for believers who know how to decipher the blueprint that the Book of Revelation lays out for "holding back the coming of Antichrist, restrain[ing] the mystery of lawlessness until he [sic] arrives. But this mystery of lawlessness is growing, growing, growing, and it climaxes with Antichrist." And it is here that Charles points to the twentieth chapter of the Book of Revelation as a key text, because "this pattern is perfectly outlined" there. Charles remarks that Chapter 20 "begins with the dragon being bound," and then released, which paves the way (seemingly) for the coming of antichrist:

> This is a quick thing. Antichrist doesn't have power for all that long, seven years, but more like three and a half years. And then in verse seven he's released, but then Christ comes back. So I would argue that this pattern is very revelatory throughout scripture. I'll point to [the Book of] Daniel as an example . . . So in Daniel, too, we have the statue, the golden head going down to the iron feet with iron and clay mixed together, partly strong, partly weak. So basically, virtually unanimous consensus [sic] that this talking about going from Babylon to the Roman Empire. And then the prophet says that s stone, a petra hits the feet, which is the Roman Empire, and grows into a great mountain that fills the whole earth.[27]

According to Charles's reading, the various symbols found in the Old Testament Book of Daniel and the New Testament Book of Revelation clearly lay out the timeline for the fearsome last battle between the Armies of the Lamb and the Armies of the Beast: indeed, the second chapter in the

Book of Daniel is "very interesting," he observes, because "in Daniel 12—this is the most explicitly end times related chapter in Daniel—explicitly Daniel asks the angel 'When will all this be fulfilled?' And I think at verse seven or something around there, the angel says 'When the power of the holy people has been shattered, all these things will be fulfilled.'" All of this (however confusing to Catholic readers) constitutes extremely interesting biblical prophecy for both Charles and Sammons because these prophecies are *actually* about an event that the New Testament, in breathless agitation, calls "The Great Apostacy." Charles switches from Daniel and Revelation at this point to suddenly consider both Jesus and St. Paul:

> Now again, looping in another element, our Lord talks in his parables, talks about the strong man being bound and his goods being plundered. But then he says he'll come back with seven more demons. Okay, now why is this interesting? Because Paul talks about the great apostacy. I think our Lord is describing the great apostacy. We know the parables about the mystery of the kingdom. He's describing the great apostacy. And we know that apostacy is worse than simply not knowing Christ. A pagan who never knew Christ is in a much better position than a pagan who once knew him and rejected him. St. Peter says explicitly ... is it St. Peter? Might be St. Peter. And in [the Letter to the] Hebrews, too, he says it'd be better that they had never known the truth than to have known it and then reject it.[28]

After many pages of being at sea (indeed, a very rough sea of a confused and confusing game of "biblical jumping" from Daniel to Revelation to St. Paul to Jesus in the Synoptic Gospels—all in total disregard for even the most basic rules of the historical criticism of the Bible), the reader finally catches sight of dry land. And that *terra firma* seems to bear the outline the Great Apostasy foretold in scripture. Both Sammons and Charles seem to believe that the End Times might very well be at hand, and that the Great Apostasy might already have begun. And they are more than willing to name names to give their followers the benefit of their biblical hermeneutics, focusing on specific contemporary persons and movements. Unsurprisingly Soviet Premier Mikhail Gorbachev appears early on in the line-up ("the mark, right? His birthmark." "Yeah, he had the mark. Come on. Yeah he had the mark [of] the beast right there." "Yeah, yeah, yeah.") But Pope Francis himself comes up immediately after the Russian who clearly had the "Mark of the Beast" on his forehead. After referencing Gorbachev, Sammons notes that a number of people he reads:

> want to suggest certain current figures, including some people have said even the Pope, like The Antichrist. And I always feel like for me, The Antichrist . . . First of all I don't think the Pope can be the Antichrist. I think the Pope can point people to The Antichrist. A final Pope. Not that the final Pope necessarily. But a pope could point people to The Antichrist. But I don't think the Pope will be The Antichrist . . . I don't think that really works.[29]

And the reason Sammons offers for not thinking that Pope Francis could be the Antichrist is because Francis is not that attractive a figure: the Antichrist "will be an impressive figure, and nobody on the world stage right now is that impressive." Just part of the Antichrist's power is his ability to attract people to himself:

> He will be an attractive figure. That's kind of the point. You see this in art and things where he looks like Christ. He's beautiful, and that's why he brings so many people to him. And I don't think we really see that yet. But that doesn't mean we can't have Antichrists in the sense of people who help lay the path, so to speak. And I just want to state that I'm willing to believe that we're in the era of the great apostasy.

Thus, while Jorge Bergoglio gets something of a "pass" on being himself the Antichrist (sort of, anyway), he still might be one of the people who "help lay the path" for the Antichrist by paving the way for the "Great Apostasy." While not being attractive enough to serve as the Antichrist working for the eternal destruction of the great mass of humankind, the pope nonetheless might still play a crucial role in leading faithful Christians into apostasy—falling away from the true faith into heresy. Indeed, precisely as Bishop of Rome (and therefore the spiritual leader of over a billion Catholics worldwide), Francis would seem to be in a prime position to do just that. But Pope Francis simply isn't impressive enough to fit the bill for leading the Forces of Darkness: "The Antichrist has not revealed himself because in my mind I'm not impressed [by any of the current world leaders]."[30]

D. "Anti-Church, Antichrist, and
Where We Stand Today"

Reading through the transcript of the conversation between Sammons and Charles is unnerving when the reader remembers that it can be accessed at an ostensibly *Catholic* online journal. And it is unnerving because the Catholic tradition of Christianity has resolutely avoided using premillennialist and postmillennialist categories in its consideration of eschatology (i.e., what will happen when—in the language of the Nicene Creed—Jesus "will come again to judge the living and the dead.") Catholic Christianity has consistently refused to speculate about the "signs of the End Times" laid out in such vivid images in the last book of the New Testament. One can presume that it's a very good bet that the vast majority of Catholics have never heard a homily at any point in their lives in which the terms "the Beast," "the Antichrist," "the Armies of the Lamb," and "Armageddon" were used. However prevalent in the conversations of premillennialist Protestant fundamentalists (and they are quite prevalent there), those terms are utterly foreign to "Catholic-speak."[31]

And they are utterly foreign to how Catholics think and speak because the *Church itself* and its sacraments play the central role in what Catholic theologians call the "Four Last Things." Precisely because Catholics believe that through their *communio* in the sacramental life of the Church, all believers—living and dead—are already united with Christ and with each other. Christ's sudden appearance, bringing with him a fearsome judgment in which most people would find themselves among the goats and not the lambs, before the thousand-year reign of Christ on earth (from the Greek—millennium, or a thousand) had no marker in the Catholic consciousness because Christ is already really present in the Church. The Catholic doctrine of "Real Presence" (in both its eucharistic and broader meanings) made the timetable adumbrated in the Book of Revelation irrelevant. Thus, one of the oldest Christian prayers found in 1st Corinthians 16:22, "*marana-tha*" (Aramaic for "Our Lord, come!") had already been fulfilled in the celebration of the sacraments. Christ is already really, truly present in the Church, and the judgment (in at least one important sense) has already taken place between those in the Church and those who are not. Living and dead believers (the Church Militant, the Church Suffering, and the Church Triumphant) already share in Christ's Real Presence in and through the Church.

At least since *Divino Afflante Spiritu*, Pope Pius XII's 1943 encyclical advancing the historical-critical study of the Bible, Catholic biblical scholars, as well all candidates studying for ordination, are expected to master the various kinds of biblical criticism for preaching and scholarship. As that epochal encyclical noted, the Bible does not necessarily mean what it says (at least in any literal sense) nor does it say what it means. Thus, Catholics were expected to master the protocols of redaction criticism, source criticism, and so on, in studying sacred scripture. Further, and more to the point, it was the duty and the privilege of the Church itself to interpret the meaning of scripture: individual believers were not free to interpret scripture in any way they saw fit. The Church alone, through those scholars rigorously trained in the arts of biblical criticism (including, of course, knowledge of the biblical languages of Greek, Hebrew, Aramaic, Old Semitic, etc.) had the right and the authority to explain what scripture "meant." Further, *Divino* simply presumed that the Bible could not be read as any kind of literal "blueprint for the End Times," offering clues as to what historical personages might (or might not) be the Antichrist, the Beast, and so forth. All of those images—so central to the story of the last days offered in the Book of Revelation—had to be interpreted according to their historical context and not understood in any simplistic, literal sense.[32]

The entire conversation between Sammons and Charles represents a total rejection (or perhaps ignorance) of the guidelines set down by church authority for interpreting holy scripture. Any mainstream Protestant, reading that conversation in *Crisis*, would immediately recognize it as a dialogue between two premillennialist Protestant fundamentalists approaching scripture in a manner that no respected Protestant biblical scholar would ever accept. One presumes that the vast majority of Catholic critics of Pope Francis would be shocked to even consider the possibility that Francis might actually be the Antichrist (even if they knew what the term meant, which is doubtful). The premillennialist logic so central to the conversation between Sammons and Charles is simply the most dramatic piece of evidence that—however vociferously they would defend themselves as "faithful Catholics"— what was going on was not a Catholic dialogue. Premillennialist biblical interpretation is so foreign to how Catholics understand scripture as to constitute a totally different language game—a language game that has no place in Catholic theology—biblical or otherwise.

But there are also other telltale signs that *Crisis* and its editor advanced a kind of fundamentalism totally foreign to Catholic Christianity; indeed, a good case could be made that Sammons and his friends might not even be Catholic fundamentalists, but Protestant sectarians who carried their approach to the Bible with them in a waterproof container when they swam the Tiber. Sammons's tendency to favor "come outer" language in his criticisms of Francis and the hierarchy betrays the sense that there is (somehow) a purer, smaller, more select church apart from the depredations of Vatican officials—the imagined "Invisible Church" of evangelical Protestants—whose location and membership is known to God alone. But such a sectarian, a-historical understanding of the True Church is a position consistently rejected by Catholic Christianity: the Donatists, the Montanists, the Spiritual Franciscans, the Hussites, the Jansenists, the Feeneyites—all of whom sought to separate themselves from sinful fellow believers to form an imagined separate conventical of "true believers"—were strongly and consistently denounced by the mainstream tradition as betraying the core principle of Catholic Christianity: communion.

Sammons's reactive, militant distrust of the paradigm of Catholicism that emerged from Vatican II is yet another telltale sign that something other than just concern for the health of the Church is going on as well. For Sammons, one of the big problems with Pope Francis is that he insists on seeing Catholicism "through a modern post-Vatican II lens" rather than remaining faithful to the primitive faith "passed on to us by our ancestors." But such an understanding of Catholic Christianity flies in the face of how Catholic theologians understand their tradition: Vatican II was a council whose magisterial pronouncements (especially its "Dogmatic Constitution on the Church") were just as normative (and binding) on Catholic consciences as the pronouncements of earlier ecumenical councils at Nicea, Chalcedon, and Trent, and just as faithful to the "primitive faith" as those earlier councils. But after 1965, there was (quite literally) no "other lens" for understanding the Church than that provided by the Second Vatican Council. Sammons's seeming desire to hold onto an earlier paradigm of Catholicism fashioned at the Council of Trent and Vatican I—a classicist, neo-scholastic understanding of the Church as an unchanging (and unchangeable) "perfect society" in which faith could be conceived as propositional—had developed into a different paradigm of Catholicism. That new paradigm was faithful to the commitments of earlier paradigms but was now reshaped into more of a democratic and biblical "pilgrim theology," in which all the People of God were priests, making eucharist with the presbyter who presided in the worship of the assembly. But such reshaping was neither novel nor disjunctive. The Church, after all, had lived long, and had undergone regular "reshapings" over the course of its two millennia-long history. And if one were a betting person, it is a very good bet that it would continue to do so until the coming of the Lord, when "God shall be all in all."

Conclusion

"Even So, In Christ"

This study of Catholic fundamentalism in the United States since the end of World War II obviously builds on the brilliant ground-breaking studies of the Protestant fundamentalist tradition written by George Marsden, Margaret Bendroth, Martin Marty, and others. Their scholarship still profoundly influences how American religious historians and historical theologians understand that complex phenomenon as a fragile coalition of militantly anti-modern believers who felt betrayed—and excluded—from mainstream Protestant belief and practice in the years after World War I. This work has taken many of their insights as axiomatically true and useful in constructing the preceding narrative.

But while the Catholic variety of fundamentalism shares many of the features explored so insightfully by Marsden and others (most obviously in the attempt to hold on to older paradigms of religious identity in the face of "modern" theological and liturgical challenges, in primitivist efforts to freeze-frame the "genuine Christianity" of some earlier period as normative for all time, and in the threats posed by pluralism itself both inside the Church and in the broader culture), there are equally obvious differences as well. Only one of the figures studied here held the kind of biblical-literalist understanding of scripture that largely defined Protestant fundamentalism as a movement. For most of the Catholics studied here, the Church itself, and not the Bible, was the screen onto which they projected their version of what Marsden termed the "fallacy of misplaced concreteness." To that extent, the core question in Catholic fundamentalism was not "who are the elect?" but rather "who are the real Catholics?"

Likewise, the threats generated by European theology and ecclesial practice play a much larger role in the Catholic version of the phenomenon. The perceived threats of higher criticism of the Bible and comparative religion coming out of European universities certainly played roles in the emergence of Protestant fundamentalism, but those threats were largely mediated by

American theologians like Walter Rauschenbusch and Charles Briggs, who were "home grown" *bêtes noires* who handily provided the face of the enemy for radically anti-modern Protestant believers. But Europe played a much more important role for the Catholics studied here, perhaps because (in some important sense) the *real* church was "over there," headquartered in Rome. The chief European threat for many of the figures and movements studied in the book was, of course, the Second Vatican Council itself; but the threats emanating from Europe can be traced to well before that Council held its first session in 1963: "Nouvelle Theologie" scholars working in France during the 1920s and 1930, and the high-level research into the liturgical practice of the early church undertaken by scholars like Josef Jungmann in the 1940s and 1950s, even if only partly understood on this side of the Atlantic, generated profound unease and worry among some of the Catholic faithful.

But very much like the Protestant anti-modernist believers who preceded them, Catholic fundamentalism was certainly not an organized theological movement or cohesive "party" in the US Church. Just like that fragile coalition of premillennialists, Biblical literalists, Holiness pietists, and devout readers of the *Scofield Reference Bible* who collectively became "Protestant fundamentalism in the United States," Catholic fundamentalism emerged helter-skelter within the household of faith, largely without planning or direct influence. Some of the chief players emerged on the east coast (Leonard Feeney and Gommar DePauw), others in the American south (Mother Angelica and Warren Carroll), and still others in the Midwest (St. Marys, Kansas). If there was anything like a cohesive master plan, it has eluded discovery.

Further, and just as importantly, the model of "Christ and Culture" (to use H. Richard Niebuhr's famous phrase) used by the various figures and movement which followed the Feeney episode were varied and put together the five characteristics that this book uses to define the phenomenon from different stances, and with different purposes in mind. While all of the forms of American Catholic fundamentalism studied here manifested some form of sectarianism, loyalty to an older paradigm of Catholic identity, an a-historical/primitivist reading of the tradition, use of the political monikers of "conservative" and "liberal" to define religious stances, and denounced their opponents in an accusatory and militant style, they did so in different registers, and used sometimes very different apocalyptic rhetoric.

DePauw and his Catholic Traditionalist Movement, Mother Angelica and her media empire at EWTN, and the faithful gathered in the small community in St. Marys, Kansas, opted for what Niebuhr termed the "Christ Against Culture" model of religion. That is, far from wanting to engage in debate to convert mainstream American or Catholic culture, these three instances of Catholic fundamentalism sought to construct an "alternative church"— St. Marys by (literally) withdrawing geographically, Mother Angelica by fashioning something like an alternative "authentic magisterium," and DePauw by drawing a very tight (and very small) circle around *true* worshippers, largely limited to the several hundred faithful who gathered on Sunday mornings in the Ave Maria Chapel in Westbury, Long Island. These forms of the Catholic fundamentalist impulse sought to maintain what they perceived to be the purity of the church (the "safe inside") from the corrupt ("impure") imposters masquerading as Catholic Christianity. Their understanding of the older "Church as Perfect Society" outlined by Cardinal Bellarmine in the years after the Council of Trent required the faithful to leave behind the values of both the mainstream Church and the mainstream culture to embrace something very close to a completely separate "total culture," adherence to which identified who the *real* Catholics were, and (conversely, and perhaps more importantly) who were not.

But the founders of Christendom College in Virginia, ChurchMilitant.com, and the current editor of *Crisis* magazine online, while using the same elements of sectarianism, primitivism, and recourse to a militantly proclaimed "conservative/liberal" political binary to denounce those they perceived to be enemies, understood their mission differently from the groups studied in Part II. They were devoted to an activist model that Niebuhr called the "Christ the Transformer of Culture" understanding of Christianity's role in the world. Far from seeking a withdrawal from the rough-and-tumble wickedness of a fallen world, they rather proactively sought to provide a clearer, purer model of how the Church should shape the world, and they were hardly timid in publicly presenting their own versions of the answer as the way for the Church to get its act together and work for the creation of a new church and a new world (in Sammons's case, quite literally). Christendom unapologetically presented its model of education as the paradigm not only for Catholic higher education but for American culture itself in forging a new form of integralism as the answer for the corruptions of modern society. Likewise, Michael Voris and Church Militant forcefully argued its own take on "righteous coercion" for correcting both a Church and a culture mired in sin and heterodoxy. And Eric Sammons repurposed the once-respected voice of *Crisis* magazine using premillennialist biblical interpretation to call a somnolent church back to its senses to prepare for the Great and Dreadful Day of the Lord.

As is hopefully apparent from the preceding pages, this author takes all of these forms of fundamentalist Christianity to be in fundamental conflict with the understandings of grace, redemption, and sacramental witness that have defined Catholic Christianity from its emergence in the early church; and to that extent they offer very different—and to a large extent, oppositional—models of how Christianity has (and should) witness to and proclaim the gospel. That tradition has always distanced itself from such sectarian happenings (as indeed it should). And that is because the Catholic tradition of Christianity has always taken its mandate from Jesus to be a resolutely public church, working in and for a world in need of grace and redemption, to some extent a redemption already won, and made available in the sacraments of the Church. There was no "safe place"—in opposition to the world—where believers could exempt themselves from the lot of all humanity. That stance is based, of course, on the New Testament itself, perhaps most memorably expressed by St. Paul in his great first epistle to the early Christians living in the Greek-speaking city of Corinth: "For as in Adam all die, even so in Christ shall all be made alive" (1 Corinthians 15:22).

Acknowledgments

As scholars instinctively know, all scholarly work is collaborative and dependent on the generosity, insight, and careful scrutiny of other scholars. This work is no different.

The initial research for this project was undertaken by a brilliant Boston College student during the summer and fall of his senior year: Sean O'Neill, an indefatigable researcher in archives both in Boston and much further afield, produced almost daily updates of his discoveries. Although I had already written about Leonard Feeney in a previous monograph, Sean uncovered many details of which I had been unaware. David Gibson, an award-winning journalist and now director of Fordham University's distinguished Center for Religion and Culture, and Cynthia Shattuck, accomplished editor, eagle-eyed literary critic, and valued friend from Cambridge days, both read what is now Chapter 1 and made extremely helpful suggestions. Mark Silk, the revered director of the Leonard E. Greenberg Center for the Study of Religion in Public Life at Trinity College Hartford and a friend of many decades since our graduate student days at Harvard, read and made trenchant (and, as always, infallibly correct) suggestions on what is now Chapter 2. John Baldovin, S.J. friend, fellow Jesuit, and much respected liturgical theologian at Boston College's School of Theology and Ministry, read Chapter 3 and made a number of important corrections to my understanding of the history of Catholic liturgy. To all of these I owe a debt that I cannot repay but only acknowledge.

M. Cathleen Kaveny of Boston College's Theology Department and Law School, Jim Bretzke, S.J. of John Carroll University, and Bernard Cook, professor emeritus of history at Loyola University New Orleans, all read the entire manuscript and offered a number of significant and extremely helpful suggestions at an important point in the evolution of the manuscript that shaped the narrative in decisive ways. All three are brilliant and accomplished scholars in their own right who took time out of their own busy research schedules to read and critique my manuscript. God has blessed me in my friends.

Paul Murphy invited me to present part of my project to the Catholic Studies Colloquium at John Carroll University: the smart scholars who are members of that wonderful faculty seminar convened by Paul helped me to rethink several important points in my argument. And, as always, my wonderful editor at Oxford University Press—Theo Calderera—offered encouragement, support, and important suggestions in the early stages of this book's evolution. When fellow scholars complain about their editorial treatment at other presses, I always respond, "I have the very best editor at the world's oldest university press, so I have no idea what you're talking about."

Finally, and by no means least, this book is dedicated to the "dream team" at the Curran Center for American Catholic Studies at Fordham University: Maria Terzulli, Angela O'Donnell, and Nick Lombardi, S.J. Over the course of many years, working on lectures, conferences, and advising extremely talented undergraduates, my "team" made the running of the Center a delight as well as an important academic enterprise. It is often said that if you love what you do, you'll never work a day in your life. These three proved that adage to be exactly right.

Notes

Chapter 1

1. George Marsden, *Fundamentalism and American Culture: The Shaping of Twentieth Century Evangelicalism, 1870–1925* (New York: Oxford University Press, 1980), 201, 204. "From its origins fundamentalism was primarily a religious movement . . . Unless we appreciate the immense implications of a deep religious commitment to such beliefs, we cannot appreciate the dynamics of fundamentalist thought and action" (3).
2. Margaret Bendroth, *Fundamentalism and Gender, 1875 to the Present* (New Haven: Yale University Press, 1993), 5. "Fundamentalist militancy grew from more than just its rejection by intellectual elites, although this did elicit considerable anger. A significant element of this militancy was generated in the masculine persona that fundamentalists identified as the true hallmark of the Christian warrior" (5–6).
3. Marsden, *Fundamentalism and American Culture*, 204, 207–209; Joel Carpenter, *Revive Us Again: The Reawakening of American Fundamentalism* (New York: Oxford University Press, 1997), 49.
4. Marsden, *Fundamentalism and American Culture*, 207–209.
5. Theodore Dwight Bozeman, *Protestants in an Age of Science: The Baconian Ideal and Antebellum American Religious Thought* (Chapel Hill: University of North Carolina Press, 1977), 4–8, 23–28. See also John Dillenberger, *Protestant Thought and Natural Science: A Historical Interpretation* (Nashville: Abingdon Press, 1960); John C. Greene, *The Death of Adam: Evolution and Its Impact on Western Thought* (Ames: University of Iowa Press, 1959), ch. 1.
6. Bozeman, *Protestants in an Age of Science*, 166–171.
7. Marsden, *Fundamentalism and American Culture*, 16–18, 55–62, 103–109; Carpenter, *Revive Us Again*, 40–49.
8. Carpenter, *Revive Us Again*, 7ff; Marsden, *Fundamentalism and American Culture*, 118–120; Bendroth, *Fundamentalism and Gender*, 48ff.
9. Marsden, *Fundamentalism and American Culture*, 215.
10. Ibid., 207.
11. Catherine Goddard Clarke, *The Loyolas and the Cabots: The Story of the Boston Heresy Case* (Boston: The Ravengate Press, 1950), 3–5, 23–25; John Deedy, "Whatever Happened to Father Feeney?" *The Critic* 31 (1973): 17–18.
12. Mark Massa, "Boundary Maintenance: Leonard Feeney, The Boston Heresy Case, and the Postwar Culture," in *Catholics and American Culture: Fulton Sheen, Dorothy Day, and the Notre Dame Football Team* (New York: The Crossroad Publishing Co., 1999), 25–27; T. Stanfill Benns, "Catacomb Catholics: Feeneyism and Traditionalism Share Heresies Concerning Grace," *BetrayedCatholics.com*, 5–6, www.betrayedcatholics.com/catacomb-catholics/.
13. Mark Silk, *Spiritual Politics: Religion and America Since World War II* (New York: Simon and Schuster, 1988), 80–81.
14. Mircea Eliade, "Roman Catholicism," in *The Encyclopedia of Religion*, ed. Mircea Eliade and Charles Adams (New York: Macmillan, 1987), 430.
15. One of the first (and still the most famous) definition of "sectarianism" was offered by Ernst Troeltsch in *The Social Teaching of the Christian Churches* (London: George Allen and Unwin, LTD, 1931), 1st English edition, 2 vols. "The church is that type of organization which . . . desires to cover the whole of humanity, The sects, on the other hand, are comparatively small groups; they aspire after personal inward perfection, and they aim at direct personal fellowship between members of the group" (I, 331). On Feeney's movement as "sectarian," see also Michael Feldberg, "American Heretic: The Rise and Fall of Leonard Feeney, S.J.," *American Catholic Studies* 123 (2012): 109–115, 113ff. Thomas O'Dea crafted a superb study of the Feeney episode that has profoundly influenced my own reading of the event: "Catholic Sectarianism: A Sociological Analysis of the So-Called Boston Heresy Case," *Review of Religious Research* 3 (1961): 49–58.

16. Massa, "Boundary Maintenance: Leonard Feeney," 21–37. "Societas perfecta" is the Latin phrase meaning "the perfect society" that had no need for change or development because it was always complete, was crafted by Cardinal Robert Bellarmine in the years after the Council of Trent (1545–1563). For historian of science Thomas Kuhn, a paradigm was the humanly constructed model that made sense of the most data gathered by scientists in their experiments. An important component of Kuhn's theory of paradigms, however, was that precisely because they were humanly constructed and therefore provisional, older paradigms would be replaced by newer ones as data increasingly showed that the older paradigms were failing in their job of "reality modeling." Thomas Kuhn, *The Structure of Scientific Revolutions*, 4th ed. (Chicago: University of Chicago Press, 2012), 3–5, 24–25, 27–34, 103–110.

17. Paul Johnson, *A History of Christianity* (New York: Atheneum, 1979), 191–192.

18. The text that offers the best single study of the term "primitivism" is Theodore Dwight Bozeman, *To Live Ancient Lives: The Primitivist Dimension in Puritanism* (Chapel Hill: University of North Carolina Press, 1988).

19. Clarke, *Loyolas and the Cabots*, 51; Brenton Welling, Jr. "Father Feeney Calls 'Liberal Catholicism 'Horrible Catholicism,'" *The Harvard Crimson*, September 30, 1949.

20. On the "parties" within American Catholicism, see Joseph Chinnici, *American Catholicism Transformed: From the Cold War Through the Council* (New York: Oxford University Press, 2021), 55–60, 74–80,81–83. The "German Triangle" referred to the area marked out by the three cities of Cincinnati, Chicago, and St. Louis, which witnessed significant settlement by German immigrants in the nineteenth and twentieth centuries. "Jansenism" (originating in the Low Countries) was a rule-based understanding of Catholicism that was carried to the United States by Irish immigrants in the nineteenth century; it emphasized sexual purity and a strict observance of the Commandments. See Richard McBrien, ed., *The HarperCollins Encyclopedia of Catholicism* (San Francisco: HarperCollins Publishers, 1989), 687–688. "Modernism" was the theological heresy ("the synthesis of all heresies") condemned by the papal encyclical *Pascendi Dominici Gregis* in 1907, which favored the replacement of traditional scholastic metaphysics (truth as "propositional") with historical criticism. See Margaret Mary Reher, *Catholic Intellectual Life in America: A Historical Study of Persons and Movements* (New York: Macmillan, 1989), 93–95. "Neo-scholasticism" was a post-nineteenth-century positivist form of theology which grossly oversimplified of the scholasticism of St. Thomas Aquinas, so that truth was presented as static, and presented in syllogisms. See Mark Massa, *The Structure of Theological Revolutions: How the Fight Over Birth Control Transformed American Catholicism* (New York: Oxford University Press, 2018), 16–18. "Americanism," a supposedly "phantom heresy" condemned in 1899 by the papal encyclical *Testem Benevolentiae*, was the belief that Catholic doctrine and practice had to adapt itself to American culture. "Ultramontanism" (from the two Latin words *ultra* and *mons*; i.e., "over the mountain") was a centralized model of Catholic authority in which all theological questions should be decided by the Vatican alone. O'Brien, ed., *HarperCollins Encyclopedia of Catholicism*, 40–42.

21. Deedy, "Whatever Happened?," 12.

22. Clarke, *Loyolas and Cabots*, 45.

23. *Harvard Crimson*, December 6, 1951, 1; Silk, *Spiritual Politics*, 74.

24. Deedy, "Whatever Happened?," 19; Clarke, *Loyolas and Cabots*, 100, 112.

25. Samuel Heilman, "Quiescent and Active Fundamentalism: The Jewish Cases," in *The Fundamentalism Project* (Chicago: University of Chicago Press, 1994), vol. 4, 183.

26. Mark Amory, ed., *The Letters of Evelyn Waugh* (London: Harmondsworth, 1982), 292–293; Silk, *Spiritual Politics*, 82.

27. Bendroth, *Fundamentalism and Gender*, 6, italics added.

28. Joseph Dever, *Cushing of Boston: A Candid Portrait* (Boston: Bruce Humphries Publishers, 1965), 143.

Chapter 2

1. *The Pilot*, September 6, 1952, 1. The Holy Office, called "The Office of the Holy Inquisition" in the sixteenth through nineteenth centuries, struck fear into the hearts of those called to appear before it (like the great astronomer Galileo). Now called "The Dicastery of the Doctrine of the Faith," it retains the same mission despite the name changes over the centuries: to safeguard the teaching of Catholic doctrine and to correct those it believes have strayed from orthodoxy.

2. Much of this paragraph is borrowed from my earlier study of the Feeney affair, "Boundary Maintenance: Leonard Feeney," in *Catholics and American Culture*, 22.

3. For example, see Michael Feldberg, "American Heretic: The Rise and Fall of Leonard Feeney, S.J.," *American Catholic Studies* 123, no. 2 (2012): 109–115; Gibson Winter, *The Suburban Captivity of the Churches* (Garden City, NY: Doubleday and Company, 1961). See also Andrew Greeley, *The Church and the Suburbs* (New York: Sheed and Ward, 1959); Dino Cinel, *From Italy to San Francisco: The Immigrant Experience* (Stanford: Stanford University Press, 1982); William Halsey, *Survival of Innocence* (Notre Dame: University of Notre Dame Press, 1979).

4. "Low tension" and "high tension" religion is well described by Roger Finke and Rodney Stark, *The Churching of America, 1776–2205: Winners and Losers in Our Religious Economy* (New Brunswick, NJ: Rutgers University Press, 2005), see especially 8–12, 43–53; Will Herberg, *Protestant, Catholic, Jew: An Essay in American Religious Sociology* (Chicago: University of Chicago Press, 1983 [1955]), 231–272; R. Laurence Moore, *Religious Outsiders and the Making of Americans* (New York: Oxford University Press, 1986).

5. Émile Durkheim, *The Division of Labor in Society*, trans. George Simpson (Glencoe, IL: Free Press, 1947), 102ff. For a superb application of Durkheim's "deviance theory" to the New England Puritans, see Kai Erikson, *The Wayward Puritans: A Study in the Sociology of Deviance* (New York: Wiley, 1966), especially 4–12. For a thorough examination of the "pure inside" versus the "polluted outside, see Mary Douglas, *Purity and Danger: An Analysis of the Concepts of Pollution and Taboo* (New York: Praeger, 1966), chs. 1 and 2. Also see Douglas's truly brilliant essay, *Natural Symbols*, Chapter 8. "The Bog Irish" (London: Routledge, 1970).

6. Kuhn, *Structure of Scientific Revolutions*, 3–5, 103–110, 138–139. This paragraph paraphrases my earlier application of Kuhn's theory in *The Structure of Theological Revolutions: How the Fight over Birth Control Transformed American Catholicism* (New York: Oxford University Press, 2018), 34–35. One of Kuhn's most famous examples of the non-cumulative nature of science focused on Isaac Newton and Albert Einstein: "The initial scoffing that greeted Einstein's theory [of general relativity]—space could not be 'curved,' as Einstein had proposed, was not wrong or mistaken, at least according to the reigning paradigm of Newtonian physics of the time. Mathematicians, physicists, and philosophers who attempted to develop a version of Einstein's theory based on Newton's model of the laws of physics were, of course, doomed to failure. What had previously been meant by 'space' was necessarily flat, homogenous, and unaffected by the presence of matter. To make the transition to Einstein's universe, the whole conceptual web whose strands are space, matter, force, and so on, had to be shifted and laid down again on nature. As Kuhn argued in, a new paradigm—like the one offered by Einstein to *replace the Newtonian one— was an entirely new way of regarding the problems of physics and mathematics, one that necessarily changed the meaning of words like 'space,' 'time,' and 'matter.'"* Massa, *Structure of Theological Revolutions*, 44, italics added; Kuhn, *Structure of Scientific Revolutions*, 148.

7. Kuhn, *Structure of Scientific Revolutions*, 24–25, 27–30.

8. Ibid., 103–110.

9. Ibid., 5, 27.

10. Massa, *Structure of Theological Revolutions*, 40–41.

11. Kuhn, *Structure of Scientific Revolutions*, 82–84. Kuhn quotes Albert Einstein, who wrote that during the period of crisis preceding his own articulation of relativity theory, "It was as if the ground had been pulled out from under one, with no firm foundation to be seen anywhere upon which one could have built." He also quotes Wolfgang Pauli, before the final articulation of the Heisenberg's Principle which replaced the Newtonian model of physics, "At the moment physics is again terribly confused. In any case, it is too difficult for me, and I wish I had been a movie comedian or something of that sort, and had never heard of physics." Both quotes are in Kuhn, *Structure of Scientific Revolutions*, 84.

12. "Orthopraxy" refers to a style of being religious in which the *practices* of the faith—church attendance, fasting on the designated days of the church's calendar, making sure to marry "inside the faith," and so forth, were more important (or at least more understood) than doctrinal correctness (orthodoxy).

13. Bendroth, *Fundamentalism and Gender*, 6. The quotation within the block is by Clarence Macartney, a prominent Presbyterian preacher turned fundamentalist, from *Ancient Wives and Modern Husbands* (Nashville: Cokesbury Press, 1934), 104.

14. Chinnici, *American Catholicism Transformed*, 5–7, 28, 59.

15. Clarke, *Loyolas and Cabots*, 45; Avery Dulles, "Leonard Feeney: In Memoriam," *America* 138 (February 25, 1978): 135.

16. Silk, *Spiritual Politics*, 71–72.

17. Dulles, "Leonard Feeney: In Memoriam," 135, 136.

18. Ibid., 136.
19. Garry Wills, *Bare Ruined Choirs: Doubt, Prophecy, and Radical Religion* (Garden City, NY: Doubleday, 1971), 15, 16. As defined by Bernard Lonergan, "classicism" was a form of theology—arguably most famously expressed in neo-scholasticism—which presumed that both the world and the truths of Christian revelation were based on unchanging laws that were always true, everywhere and for all time. For classicist believers like Feeney, human nature and right action were necessarily static realities because they rested on immutable laws found in nature, whose author was God. And precisely because God created human reason as well, the purposes of human acts (the "rightness" and "wrongness" of specific actions) could be appropriated through the rational study of an unchanging natural law. Bernard Lonergan, "The Transition from a Classical Worldview to Historical Mindedness," in *Law for Liberty: The Role of Law in the Church Today*, ed. James E. Biechler (Baltimore: Helicon Press, 1967), 127.
20. Richard McCormick, "Moral Theology from 1940 to 1989: An Overview," in *Corrective Vision: Explorations in Moral Theology* (Milwaukee: Sheed and Ward: 1994), 1–7; James F. Keenan, *A History of Catholic Moral Theology in the Twentieth Century* (New York: Continuum, 2010), 118–122.
21. Dulles, "Leonard Feeney: In Memoriam," 136.
22. Ibid., 137.
23. Ibid., 137.
24. Robert Conner [pseudonym for Robert Colopy], *Walled In: The True Story of a Cult* (New York: 1979), 253; Silk, *Spiritual Politics*, 73.
25. Clarke, *Loyolas and Cabots*, 45.
26. Avery Dulles, "On Keeping the Faith," *From the Housetops* 1 (1946): 60–62; Margaret T. O'Brien, "Secularism in American Colleges," *From the Housetops* 1 (1946): 40; Clarke, *Loyolas and Cabots*, 50–51. For much more detail see: James O'Toole, "Oral History Interview of Reverend Avery Dulles," (June 21, 1982), 2–5, 11–13, 16 ff., Archives of the Archdiocese of Boston.
27. William O'Connell, "The Catholic Priest and the Catholic School," *Sermons and Addresses* (Boston: Pilot, 1931), 10, 51–53.
28. *Boston Globe*, February 16, 1948; *Harvard Crimson*, April 21, 1949, front page.
29. "Heresy is Charged to Church Leaders," *Life*, May 2, 1949, 53; "Abp. Cushing's Brighton Home Picketed by 38," *Boston Globe*, July 3, 1949; Roland Bainton, *Here I Stand: A Life of Martin Luther* (Nashville: Abingdon Press, 1950), 183; "The Boston College Case," *America* 81 (September 17, 1949): 629; "The Competing Claims of Truth and Obedience" in Silk, *Spiritual Politics*, 79.
30. "Archbishop Upheld in 'Heresy' Dispute," *Boston Herald*, April 22, 1949; "Heresy is Charged," *Life*, May 2, 1949.
31. Maluf's accusation of heresy was covered in both the Boston and national newspapers. See "Four Fired B.C. Professors Charge Heresy," *The Waltham Massachusetts News-Tribune*, April 14, 1949, front page; "Fr. Feeney Defends Teachers B.C. Fired," *The Boston Herald*, April 14, 1949. In the same edition, see "Noted Jesuit Writer Defends 4 Teachers Fired by B.C. Head." See also "The Boston College Case," *America* 81 (September 17, 1949): 629; "Heresy is Charged," *Life*, May 2, 1949, 53; "Archbishop Upheld in 'Heresy' Dispute," *The Boston Herald*, April 22, 1949; "Letter of John B. Sheerin to Richard Cushing, April 19, 1949," Archive of the Archdiocese of Boston; John Henry Newman, *An Essay on the Development of Christian Doctrine* (London: J. Toovey, 1846), ch. 1, sec. 1, pt. 7.
32. Clarke, *Loyolas and Cabots*, 270–271. "Solemnly professed" Jesuits (those who took four vows after many years in the order, including a special regarding missions at the direction of the pope), could not be dismissed from the order without a formal canonical (church) trial at which the accused had a right to a canon lawyer in constructing his defense.
33. "Easter duty" refers to the church law that requires faithful Catholics to receive communion at some point between Ash Wednesday and Pentecost Sunday (forty days after Easter) to be considered "Catholics in good standing." "Interdict" is a broader form of excommunication, laying disciplinary strictures of a group of people rather on only one individual. Thus, while individuals can be excommunicated, interdict is the disciplinary charge placed on groups in parishes, and sometimes even on dioceses which cause scandal or hold false teaching. It was a form of "social excommunication" extremely rare in the United States. The announcement if the new Catechism issued by the Confraternity of Christian Doctrine was announced in *The Boston Herald*, April 22, 1949, 1, 8.
34. "Book Upholds Archbishop," *The Boston Herald*, April 22, 1949. Italics in the quote from the new catechism are added by the author and are not in the original.

35. "Father Feeney's Excommunication," *Time*, October 13, 1952. Block quote from the article in the "Religion" section.

36. "Memoranda on Extra-Curricular Activities of the Feeney Group, December 10, 1952, reported by Isabel Currier," Archives of the Archdiocese of Boston, Braintree, Massachusetts.

37. *New York Times*, May 20, 1949.

38. Clarke, *Loyolas and the Cabots*, 255, 257; Currier, "Memoranda," 2.

39. "Letter of Isabel Currier to the Right Reverend Walter J. Furlong, Chancellor," attached to document "Hatred Inspires Hatred for Father Feeney and Followers," Archives of the Archdiocese of Boston; "Father Feeney's Excommunication," *Time*, October 13, 1952, 78–79.

40. "I Preach Hatred," *Time*, October 13, 1952, 78.

41. "Anti-Jewish Placard Provokes Fight in Boston; Police Intervene," September 8, 1955, Archive, Jewish Telegraph Agency; "Letter of Isadore Zack to Isabel Currier, June 19, 1952," Archives of the Anti-Defamation League of B'nai B'rith.

42. Feldberg, "American Heretic," 109–111.

43. "Archbishop Gives Final Warning to Fr. Feeney in Boston Heresy Case," *Newark (New Jersey) Advocate*, September 13, 1952; "Pope Pius Rules on Fr. Feeney," *The Boston Herald*, September 5, 1952; "Holy Office Issues Sentence Declaring Fr. Leonard Feeney Has Incurred Excommunication," Immediate Release: February 19, 1953, issued by N.C.W.C News Service, 2; "Father Feeney's Excommunication: The Final Punishment Falls on an Unruly Priest," *Time*, October 13, 1952, 78–79.

44. "Holy Office Issues Sentence," N.C.W.C. News Service, February 19, 1953, 1, 2.

45. Richard McBrien, *Do We Need the Church?* (New York: Harper & Row, 1969), 112; Silk, *Spiritual Politics*, 83 (for "unwitting Catholics").

46. *Lumen Gentium* 8. *Vatican Council II, The Conciliar and Post-Conciliar Documents* (Northport, NY: Costello Publishing Company, 1980), 357, italics added.

47. See "The Church of Christ and the Churches," *America* 623 (August 8, 2007), www.amer icamagazine.org/issue/623/article/church-christ-and-churches; "The Subsisting Church," *Commonweal*, www.commonwealmagazine.org/subsisting-church.

48. Deedy, "Whatever Happened?," 17; Massa, *Catholics and American Culture*, 32.

Chapter 3

1. "Catholic Priest Decries Church Reform, Feels Church is Undermined From Within," *The (Nyack, New York) Journal News*, April 24, 1967, 1; "Robber Council," *Introibo ad Altare Dei*, introiboadalataredei2.blogspot.com/2018; "60%" from *The National Observer*, May 10, 1965, front page.

2. "Tower of Trent Hall of Honor," *DailyCatholic.org*, www.dailycatholic.org/issue/04May, 1–2; *Time* 85 (January 28, 1966): 55.

3. Gommar DePauw was hardly the first member of his family to arrive in the New World: in the eighteenth century his ancestor, Michael DePauw, employed by the Dutch East India Company, owned land in both Manhattan and Staten Island. Another ancestor, Charles DePauw, served as personal aide-de-camp to Lafayette during the American Revolution, while yet another—Washington Charles DePauw—moved west to the "middle border" (now the state of Indiana)—where his largess helped found the Methodist-affiliated DePauw University in Greencastle. His maternal grandparents immigrated in 1911, settling in Patterson, New Jersey. "Tower of Trent Hall of Honor," *DailyCatholic.org*, www.dailycatholic.org/issue/04May, 2; Albert Marcello, "Reclaiming a Lost Voice in Catholic Moral Theology," *Homiletic and Pastoral Review* (August 28, 2020): 1–2.

4. "Into Uncertain Life: The First Sunday of Advent, 1964," in Mark Massa, *Catholics and American Culture: Fulton Sheen, Dorothy Day, and the Notre Dame Football Team* (New York: Crossroad, 1999), 148–149; Frederick McManus, "Vatican Council II," *Worship* 40 (March 1963): 146–148; Daniel O'Hanlon "The Development of Worship at the Second Vatican Council," *Worship* 40 (March 1966): 130–136; James D. Crichton, *Changes in the Liturgy: Considerations on the Instructions of the Sacred Congregation of Rites for the Proper Implementation of the Constitution on Sacred Liturgy* (Staten Island, NY: Alba House, 1965), 4–6.

5. The *Missale Romanum* of 1570, the result of the call of the Council of Trent to establish some order in the worship of the western church, was itself just the most recent of a number of reforms in the celebration of mass over the course of a millennium: the *Gelasian Sacramentary* of 510; the *Gregorian Sacramentary* of 600; the *Ordo Romanus Primus* of 700; the Mozarabic *Liber Sacramentorum* of 794; and others. The list is long and varied, and it gives the sense of

a living tradition of worship dedicated to geographical adaptation rather than liturgical uniformity. See the excellent historical overview provided by Gregory Dix, *The Shape of the Liturgy* (New York: Seabury Press, 1982), 546–612; Josef Jungmann, *The Mass of the Roman Rite: Its Origins and Development*, trans. Francis Brunner (New York: Benziger Brothers, Inc., 1950), 133.

6. "The Divine Liturgy of St. Ambrose," https://web.archive.org//rwrv.org/files/AmbrosianMass.pdf; *We Give You Thanks and Praise: The Ambrosian Eucharistic Prefaces*, trans. Alan Griffiths (Norwich, UK: Canterbury Press, 2000); *The Revised Divine Liturgy According to Our Holy Father Ambrose of Milan*, 2 vols. (Amazon: Createspace, 2014); William Bonniwell, *A History of the Dominican Liturgy* (New York: Joseph F. Wagner, Inc., 1944), 28–35; B. Luykx, "Essai sur les sources de l'Ordo missae Premontre," *Analecta Praemonstratensia* XXII–XXIII (1946–1947): 35–90.

7. Germain Morin, "Depuis quand un canon fixe a Milan?," *Revue Benedictine* (1939): 101–108; Jean Michel Hanssens, S.J., *Institutiones liturgiae de ritibus orientalibus* (Rome: Gregorian University, 1930), 407–413; Jungmann, *Mass of the Roman Rite*, 138.

8. Jungmann, *Mass of the Roman Rite*, 138ff.

9. *Missale Romanum: Edition Princeps, 1570*, ed. Manlio Sodi and Achille Triaca (Vatican City: Libreria Edititrice Vaticana, 1988); Lukasz Celinski "Per una riletturs della storia della formazione del Messale Romano: Il caso del Messale di Clemente V," www.academia.edu/31464425; Thomas Drolesky, "Presaging a Revolution," *Christ or Chaos*, www.christorchaos.com/PresagingaRevolution.html; "Papal Decree *Maxima redemptionis nostrae mysteria*," *Acta Apostolica Sedis* 47 (1955): 838–847.

10. Sue Eveslage, "What in the Name of God?," *American Free Press (Cincinnati, Ohio)*, November 1968, front page.

11. "A Lonesome Crusade," *Washington Post*, July 17, 1966, E6, photos are on page E6.

12. Quotations in this paragraph are taken from "Priest Says Bishops Rebel Against Pope," *The (Providence, Rhode, Island) Evening Bulletin*, January 24, 1967, front page. See also "DePauw Ducks as Shehan Drops Boom," *National Catholic Reporter*, February 2, 1966, front page; "Litugical Beatniks," *Tower of Trent Hall of Honor*, 5, quoting DePauw in the *St. Louis Globe-Democrat*.

13. Jungmann, *Mass of the Roman Rite*.

14. English translation of *Quo Primum* in "Our Origin and General Aim," www.latinmass-ctm.org/about/origin.htm, 1, italics added by DePauw.

15. "Loathsome," *Introibo ad altare Dei*, introiboadaltaredei2.blogspot.com/2018; William D. Dinges, "Roman Catholic Traditionalism in the United States," in *Fundamentalisms Observed*, ed. Martin Marty and R. Scott Appleby (Chicago: University of Chicago Press, 1991), 70–72; Gommar DePauw, *The "Rebel Priest" of the Catholic Traditionalist Movement* (New York: Catholic Traditionalist Movement, 1967), 7, 9. For sympathetic voices supporting DePauw, see also James Wathen, *The Great Sacrilege* (Rockford, IL: TAN Books, 1971) and Michael Davies, *Pope Paul's New Mass* (Dickinson, TX: Angelus Press, 1980).

16. "Catholic Unit Fighting Change in Liturgy Renews U.S. Drive," *New York Times*, January 6, 1966, 1, 6.

17. Michael Cuneo, *The Smoke of Satan: Conservative and Traditionalist Dissent in Contemporary American Catholicism* (New York: Oxford University Press, 1997), 90. See also "A Lonesome Crusade," *Washington Post*, July 17, 1966, E1, E5.

18. James Likoudis and Kenneth Whitehead, *The Pope, the Council, and the Mass* (W. Hanover, MA: Christopher Publishing House, 1981), 97–104; DePauw, *The "Rebel" Priest*, 7ff.

19. "Apostolic Constitution Issued by His Holiness Pope Paul VI on the New Roman Missal," April 3, 1969, www.vatican.va/content/paul-vi/apost-documents/hf_p-vi_apc_1969_missale-romanum.html; "Text of the Ordinary Form/Mass of Paul VI/*Novus Ordo Missae*," www.latinliturgy.com/imtexts.

20. "They Came for Miles to Hear Latin Mass," *Long Island Press*, July 1, 1968, front page.

21. "A Lonesome Crusade," *Washington Post*, July 17, 1966, E5.

22. Kenneth Briggs, "Ultra traditionalist Catholics Back Suspended Prelate," *New York Times*, November 9, 1976, 39, 40.

23. Ibid., 40.

24. Briggs, "Ultra traditionalists," 40.

25. Garry Wills, *Bare Ruined Choirs: Doubt, Prophecy, and Radical Religion* (Garden City, NY: Doubleday, 1971), 21. The reference to Miss Havisham is, of course from Charles Dickens's

novel *Great Expectations*. Early in that novel the young lead character, Pip, is invited into the dilapidated mansion of Miss Havisham (Satis House), where he discovers a "house of arrested clocks": all the windows of Satis House are boarded over, and all clocks stopped at the minute when Miss Havisham's lover failed to show up for their wedding decades before.

26. Lonergan, "The Transition from a Classical Worldview," 127.
27. Ibid., 127, 128.
28. Ibid., 30.

Chapter 4

1. Colleen Dulle, "Explainer: The Story Behind Pope Francis' Beef With EWTN," *America*, September 30, 2021, 2; "From the Bible Belt, EWTN Shapes World Catholic News," *National Catholic Reporter*, January 15, 2019, https://www.ncronline.org/news/media/media/bible-belt-ewtn--world-catholic-new; "Mother Angelica," *Encyclopedia of Alabama*, http://www.encyclopediaofalabams.org/article/h-1400.
2. Peter Applebome, "Scandals Aside, TV Preachers Thrive," *New York Times*, October 8, 1989, https://query.nytimes.com/gst/fullpage.html.
3. "Religious Catalog Featured Highlights," *EWTN*, http://www.ewtn.com/cataloguefeatured/; "Support EWTN," *EWTN*, https://www.ewtn.com/donatenow/.
4. "EWTN Radio—Solid Catholic Talk & Info—SiriusXM Radio," *SiriusXM.com*, http://www.siriusxm.com/ewtnradio; "EWTN Radio Affiliates and Channels Map/EWTN," *EWTN*, https://www.ewtn.com/radio/affiliates-map; "EWTN News Nightly/EWTN," *EWTN*, https://www.ewtn.com/tv/shows/ewtn-news-nightly.
5. Heidi Schlumpf, "How Mother Angelica's 'Miracle of God' Became a Global Media Empire," *National Catholic Reporter*, July 19, 2019; "Mother Angelica," *The (London) Times*, March 29, 2016, 45; "Mother Angelica, Television Nun—Obituary," *The (London) Telegraph*, March 29, 2016; "Mother Angelica Biography," Poor Clares of Perpetual Adoration: Our Lady of the Angels Monastery, https://web.archive.org/web/loamnuns.com/mother-angelica-biography.html.
6. Raymond Arroyo, *Mother Angelica: The Remarkable Story of a Nun, Her Nerve, and a Network of Miracles* (New York: Doubleday, 2005), 5, 6–7, 15, 19, 20–21, 31–32.
7. W. Jason Wallace, "Eternal Word Television Network (EWTN)," *Encyclopedia of Alabama*, http://encyclopediaof alabama.org/article/h-1399; Dan O'Neill, *Mother Angelica: Her Life Story* (New York: Crossword Publishing Company, 1986), 50–51; "EWTN Celebrates Mother Angelica's 90th Birthday," *Catholic News Agency*, http://wwew.catholicnewsagancy.com/news/ewtn-celebrates-mother-angerlicas-90th-birthday/.
8. To get a sense of Mother Angelica's style of presenting Catholicism on the air, see the following videos, all produced by EWTN and found under the title "Mother Angelica Live Classics": "The Presence of God," April 5, 1994; "The Miracles of Jesus," April 16, 1996; "The Gift of Knowledge," June 29, 1999; "What is Heaven Really Like?" November 9, 1999; "Heaven and Angels," December 14, 1997; "The First Beatitude and Hell," August 1, 2000; "The Silver Lining," October 11, 2011; "Keep Your Eyes on God," July 7, 2014. The block quote is from Tim Lacy, "Mother Angelica, the Culture Wars, and the Catholic Church," *U.S. Intellectual History Blog*, April 1, 2016, https://s-usih.org/2016/04/mother-angelica-the-culture-wars-and-the-catholic-church/.
9. Greg Garrison, "Mother Angelica Will Be Buried Friday at Her Alabama Monastery," March 30, 2016, *Advance Local*, https://al.com/living/index.ssf/2016/03/mother_angelica_will_be_buried.html; Joel Mathis, "Chaput to Officiate at Mother Angelica's Funeral," *Philadelphia*, March 30, 2016, http://www.phillymag.com/news/2016/0330/chaput-mother-angelica-funeral/.
10. Katherine Stewart, "How Big Money is Dividing American Catholicism," *The New Republic*, March 9, 2021, https://newrepublic.com/article/161262/big-money-dividing-american-catholicism/.
11. Heidi Schlumpf, "On Pope Francis, EWTN, and Cracking Down on Criticism," *National Catholic Reporter*, October 21, 2021, https://ncronline.org/news/opinion//ncr-connections/pope-francis-ewtn-and-cracking-down-criticism/; Mark Massa, "Catholicism as a Cultural System: Joe McCarthy, Clifford Geertz, and the 'Conspiracy So Immense,'" in *Catholics and American Culture: Fulton Sheen, Dorothy Day, and the Notre Dame Football Team* (New York: Crossroad, 1999), 57–82. On Monk, see Mark Massa, "Catholic Otherness," in *Anti-Catholicism in America: The Last Acceptable Prejudice* (New York: Crossroad, 2003), 22–23.
12. Heidi Schlumpf, "EWTN: Connected to Conservative Catholic Money, Anti-Francis Elements," *National Catholic Reporter*, July 17, 2019, https://www.ncronline.org/culture/ewtn-connected-to-conservative-catholic-money-anti-francis-elements/2-3.

13. Ibid., 2–5.
14. On the Protestant "interlocking directorate," see John Bodo, *The Protestant Clergy and Public Issues, 1812–1848* (Princeton: Princeton University Press, 1954); Charles Cole, *The Social Ideals of the Northern Evangelists, 1826–1860* (New York: Columbia University Press 1954); and especially Charles Foster, *An Errand of Mercy: The Evangelical United Front, 1790–1837* (Chapel Hill: University of North Carolina Press, 1960).
15. Ibid., 4–5.
16. Nico Spuntoni, "Muller: Not even the Pope Can Decide to Bless Gay Couples," *The Daily Compass: Made for the Truth*, March 4, 2023, https://newdailycompass.com/en/mueller-not-even-pope-can decide-to-bless-gay couples/; Schlumpf; "EWTN Connected to Conservative, Anti-Francis Elements."
17. Jay Reeves, "Catholic View of Pope's Death," *Los Angeles Times*, April 6, 2005, https://artic les/latimes.comn/2005/apr/06/entertainment/et-tvpope6. The "Gloria" at a Catholic eucharist is recited/sung just before the scripture readings and begins with the song of the angels in Bethlehem ("Glory to God in the highest . . ."). The *Agnus Dei* is recited or sung before the reception of communion and is a three-fold prayer ("Lamb of God, who takes away the sin of the world . . ."). The same is true of the "*Domine non sum dignus*" ("Lord, I am not worthy . . .").
18. Gustav Niebuhr, "Use of Actress in Jesus Role Stirs Dispute," *Washington Post*, September 11, 1993, https://www.washingtonpost.com/archive/politics/1993/09/11/use-of-actress-in-jesus-role-stirs-dispute.
19. Christine Niles, "Mother Angelica's Legendary Rant Against the Liberal Church," *Church Militant*, March 28, 2016, https://www.churchmilitant.com/news/article/mother-angelicas-legendary-1993-rant-against-liberal-church/.
20. The *Enchiridion Symbolorum* contains the major Greek and Latin statements of faith, including documents promulgated by councils and synods, as well as the most important papal teaching from Clement I to Paul VI. The most recent (English) version was published in 1957 as *Sources of Catholic Faith*. The theological notes witness to various levels of teaching authority that could be attached to specific documents or statements. Those labeled *de fide definite* claimed the highest level of teaching authority, so that Catholics were *required* to believe them. Their teaching authority claimed a considerably higher level of authority than statements labeled *theologice certa* ("theologically certain") or *proxima fidei* ("border on the faith"). The lowest level was that of "probable opinion." McBrien, ed., *HarperCollins Encyclopedia of Catholicism*, 464–465, 920–921.
21. Cardinal Roger Mahony, Archbishop of Los Angeles, "Gather Faithfully Together: A Guide for Sunday Mass. A Pastoral Letter on the Liturgy," September 4, 1997, 1–2, 4, 5, 12.
22. John Allen, "Mahony Appeals to Rome About Angelica," *National Catholic Reporter*, January 30, 1998, https://natcath.org/NCR_Online/archives2/1998a/013098/mahony.htm; Jim Russell, "Cardinal Mahony Wrecks the REC," *Crisis*, February 14, 2019, https://www.crisismagazine.com/opinion/cardinal-mahony-wrecks-the-rec. The levels of confusion here are dense and complicated. Part of the confusion is that Mother Angelica regularly (and incorrectly) referred to the "Catholic doctrine of transubstantiation" regarding Christ's presence in the eucharist. But the Catholic Church has no doctrine of transubstantiation, but rather the doctrine of Christ's "Real Presence" in the consecrated bread and wine. Transubstantiation was simply one theological way (among several others) that one might explain *how* Christ was present in the elements of bread and wine after the words of consecration ("This is my body . . ."). The finer points of Aristotelian philosophy and medieval nominalism seems to have eluded Mother Angelica. See McBrien, ed., *HarperCollins Encyclopedia of Catholicism*, 1080, 1264; *Sacrosanctum Concilium* ("The Constitution on the Sacred Liturgy"), n. 7 on p. 163, in *Vatican Council II: The Conciliar and Post-Conciliar Documents*.
23. "Real Presence," 1080, and "Transubstantiation," 1264, in McBrien, ed., *HarperCollins Encyclopedia of Catholicism*; *Sacrosanctum Concilum* ("The Constitution on the Sacred Liturgy"), n. 7 in Austin Flannery, O.P., ed., *Vatican Council II: The Conciliar and Post-Conciliar Documents* (Northport, NY: Costello Publishing Company, 1975), 163.
24. Allen, "Mahony Appeals to Rome."
25. Ibid. See also David Finnegan, "News Story: Cardinal Mahony, Mother Angelica in Flap Over Liturgical Changes," *Religion News Service*, January 1, 1997, https://religionnews.com/1997/01/01/news-story-cardinal-mahony-Mother-angelica-in-flap-over-liturgical-changes/.
26. Ibid.
27. Ibid.

28. John Allen, "EWTN's Bishop Says Priests Must Face the People," *National Catholic Reporter*, November 19, 1999, https://natcath.org?NCR_Online/archives2/1999d/111999/111999/111999g.htm.

29. Ibid.

30. Brian Williams, "Mother Angelica on the Latin Mass," *The Liturgy Guy*, March 28, 2017, https://liturgyguy.com/2017/03/28/mother-angelica-on-the-latin-mass/comment-page-1.

31. Ibid., 2.3.4.

32. Michael Sean Winters, "It's Time for U.S. Bishops to Reconsider Relationship with EWTN," *National Catholic Reporter*, September 27, 2021, https://www.ncronline.org/news/opinion/its-time-us-bishops-reconsider-relationship-ewtn/. The Latin word *magisterium* (from *magister*, teacher) refers to the official teaching of the Catholic Church, usually set forth by the hierarchy, which are the bishops, and—finally—the pope.

33. Dulle, "Explainer: The Story Behind Pope Francis' Beef with EWTN," 3.

34. Winters, "It's Time for U.S. Bishops to Reconsider."

35. "*Dubia*"—the Latin (plural) word for "doubts"—refers to a document published on November 14, 2016, and signed by Burke and three other cardinals, raising serious doubts as to Pope Francis's teaching in *Amoris Laetitia*, and voicing their concern that the Pope's teaching would cause grave scandal and confusion among the Catholic faithful on five points. One of those points of concern was that the Pope's letter raised the question of letting confessors decide whether someone living in an "adulterous union" (Burke's words) could receive the sacraments, which the *Dubia* document stated would lead to "scandal" among the faithful. Burke subsequently sent a letter to his brother bishops around the world, asking them to press the pope on the "conspiracy of silence" inside the Vatican regarding the suppression of the investigations of the sexual abuse of minors because of the "homosexual agenda in the church," abetted by the Vatican itself. A subsequent investigation of these concerns revealed that there was no substance to the charges. But Burke himself was a repeated guest on Arroyo's show, even after the investigation revealed that the charges were without substance. See "Dubia Cardinals Ask Bishops to Confront 'Conspiracy of Silence,'" *Catholic News Agency*, February 20, 2019, https://www.catholicnews agency.com/news/40610/dubia-cardinals-ask-bishops-to-confront-conspiracy-of-silence/; Elizabeth A. Mitchell, "The Dubia Were Answered," *The Catholic Thing*, May 11, 2019, https://www.thecatholicthing.org/2019/05/11/the-dubia-were-answered/; "Cardinal Burke on Amoris Laetitia Dubia: 'Tremendous Division' Warrants Action," *National Catholic Register*, https://www.ncregister.com/news/cardinal-burke-on-amoris-laetitia-dubia--tremendous-division-warrants-action/. "*Fugitivus*" (Latin for "fugitive" or "absent without permission") in Catholic Canon Law refers to the act of being absent without proper permission from one's religious superior. After Vigano's public letter calling on Pope Francis to resign, he vanished from sight. As the *Washington Post* reported it: "After [Vigano's] letter was published, he turned off his phone, told friends he was disappearing. Nine months later . . . Vigano refused to disclose his location. But his comments indicate that, even in hiding, he is maintaining his role as the fiercest critic of the pope." Chico Harlan and Stefano Pitrelli, "He Called on the Pope to Resign. Now this Archbishop Is in an Undisclosed Location," *The Washington Post*, June 10, 2019; Philip Pullella, "Vatican Takes Gloves Off, Accuses Papal Critic of 'Calumny, Defamation,'" *Reuters*, October 7, 2018, https://www.reuters.com/article/uk-pope-abuse-mccarisck/vatican-takes-off-gloves-accuses-papal-critic-of calumny-defamation/.

36. Ibid., 1, 2; Heidi Schlumpf, "The Rise of EWTN: From Piety to Partisanship," *National Catholic Reporter*, July 16, 2019, https:///www.ncronline.org/news/media/rise-of-ewtn-piety-partisanship/. See also the account at *Bishops Accountability*, https://www.bishopsaccountability.org/news2019/ 07_08/2019_07_07_16_schlumpf_theRise.htm.

37. Clemente Lisi, "Pope Francis Lashes Out at Criticism from the Catholic Press, Calls It 'Work of the Devil,'" *Religion Unplugged*, September 22, 2021, https://religionunplugged.com/news/2021/9/21/pope-francis-lashes-back-at   his-critics-in-the-catholic-press-calls-it-the-devilswork/.

38. Ibid.

39. The nineteenth-century "Princeton School" was the only Protestant tradition offering a much more specific understanding of how—and in what ways—the Bible was "inspired." Thus, Princeton Seminary giants like Charles Hodge, Benjamin Warfield, and Archibald Alexander developed a Presbyterian "Old School" theory of the literal inerrancy of the "Original Autographs" (the actual parchment on which Moses, David, etc., wrote), but now lost: it was this theory that attempted to explain why there were errors in scripture. But Princeton Seminary professors

honed this theory of the Original Autographs in response to the higher criticism of the Bible imported from Germany by biblical scholars like Charles Augustus Briggs at Union Theological Seminary. It was thus "reactive" in a literal sense: earlier in the nineteenth century there was no need for such a theory because biblical higher criticism was unknown in the US. And mainstream Protestantism in both the nineteenth and twentieth centuries rejected the "Princeton Theology" in any case as obviously a modern creation, and not part an authentic part of the Reformation heritage (Marsden, *Fundamentalism and American Culture*, 102–108); Mark Massa, *Charles Augustus Briggs and the Crisis of Historical Criticism* (Minneapolis: Fortress Press, 1990), 59–63.

40. Lonergan, "The Transition from a Classical Worldview," 127, 128; Massa, *Structure of Theological Revolutions*, 24–25.
41. H. Richard Niebuhr outlined five possible models of how Christianity might relate to human culture: Christ of Culture, Christ Above Culture, Christ the Transformer of Culture, and Christ and Culture in Paradox. But he opened his now-classic book by examining "Christ Against Culture," the model of sectarian Christianity adopted by a range of groups: the Amish, Jehovah's Witnesses, and others. But he argued that the Roman Catholic Church had consistently rejected that sectarian model, which set its face against human culture in favor of the Christ Above Culture paradigm, which sought to serve and educate human culture, in a sense "completing" its best impulses by fulfilling them with teaching "from above." *Christ and Culture* (New York: Harper Torchbooks, 1951), 45–82, 116–148; Eliade, "Roman Catholicism," 430.
42. Marsden, *Fundamentalism and American Culture*, 207.
43. The USCCB (the US Conference of Catholic Bishops) releases a document before each presidential election to prepare to vote. That document—*Forming Consciences for Faithful Citizenship*—lists forty-seven issues that Catholics should consider when voting. A related document, a "Catholic Voter Guide" for the 2020 election, compared the two candidates. In the section "Here Are the Issues," Joe Biden "Aligned with Catholic Teaching" on thirty-eight issues and did not align on seven. In contrast, Donald Trump "aligned" on eleven issues, but did not align twenty, and remained "inconclusive" on a further sixteen issues. Biden failed to align on the issues of abortion, church teaching against the intentional targeting noncombatants, and church teaching that marriage was always between a man and a woman. Trump, on the other hand, aligned with church teaching on abortion but failed to align with church teaching on torture, the necessity of creating jobs for the poor, and restrictions on the availability of assault weapons. Further, in Trump's category was a long list of issues on which the candidate was "inconclusive," including affordable health care, addressing the causes of migration, and addressing the urgent needs of the poor. Arguably the most telling fact of that comparative list was that it fell under the consistent teaching of the Bishops' Conference that Catholics were to avoid being "single issue voters"—and thus the comparative listing of the two candidates (https://www.catholicvoterguide.com).
44. Schlumpf, "The Rise of EWTN."

Chapter 5

1. Alasdair MacIntyre, *After Virtue: A Study in Moral Theory* (Notre Dame, IN: University of Notre Dame Press, 1981), 263.
2. McBrien, ed., *HarperCollins Encyclopedia of Catholicism*, 153–156, 156, 890.
3. Rod Dreher, *The Benedict Option: A Strategy for Christians in a Post-Christian Nation* (New York: Penguin Publishing Group, 2017), dust jacket text.
4. Both the Chaput and Brooks quotes are taken from Emma Green, "The Christian Withdrawal Experiment," *The Atlantic Monthly*, January/February 2020, www.theatlantic.com/magazine/archive/2020/01/retreat-christian-soldiers, 2.
5. "Magnificent" from "Early Threads in the History of St. Mary's [School]," https://stmarys-p.prod.fsspx.org/en/Prologueearly-threads-history-st-marys; Green, "Christian Withdrawal Experiment," 1–2. The town, from its founding by the Jesuits, never used the apostrophe in its name: it was always "St. Marys," not "St. Mary's."
6. Green, "Christian Withdrawal Experiment," 3.
7. Marsden, *Fundamentalism and American Culture*, 207.
8. Statistics on the population, wages, and gender identities of St. Marys, Kansas are from: "St. Marys, Kansas (KS66536) profile: Population, maps, real estate. Homes" at www.city-data.com/St.-Marys-Kansas.Html. On Pius X, see Johnson, *A History of Christianity*, 469–475, 503–510. The "Modernist Crisis" within the Catholic Church occurred in the first decade of the twentieth century, caused by the efforts of Catholic intellectuals to reconcile Catholic theology with

modern rationality, especially by modern conceptions of history. McBrien, ed., *HarperCollins Encyclopedia of Catholicism*, 877–878.

9. Marcellefebvre.info, http://marcellefebvre.info; "The Society of Saint Pius X Reaches Milestone of 700 Priestly Members," https://sspx.org/en/news-events/news/society-saint-pius-x-reaches-milestone-700-priestly-members; B. A. Cathey, "The Legal Background to the Erection and Alleged Suppression of the Society of St. Pius X," in *Apologia Pro Marcel Lefebvre*, ed. Michael Davies (St. Marys, KS: Angelus Press, 1979), appendix V, 443ff. "Indifferentism" is the false teaching, condemned by Vatican I, that specific membership in any Christian denomination was a secondary concern, all of them being basically equal in terms of teaching authority. See McBrien, ed., *HarperCollins Encyclopedia of Catholicism*, 662; "Conservative Theologians Accuse Pope of Spreading Heresy," *New York Times*, September 23, 2017.

10. "Short History of the Society of St. Pius X," https://web.archive.org/web/201509240311 048///www.holycrossseminary.com/Most_Asked_Questions_Appendix_III_page2.htm/; F. Charriere, "Decree Establishing the International Priestly Society of St. Pius X," photographically reproduced in Davies, *Apologia*, trans. Michael Davies, *An Open Letter to Confused Catholics*, trans. SSPX (St. Marys, Kansas: SSPX, 1992), 140.

11. "The 1974 Declaration of Archbishop Lefebvre," http://archives.sspx.org/archbishop_lefebvre/1974_declaration _of_archbishop_lefebvre.htm; Peter Vere, *A Canonical History of the Lefebvre Schism* (Ontario: St. Paul University, 1999); Marcel Lefebvre, "La Declaration du 21 novembre 1974," in *The Collected Works of His Excellency Archbishop Marcel Lefebvre*, vol. 1 (Dickenson, TX: Angelus Press, 1985), 34.

12. "*Bruta figura*" is an Italian term meaning "leaving a bad image," or any action that brings dishonor to the individual doing it. "Short History of the Society of Saint Pius X," 2; "Fr. Gueard des Lauriers to Msgr. Lefebvre: You Act like Pontius Pilate," https://www.traditioninaction.org?HotTopics/f045ht_Lauriers0.1.htm; Davies, *Apologia*, 51.

13. "The Ordinations of 29 June 1976," http://www.sspxasia.com/Documents/Archbishop-Lefebvre/Apologia/ Vol_One/Chapter_11.httm; Paul VI, "Lettre de S.S. Le Pape Paul VI a Mgr. Lefebvre, June 29, 1974," "*La Documentation Catholique*, No. 1689," trans., in Davies *Apologia*, 113; Marcel Lefebvre, "Letter to Pope Paul VI, June 22, 1976," trans., in Davies, *Apologia*, 196; Secretariat of State, "Letter from Mgr. Benelli to Mgr. Lefebvre, June 25, 1976," trans., in Davies, *Apologia*, 197–199.

14. Canon 1013 of the old (1917) *Code of Canon Law* stated that "No bishop is permitted to consecrate anyone a bishop unless it is first evident that there is a pontifical mandate (https://www.vatican.va/archive/ENG1104_P03 Htm), while canon 1382 in the same *Code* states that "a bishop who consecrates someone a bishop without a pontifical mandate and the person who receives the consecration from him [both] incur a *latae sentientiae* [i.e., automatic] excommunication reserved to the Holy See" (https://vatican.va/archive/ENG1104/_P54..htm).

15. "The situation is such, the work placed in our hands by the good Lord is such, that faced with this darkness in Rome, faced with the Roman authorities' pertinacity in error, faced with this refusal to return to truth or tradition on the part of those who occupy the seats of authority in Rome, faced with all these things, it seems to us that the good Lord is asking for the Church to continue. This is why it is likely that before I give account of my life to the good Lord, I shall have to consecrate some bishops." Marcel Lefebvre, "Sermon on June 29, 1987," http://www.sspx.Com/Documents/Archbishop-Lefebvre/Bishops-to-save-the-Church.htm.

16. "Decree of Excommunication on Marcel Lefebvre," http://www.cin.org/users/james/files/l-excomm.htm; "Apostolic Letter *Eclessia Dei* (July 2, 1988) John Paul II," https://web.archive.org/web/20150129194411/www.vatican.va/holy_father/john_paul_II/motu_proprio/documents/hf_jp-ii_motu-proprio_02071988_ecclesia_Dei_en.html. In John 18:14, Caiphas, high priest the year Jesus was crucified, stated that "it is better that one man should die rather than the whole people perish"—a theological observation that was true in ways that Caiphas himself did not understand.

17. "Interview with Bishop Bernard Fellay," March 21, 2016, https://sspx.org/en/interview-bp-bernard-fellay; "Vatican Official Confirmed: Agreement with SSPX is Close: News Headlines," www.catholiculture.org.

18. *Unitatis Redintegratio*, ch. I, no. 2; Flannery, *Vatican Council II*, 455.

19. "*Nostra Aetate*, No. 4," in *Vatican Council II*, 741.

20. See "Truth and Error Cannot Go Hand in Hand," 3, in *We Must Maintain Tradition and Pass It On*, FSSPX News, February 11, 2022. A transcript of a conference given by Don Davide Pagliarani, Superior General of the Society of St. Pius X, https//stas.org/en/news-events/

we-must-maintain-tradition-and-pass-it-71504; Marcel Lefebvre, "1983 Open Letter to Pope John Paul II," https://sspx.org/en/1983-open-letter-pope-john-paul-ii. "Supersessionism" is the theological belief that after Jesus's death and resurrection, the Christian Church itself replaced the nation of Israel as "God's chosen people." Thus, the church "superceeded" the nation of Israel as enjoying God's special blessing.

21. James M. Markham, "Fugitive Nazi Collaborator Seized from a Cat," *New York Times*, May 25, 1989. The *Times* reported that Touvier had been on the run since 1974, being hidden by French right-wing Catholics from one religious refuge to another. He had been sentenced to death *in absentia* in 1945 for six "crimes against humanity," including directly overseeing the deportation of French Jews to extermination camps.

22. Southern Law Poverty Center, "Behind the Bishop: The Anti-Semitism of the SSPX," *Hate Watch*, February 26, 2009, https://www.splcenter.org/hatewatch/2009/02/26/behind-the-bishop-anti-semitism-sspx; Heidi Beirich, "Pope Welcomes Holocaust-Denying Bishop Back After Excommunication," *Hate Watch*, January 26, 2009, https:////www.splcenter.org/hatewatch/2009/01/26/pope-welcomes-Holocaust-denying-bishop-back-after-excommunication, 1; "The Society of St. Pius X: Mired in Anti-Semitism," *The (Jewish) Anti-Defamation League News Release*, March 20, 2009, https://www.adl.org//resources/news/Society-of-st-pius-x-mired-antisemitism.

23. "The Society of St. Pius X: Mired in Anti-Semitism," 3.

24. Beirich, "Pope Welcomes Holocaust-Denying Bishop," 2.

25. "The Society of St. Pius X: Mired in Anti-Semitism," 2.

26. "The Society of St. Pius X: Mired in Anti-Semitism," 3.

27. Ibid., 3–4.

28. Sydney Ahlstrom, *A Religious History of the American People* (New Haven: Yale University Press,1972), ch. 30, "The Communitarian Impulse." On the Harmony and Zoar communities, see 496–497; on Brook Farm and Fruitlands, see 500–501; on Oneida, see 498–499.

29. Green, "Christian Withdrawal Experiment," 6–7.

30. Statics based on the 2020 Census Bureau Profile, St. Marys, Kansas, *2020 Decennial Census*, Population, 1; Median age, 3; Education, 3–4, https://data.census.gov/cedsci/profile?g=1600000US2062400.

31. In response to the basketball hubbub, the SSPX put out a statement which said: "Teaching our boys to treat ladies with deference, we cannot place them in an aggressive athletic competition where they are forced to play inhibited by their concern about running into a female referee." Green, "Christian Withdrawal Experiment," 7.

32. Wills, *Bare Ruined Choirs*, 15, 16. See also Massa, *Catholics and American Culture*, 2–3.

33. Green, "Christian Withdrawal Experiment," 8–9.

34. Ibid., 9.

Chapter 6

1. Alan Anderson, "'One Man Can Make a Difference:' Review of *One Man Perched on a Rock: A Biography of Dr. Warren Carroll*," *Catholic World Report*, July 22, 2018, https://www.catholicworldreport.com/2018/07/22/one-man-can-make-a-difference/.

2. "About Dr. Warren Carroll," *Dr. Warren Carroll Lecture Series*, media.christendom.edu/dr-warren-carroll-lectures/.

3. "The First 35 Years (1977–2012): A History of Christendom College," 1, https://www.christendom.edu/ about/a-history-of-christendom-college/.

4. Ibid., 2, 3. The classic study is Peter Brown, *The Rise of Western Christendom* (Oxford: Blackwell Publishers, 1996). See also Stanley Hauerwas, *After Christendom? How the Church is to Behave if Freedom, Justice and a Christian Nation Are Bad Ideas* (Nashville: Abingdon Press, 1999); Douglas John Hall, *The End of Christendom and the Future of Christianity* (Valley Forge, PA: Trinity Press International, 1997).

5. Diarmaid MacCulloch, *A History of Christianity: The First Three Thousand Years* (London: Penguin Publishing Group,2010), 572; Thomas J. Curry, *Farewell to Christendom: The Future of Church and State in America* (New York: Oxford University Press, 2001), 9.

6. Thomas Jefferson, "Notes on Religion, October, 1776," in *The Complete Jefferson, Containing His Major Writings, Published and Unpublished*, assembled and arranged by Saul K. Padover, with illustrations and analytic index (New York: Duell, Sloan, & Pearce, Inc., 1943), 944.

7. Troeltsch, *Social Teaching of the Christian Churches*, 34–39, 201–218, 246–278. On the "voluntary principle," see Finke and Stark, *The Churching of America*, 3–7.

8. Sidney Mead, "Denominationalism: The Shape of Protestantism in America," in *The Lively Experiment: The Shaping of Christianity in America* (New York: Harper and Row, Publishers 1963), 104. See also Sidney Mead, *The Old Religion in the Brave New World: Reflections on the Relation Between Christendom and the Republic (The Jefferson Memorial Lectures)* (Berkeley: University of California Press, 1977), 58–80.

9. It was the Treaty of Thessalonica of 380 that made Catholic Christianity the official religion of the Roman Empire, and not (as is often mistakenly argued) the Treaty of Milan of 313, which simply recognized the right of Christians to gather unmolested within the territories of the Roman Empire. The Latin phrase *cujius regio, ejius religio* means "whose kingdom, his religion" (i.e., the territory established the religion of its ruler as its official religion).

10. Mead, "From Coercion to Persuasion: Another Look at the Rise of Religious Liberty and the Emergence of Denominationalism," in *The Lively Experiment*, 18.

11. John Conley, "Religious Freedom as Catholic Crisis," in *The Human Person and a Culture of Freedom*, ed. Peter Pagan Aguilar and Terese Auer (Washington: Catholic University of America Press, 2009), 226–241, 228–229. The Latin phrase in the *Codex of Canon Law* was "*error non habet ius*," and it remained part of the official teaching of the Catholic Church until the new *Code* was published in 1983. See John Cogley, "Freedom of Religion: Vatican Decree Supplants Ancient Doctrine that 'Error Has No Rights,'" *New York Times*, December 8, 1965.

12. Conley, "Religious Freedom," 229–230.

13. Massa, *Catholics and American Culture*, 143–146.

14. John Courtney Murray, "Leo XII on Church and State: The General Structure of the Controversy," *Theological Studies* 14 (1953): 1–30; John Courtney Murray, "Leo XIII: Separation of Church and State," *Theological Studies* 14 (1953): 145–214; John Courtney Murray, "Leo XIII: Two Concepts of Government," *Theological Studies* 14 (1953): 551–567; John Courtney Murray, "Leo XIII: Two Concepts of Government: Government and the Order of Culture," *Theological Studies* 15 (1954): 1–33; John Courtney Murray, "Leo XIII and Pius XII: Government and the Order of Religion," in *Religious Liberty: Catholic Struggles with Pluralism* ed. Leon Hooper (Louisville: Westminster/John Knox, 1993), 49–125; John Courtney Murray, *We Hold These Truths: Catholic Reflections on the American Proposition* (New York: Sheed and Ward, 1960), 48–56, 69–71.

15. J. Leon Hooper and Todd David Whitmore, *John Courtney Murray and the Growth of Tradition* (Kansas City: Sheed & Ward, 1996), viii–xii, 276.

16. Todd David Whitmore, "The Growing End: John Courtney Murray and the Shape of Murray Studies," in *John Courtney Murray and the Growth of Tradition*, xii–xiii.

17. "*Dignitatis humanae*, 'Chapter 1: "The General Principle of Religious Freedom,'" in Flannery, ed., *Vatican Council II*, 800.

18. Bozeman, *To Live Ancient Lives*. By "primitivism" Bozeman meant the attempt to reconstruct the Primitive Church described in the acts of the Apostles in contemporary culture. This is always what he terms a "historical heresy"; that is, it rests on the mistaken belief that such a project is possible, because those who attempt it live (almost literally) in a different world than the one they're attempting to reconstruct. On the "pure inside" versus the "unclean outside," see Douglas, *Purity and Danger*, chs. 1 and 2.

19. Alan L. Anderson, "Review of Laura S. Gossin's *One Man Perched on a Rock: A Biography of Dr. Warren Carroll*," *Catholic World Report*, July 22, 2018, www.catholicworldreport.com/2018/07/22/one-man-can-make-a-difference/.

20. Ryan Cornell, "Christendom College Ranked Sixth for Best Value," *Northern Virginia Daily*, November 17, 2013; "Christendom College Began Its 45th Anniversary Year by welcoming a Record-Breaking Student Body," *Arlington Catholic Herald*, September 28, 2022.

21. "Rankings and Endorsements," www.christendom.edu/news/rankings-endorsements/.

22. "Christendom College," https://cardinalnewmansociety.org/college/christendom-college/, italics added; "Admission rate at Christendom College," *Princeton Review*, https://www.princetonreview.com/college/christendom-college-1023926.

23. "Faithful to the Core, The Core Curriculum at Christendom College," www.christendom.edu/academics/the-core-curriculum/. The "*Mandatum*" (Latin) or Mandate is an official acknowledge by someone in church authority that theologians claiming to teach Catholic theology is orthodox and is in fact teaching what the Church mandates. According to Canon 812 of the 1983 *Code of Canon Law*, any Catholic professor teaching theology should receive such a mandate from their local ordinary (usually a bishop). This requirement was first elucidated

by Pope John Paul II in his 1990 apostolic constitution, *Ex Corde Ecclesiae*. See *The Catholic Encyclopedia*, encyclopedia.com/religion/encyclopedias-almanacs-transcripts-and-maps/manadatum-academic.

24. "Faithful to the Core," 3.
25. Ibid., 3.
26. Ibid., 3.
27. Ibid., 4–5.
28. Simcha Fisher, "Are Women Safe in Christendom's Bubble?," *Simchafisher.com*, https://www.simchafisher.com/2018/01/16/are-women-safe-in-christendom's-bubble-part-1/2.
29. Ibid., 2–3.
30. Simcha, "Are Women Safe?," 5–6.
31. Ibid., 6.
32. Ibid., 9.
33. Ibid.
34. "As Alumni Claim Sexual Assault is Mishandled, Christendom College Vows to Improve," *Catholic News Service*, February 5, 2018, https://www.catholicnewsagency.com/news/37687/as-alumni-claim-sexual-assault-Is-mishandled-christendom-college-vows-to-improve, 4.
35. Simcha Fisher, "Are Women Safe in Christendom's Bubble? Part II," *Simchafisher.com*, https://www.simchafisher.com/2018/01/16/are-women-safe-in-christendom's-bubble-part-ii, 9.
36. Ibid., 25, italics added.
37. Ibid., 11.
38. Bozeman, *To Live Ancient Lives*, 2–11.
39. Sacvan Bercovitch, *The Puritan Origins of the American Self* (New Haven: Yale University Press,1975), 49–58.
40. Charles Taylor has written quite brilliantly on "social imaginaries": "what I'm trying to get at with this term is something much broader and deeper than the intellectual schemes people may entertain when they think about reality. I am thinking rather of the ways in which they *imagine* their social existence, how they fit together with others, how things go on between them and their fellows, the expectations which are normally met, and the deeper normative notions and images which underlie these expectations" (171). But these imaginaries *don't* exist "out there" in history apart from the imaginations of those who share them. To believe such imaginaries to be actually embodied in the structures of the historical process is to misunderstand their origin and content: they are intellectual *constructs* imposed on historical activity, not derived from it. Charles Taylor, *A Secular Age* (Cambridge: Belknap Press of Harvard University Press, 2007).
41. Eliade, "Roman Catholicism," 430.
42. Steven Millies, "What is Catholic Integralism? One of the Oldest Ideas in Christianity Has Come to Renewed Prominence," *U.S. Catholic*, October 2019, https://uscatholic.org/articles/201910/what-is-catholic-integralism/1.
43. William Galston, "What is Integralism: The Catholic Movement that Wants to Use Government Power in the Name of Public Morality," *Persuasion*, November 2, 2022, https://www.persuasion.community/p/what-is-integralism, 1.
44. As quoted by William Galston from an article ("Integralism in Three Sentences") by Pater William Waldstein, posted on the integralist website, *The Josiahs*; Galston, "What is Integralism?," 3.
45. Galston, "What is Integralism?," 4–5.
46. "Rankings and Endorsements—Christendom College," www.christendom.edu/about/a-history-of-Christendom-college/, 3–5.
47. Ibid.

Chapter 7

1. "Limiting God," https://www.churchmilitant.com/video/episode/limiting-god/. The chapter title is from the words of Jesus in St. Matthew 11:12: "From the days of John the Baptist until now, the kingdom of heaven has been subject to violence, and the violent bear it away."
2. Niraj Warikoo, "Views on Provocative Real Catholic TV Station Anger Detroit Archdiocese and Others," *Detroit Free Press*, February 13, 2012, https://www.freep.com/article/20120213/views-on-provocative-Real-Catholic-TV-Station-anger-Detroit-Archdiocese-and-others/; "Biography of Michael Voris," https:// www.realcatholictv.com/about/bio.php. Church Militant's budget in 2018 is included in Christopher White, "Church Militant Founder May

Face Legal Reckoning for Defamation," *National Catholic Reporter*, April 30, 2021, https://ncronline.org/culture/church-militant-founder-may-face-legal-reckoning-defamation/.

3. Alexander Slavsky, "University of Notre Dame Offers Pro-LGBT Retreat, Distorts Church teaching," *Church Militant*, January 26, 2018, https://www.churchmilitant.com/news/article/notre-dame-caves-to-dissent-with-another-LGBT-retreat; Southern Poverty Law Center, "Ultra-Orthodox Catholic Propaganda Outlet Pushes Anti-LGBTQ Agenda," *Hate Watch*, https://www.splcenter.org/hatewatch/2018/0817/untra-orthodox-catholic-propaganda-outlet-pushes-anti-lgbtq/.

4. Kathryn Joyce and Ben Lorber, "Exclusive: Self-Described 'Christian Fascist' Movement is Trying to Sabotage LGBTQ Pride Month," *Salon.com*, June 9, 2022, https://www.salon.com/2022/06/09/exclusive-self-described-christian-fascist-movement-is-trying-to-sabotage-lgbtq-pride-month/; Michael Voris, "Weak Men Suck. And They are Destroyers," *The Vortex* (transcript), August 10, 2022, https://www.churchmilitant.com/video/episode/vortex-wea-men-suck.

5. Voris, "Weak Men Suck." "Charging Charlie" is on page 4 of the transcript and "John Joseph" is on page 7.

6. Fern Shen, "Church Militant Sues Baltimore, Calls Cancellation of Pier Six Event Free Speech Infringement," *Baltimore Brew*, September 14, 2021, https://www.baltimorebrew.com/2021/09/14/curch-militant-sues-baltimore-calls-cancellation-of-pier-six-event-free-speech infringement/.

7. Ibid., 2.

8. Robert Allen, "How a Right-Wing Ferndale Fringe Group is Building a Multimedia Empire," *Detroit Free Press*, February 18, 2017, https://www.freep.com/story/news/local/michigan/oakland/2017/02/18/church-militant-Growing-influence/.

9. Kathryn Joyce, "Political Violence Must Always Be an Option, Says Far-Right Catholic Outlet," *Salon.com*, November 8, 2022, https://salon.com/2022/11/8/political-violence-must-always-be-an option-says-far-right-catholic- outlet.

10. Michael Sean Winters, "Church Militant's Nonsense Not Authentically Catholic," *National Catholic Reporter*, May 11, 2017, https://www.ncronline.org/blogs/distinctly-catholic/church-militants-nonsense-not-authentically-catholic/; Shen, "Church Militant Sues Baltimore."

11. Allen, "How a Right-Wing Ferndale Fringe Group," 2.

12. Ibid., 4. On supersessionism, see McBrien, ed., *HarperCollins Encyclopedia of Catholicism*, 706–707.

13. Ibid., 2.

14. Joyce, "Political Violence." See also Hemant Mehta, "Catholic Extremist: When Politics Fails Us, Violence 'Must Always be an Option,'" *Only Sky Media*, November 9, 2022, https://onlysky.media/hemant-mehta/catholic-michael-voris-abortion-violence-must-always-be-an-option/; Deacon Greg Kandra, "Church Militant on Election Day: 'Violence Is Not Immoral. It Must Always Be An Option," *The Deacon's Bench*, November 8, 2022, https://thedeaconsbench.com/church-militant-on-election-day-violence-is-not-immoral-it-must-always-be-an-option/

15. Ibid., 3.

16. Ibid., 2.

17. Jerod Macdonald-Evoy, "The 'Groyper Army' is Looking to Make White Nationalism Mainstream," *AZ Mirror*, February 22, 2022, https://www.azmirror.com/2022/02/22//rthe-groyper-army-is-looking-to-make-white-nationalism-mainstream; Institute for Strategic Dialogue, "Groypers," https://www.isdglobal.org/wp-content/uploads/2022/10/ Groypers-external-October-2022-1.pdf. On the political goals of the "Groyper Army," see https://www.hsgac.senate.gov/imo/media/doc/Testimony-greenblatt-2021-08-05.pdf. On Fuentes at the Charlottesville rally, see https://abcnews.go.com/US/group-afpac-twitter-grow-movements/story?id=76418773. On Fuentes as host of the *America First* podcast, see https://luskincenter.history.ucla.edu/wp-content/ uploads/sites/66/2021/03/Public-From-Student-Politics-to-Capital-Insurerection-The-Intensification-of-Extremism -at-UCLA-and-Beyond.pdf.

18. Kathryn Joyce and Ben Lorber, "'Traditional' Catholics and White Nationalist 'Groypers' Forge a New Far-Right Youth Movement," *Salon.com*, May 13, 2022, https://www.salon.com/2022/05/13/trad-catholics-and-And nationalist-groypers-forge-a-new-far-right-youth-movement/; Joyce and Lorder, "Exclusive: Self-Described 'Christian Fascist' Movement," 3.

19. Michael Voris, "A Disgrace to the Chair of Peter: The Church Belongs to Almighty God, Not to the shepherds," *The Vortex* (transcript), February 23, 2016, https://www.churchmilitant.com/Video/episode/a-disgrace-to-the-chair-of-peter/.

20. Ibid., 3.
21. Ibid., 3; Scott Detrow, "Pope Says Trump 'Is Not Christian,'" *All Things Considered*, February 18, 2016, https://npr.org/2016/02/18/4672293/pope-says-trumpis-not-christian/. Trump, of course, immediately responded, "If and when the Vatican is attacked by ISIS, which as everybody knows is ISIS' ultimate trophy, I can promise you that the Pope would have only wished and prayed that Donald Trump would have been President because this would not have happened."
22. Voris, "Disgrace to the Chair of Peter," 3.
23. "Universal Ordinary" referred to the fact that the Pope (as Bishop of Rome) could offer official (magisterial) teaching that took precedence over the teaching of all the other bishops of the Church. See McBrien, ed., *HarperCollins Encyclopedia of Catholicism*, 805–807.
24. Michael Voris, "CM Statement on the Pope," *The Vortex*, August 27, 2018 https://www.churchm ilitant.com/video/episide/vort-cm-statement-on-the-pope/.
25. Ibid., 3.
26. Ibid., 2.
27. Nicole Winfield, "Vatican Official Warns Pope of Corruption," *Seattle Times*, January 26, 2012; John Allen, "New Nuncio is No Stranger to Politics," *National Catholic Reporter*, September 27, 2011; Gianluigi Nuzzi, *Merchants in the Temple* (New York: Henry Holt and Company, 2015), 25; Austen Ivereigh, *The Great Reformer* (New York: Macmillan, 2014), 343; *Biography of Archbishop Carlo Maria Vigano* (Franciscan Foundation for the Holy Land, 2015), https://www.ffhl.org/wp-content/uploads/2015/03/Vigano_Biography.pdf; "Archbishop Carlo Maria Vigano," *Catholic Hierarchy*, http://www.catholic-hierarchy.org/bishop/bvigano.html.
28. Michael O'Loughlin, "Vigano's Accusations: What We Know and What Questions They Raise," *America*, August 26, 2018, https://www.americamagazine.org/faith/2018/08/26/viganos-accussations-what-we-know-and-what-what-questions-they-raise/; Harriet Sherwood, "Pope Francis Failed to act on U.S. Abuse Claims, Says Former Vatican Envoy," *The Guardian*, August 26, 2018, https:///www.theguardian.com/world/2018/aug/26/pope-Francis-failed-to act-on abuse-claims-says-former-vatican-envoy; Nicole Winfield, "Pope on McCarrick Claims: I Won't Say a Word About It," *The Kansas City Star*, August 26, 2018; Jason Horowitz, "Defending Pope Francis, Vatican Allies May Strengthen Vigano's Hand," *New York Times*, September 2, 2018, https://www.nytimes.com/2018/09/02/World/Europe/pope-francis-archbishop-vigano-kim-davis.html.
29. Laurie Goodtsein and John Horowitz, "Why Was He Allowed at Gala Events?" *The New York Times*, September 1, 2018, https://www.nytimes.com/2018/09/01/world/europe/pope-francis-benedict-mccarrick.html.
30. O'Loughlin, "Vigano's Accusations," 3.
31. Cardinal Marc Ouellet, "Cardinal Ouellet: Vigano in 'Open and Scandalous Rebellion' Against the Pope," *Catholic News Service*, October 7, 2018, https://www.catholicnewsagency.com/news/39577/Cardinal-ouelette-vigano-in-open-and-scandalous-rebellion-against-pope-francis, 2, 5.
32. Ibid., 8; Daniel Burke, "The 'Coup' Against Pope Francis," *CNN*, August 27, 2018, https://www.cnn.com/2018/08/27/us/vigano-pope-resign-abuse-analysis/index.html; Richard Perez-Pena, "Pope Francis, The Accusations, and the Back Story," *New York Times*, August 27, 2018, https://www.nytimes.Com/2018/08/27/world/Europe/pope-francis-vigano-mccarrick.html.
33. Jaweed Kaleem, "Who Is Carlo Maria Vigano, the Man Accusing Pope Francis of Covering Up sex Abuse?," *Los Angeles Times*, August 28, 2018, https://www.latimes.com/nation/la-fg-pope-francis-papal-nuncio-20180828-story-html; Chico Harlan and Stefano Pitrelli, "He Called on the Pope to Resign: Now this Archbishop is in an Undisclosed Location," *Washington Post*, June 10, 2019.
34. Ibid.; Jason Horowitz, "The Man Who Took on Pope Francis: The Story Behind the Vigano Letter," *New York Times*, August 28, 2018, https://www.nytimes.com/2018/08/28/world/eur ope/archbishop-carlo-maria-vigano-Pope-francis.html.
35. In 1884, Pope Leo XIII ordered certain prayers to be recited after "low mass" to insure the independence of Vatican City. One of those was the Prayer to St. Michael the Archangel: "St. Michael the archangel, defend us in battle. Be our protection against the wickedness and snares of the devil. May God rebuke him, we humbly pray. And do thou, O Prince of the Heavenly Host, by the power of God, thrust into Hell Satan and all evil spirits who wonder through the world for the ruin of souls. Amen." *Liber Usualis*, Abbey of Solesmes, 1961, 1655.
36. Allen, "How a Right-Wing Ferndale Fringe Group"; Warikoo, "Views on Provocative Real Catholic TV"; The Archdiocese of Detroit, "Regarding Real Catholic TV and Its Name,"

December 15, 2011, https://aod.org/announcements-newsroom/2011/december/regarding-rctv-and-its-name; Michael Voris, "On Claims of Disobedience," *ChurchMilitant.com*, August 11, 2020, https://www.churchmilitant.Com/main/generic/on-claims-of-disobedience.

37. Allen, "How a Right-Wing Ferndale Fringe Group," 3.
38. Eliade, "Roman Catholicism," 430.
39. Marsden, *Fundamentalism and American Culture*, 207, italics added.
40. "Broke their vows" in quotation marks because, save for a few religious order priests appointed to be bishops, diocesan priests who became bishops had no vows, but rather promises to obey their ordinary when they were ordained presbyters, and to live in communion with the Bishop of Rome as bishops.
41. Joyce and Lorber, " 'Traditional' Catholics and White Nationalist 'Groypers' "; Mehta, "Catholic Extremist."
42. Romans 7:23.
43. See the entries for "church militant," "church suffering," and "church triumphant" in McBrien, ed., *HarperCollins Encyclopedia of Catholicism*, 317, and "communion of saints," on page 339. This understanding of the phrase "church militant" is wonderfully expressed in Ralph Vaughn Williams's great hymn, "For All the Saints."
44. Bendroth, Fundamentalism and Gender, 6.
45. For a discussion of both Baconian Realism and paradigm revolutions, see Chapter 1 of this book. See also Marsden, *Fundamentalism and American Culture*, 118–129.
46. Niraj Warikoo, "Head of Conservative Religious Media Outlet Church Militant Resigns," *Detroit Free Press*, November 21, 2023, https://www.freep.com/story/local/michigan/oakland/2023/11/21/michael-voris-founder-and-president-of-church militant-resigns.
47. Ibid., 1.
48. Mike Lewis, "Michael Voris Forced Out at Church Militant," *WherePeterIs*, November 21, 2023, https://wherepeteris.com/michael-voris-forced-out-at-church-militant/.

Chapter 8

1. Jessica Kramer, "Conservatism's Inevitable Conversion to Catholicism," *Crisis* magazine, July 16, 2021, 2, https://crisismagazine.com/opinion/conservatisms-inevitable-conversion-to-cath olisism.
2. Matthew Bunson, "50 Catholic Converts: Notable Churchgoers of the Last Century," *National Catholic Register*, April 15, 2017, https://www.ncregister.com/commentaries/50-catholic-conve rts-notable-churchgoers-of-the-last-century.
3. See Chapter 2, "Young Man Merton: Thomas Merton and the Postwar 'Religious Revival," and Chapter 5 " 'The Downward Path': Dorothy Day, Anti-Structure, and the Catholic Worker Movement," in my Massa, *Catholics and American Culture*. The Pew Research Center estimates that just two percent of Catholics in the US Church are converts: David Masci and Gregory Smith, "7 Facts About American Catholics," October 10, 2018, https://www.pewresearch.org/short-reads/2018/10/7-facts-about-american-catholics
4. Anne C. Rose, "Some Private Roads to Rome: The Role of Families in American Victorian Conversions to Rome," *Catholic Historical Review* 14 (Winter 1996): 35–57; Patrick Allitt, *Catholic Converts: British and American Intellectuals Turn to Rome* (Ithaca, NY: Cornell University Press, 1997), esp. chs. 14–17; Jenny Franchot, *Roads to Rome: The Antebellum Protestant Encounter with Catholicism* (Berkeley: University of California Press, 1994).
5. See Chapter 5 of this text.
6. Kramer, Conservatism's Inevitable Conversion to Catholicism," 1, 2.
7. Ibid., 3.
8. "The 40 Year Impact of Crisis Magazine," *Crisis* magazine, November 1, 2022, https://crisism agazine.com/opinion/the-forty-year-impact-of-crisis-magazine; Sean Michael Winters, "*Crisis* Magazine Returns," *National Catholic Reporter*, May 10, 2011, https://www.ncronline.org/blogs/distinctly-catholic/crisis-magazine-returns.
9. "About Deal Hudson," https://dealhudson.blog/about; Michael S. Rose, "The Crisis at *Crisis* Magazine, (Part II)" *New Oxford Review*, November 2004, https://www.newoxfordreview.org/documents/the-crisis-at-crisis-Magazine-part II; "About the Christian Review," https://thechri stianreview.com/about-the-christian-review.
10. "Eric Sammons," https://ericsammons.com/about/; "The Forty Year Impact of *Crisis* Magazine."
11. "And after this I saw another angel coming down from heaven, having great authority. And he called out with a mighty voice: 'Fallen, fallen is Babylon the great! It has become a dwelling place

of demons, a haunt of every foul spirit. For all nations have drunk the wine of her impure passion, and the kings of the earth have committed fornication with her.' Then I heard another voice from heaven saying, 'Come out of her, my people, lest you take part in her sins, lest you share in her plagues.'" Book of Revelation 18:1–5.

12. Eric Sammons, "The Rebranding of the Latin Mass Movement," *Crisis* magazine, December 15, 2022, https://crisismagazine.com/editors-desk.

13. Ibid., 2.

14. Eric Sammons, "Be Angry," *Crisis* magazine, July 8, 2023, https://crisismagazine.com/editors-desk/be-angry/.

15. Eric Sammons, "10 Years of Confusion, Political Ideology, and Scandal," *Crisis* magazine, May 13, 2023, https://crisismagazine.com/editors-desk/10-years-of-confusion-political-ideology-and-scandal.

16. Charles Curran, "Invincible Ignorance of the Natural Law According to St. St. Alphonsus: An Historical-Analytic Study from 1784 to 1765," STD Dissertation, Academia Alfonsiana, 1961.

17. Sammons, "10 Years of Confusion, Political Ideology, and Confusion," 2.

18. Ibid., 2.

19. Elizabeth A. Mitchell, "The Dubia Were Answered," *The Catholic Thing*, May 11, 2019, https://www.thecatholicthing.org/2019/05/11/the-dubia-were-answered/; Harlan and Pitrelli, "He Called on the Pope to Resign"; Philip Pullella, "Vatican Takes Gloves Off, Accuses Papal Critic of 'Calumny, Defamation,'" *Reuters*, October 7, 2018, https://www.reuters.com/uk-pope-abuse-mccarrick/vatican-takes-off-gloves-accuses-papal-critic-of calumny.

20. Eric Sammons, "The Devilishly Heretical Fr. James Martin," *Crisis* magazine, January 23, 2023, https://crisismagazine.com/editors-desk.

21. Ibid.

22. On the Plymouth Brethren, one of proto-groups that led to the formation of the fragile coalition that became American Protestant fundamentalism, see Ernest Sandeen, *The Roots of Fundamentalism: British and American Millennialism* (Chicago: University of Chicago Press, 1970). On dispensationalism, see C. Norman Krause, *Dispensationalism in America: Its Rise and Development* (Richmond, VA: John Knox Press, 1958).

23. Catholic Christianity has, by and large, avoided talking about the "end times" of Jesus's return in either premillennialist or dispensationalist language, save for figures like the medieval Joachim of Fiore, whom was condemned by the Church in 1215. For Catholics, the "Four Last Things" are death, judgment, heaven, and hell.

24. Eric Sammons and Joshua Charles, "An Age of Antichurch and Antichrists (Part II)," *Crisis* magazine, podcast recorded on July 20, 2023, https://crisismagazine.com/podcast/an-age-of-antichurch-and-antichrists-part-ii-guest-joshua-charles/.

25. Marsden, *Fundamentalism and American Culture*, 30–31, 45, 48, 119, 168–169, 272; Ernest Sandeen, *The Roots of Fundamentalism: British and American Millenarianism* (Chicago: University of Chicago Press, 1970); *The Scofield Reference Bible III, KJV: How to Use This Bible* (New York: Oxford University Press, 2003).

26. Sammons and Charles, "An Age of Antichurch," 4.

27. Ibid., 5.

28. Ibid., 5.

29. Ibid., 11.

30. Ibid., 12.

31. The prefix in the terms "premillennialist" and "postmillennialist" ("pre" and "post") refer to the relation of Jesus's appearing to the thousand years of peace and plenty (the millennium) that cover the earth. Protestant premillennialists tend to be pessimistic about history and the final judgment: history will decline into chaos, which will provoke Christ's Second Coming and the judgment that is part of it. Few will be saved, and the vast majority will be damned, after which Satan and the Antichrist will be cast into the Lake of Fire, with the millennium following. Protestant postmillennialists tend to be optimistic about history and Christ's Second Coming: history will gradually get better because of the Christian efforts to build the Kingdom of God on earth, so that Christ will appear to crown those efforts. In this model of the end times, Christ appears *after* the millennium has taken place. Protestant fundamentalists are overwhelmingly premillennialist. See George Marsden, "Defining Fundamentalism, *Christian Scholars Review* I (Winter

1971): 141–151; LeRoy More, Jr., "Another Look at Fundamentalism: A Response to Ernest R. Sandeen," *Church History* XXXVII (June 1968): 195–202; Wilbur M. Smith, "The Second Coming of Christ," The Best of D. L. Moody (Chicago: Moody Press, 1971): 193–195. The most famous recent premillennialist author is Hal Lindsey, whose 1970 book, *The Late Great Planet Earth* (Grand Rapids, MI: Zondervan), has sold over ten million copies.

32. McBrien, ed., *HarperCollins Encyclopedia of Catholicism*, 423. On redaction and source criticism, see McBrien, ed., *HarperCollins Encyclopedia of Catholicism*, 173.

Index

For the benefit of digital users, indexed terms that span two pages (e.g., 52–53) may, on occasion, appear on only one of those pages.